DATE DUE

JY 2 9 '99			

DEMCO 38-296

Peonies

Peonies

by
Allan Rogers

illustrated
and with an
essay on landscaping
by
Linda Engstrom

Timber Press
Portland, Oregon

Reprinted 1996

Printed in Hong Kong

TIMBER PRESS, INC.
The Haseltine Building
133 S.W. Second Avenue, Suite 450
Portland, Oregon 97204, U.S.A.

Library of Congress Cataloging-in-Publication Data

Rogers, Allan.
    Peonies / by Allan Rogers ; illustrated and with an essay on
landscaping by Linda Engstrom.
        p.   cm.
    Includes bibliographical references (p.   ) and index.
    ISBN 0-88192-317-6
    1. Peonies.   I. Title.
SB413.P4R64   1995
635.9'33111–dc20   94-48535
                                                         CIP

To my wife, Dorothy,
who worked for this book untold hours,
both directly and indirectly,
who cheered me up
when I became discouraged,
and who put up with me
for fifty years, and counting.

Contents

Color photographs follow page 132

Foreword

Peonies—those buxom, flaunting flowers—are enjoying a horticultural renaissance. Though everybody's granny grew them, modern gardeners lacked patience with perennials better suited in habits and timing to a more leisurely age. As heritage plants regain our favor and foliage plays an increasingly important role in our gardens, peonies are reclaiming their lost status. As our interest is roused, we want to know more about these plants, which captured the hearts of our ancestors. When we look for information, however, a cursory paragraph or two is all we find. When we look for plants, we are apt to be offered nameless collections or peonies sold by color, listed simply as "pink" or "white flecked with red." To learn about their development and preferences in detail, we must comb through the garden books of our grandparents and their great-greats.

This book—the first comprehensive book about peonies to appear in decades—comes as a treasure trove for peony lovers. In it, we find not only an enormous amount of detailed and specific information about growing peonies in North America, but also how they are tended and marketed elsewhere, in Japan, China, Germany, the Netherlands, England, even New Zealand and Australia. Peony societies and commercial growers, academics and gifted gardeners the world round contributed experiences, ideas, and insights to these pages. We are shown not only garden hybrids of all sorts but species peonies, a relatively abstruse interest which is becoming more popular each year. An unmatched resource—Appendix I's lists of herbaceous and tree peony species and cultivars, along with their commercial sources—would alone be worth this book's price several times over for the peony devotee. Rogers takes us deeper, however, offering historical overviews as well as a fascinating look at new directions in hybridizing and the peonies of tomorrow.

The amateur is well served here, but so too is the would-be commercial grower. Rogers offers the equivalent of a full course in every aspect of peony raising, from culture to propagation. Too often our highly skilled nursery people retire without passing on their knowledge to the next generation. The Rogers children have chosen to continue the family nursery, it is true, but Al has made his lifetime of accumulated information available for all of us to draw upon. This is a typical act for this generous soul, who actively promotes horticulture throughout the country and especially in his own region. Thanks to his background in professional education, he is able to communicate his expertise effectively.

He also unwittingly communicates his own generosity of heart and spirit. Some years back, Al Rogers discovered that a private collection of thousands of tree peonies had outlived its owner and was threatened by the bulldozer. Most were dead or too damaged to save after years of neglect, but some 700 were rescued. Put to pasture like weary old horses, they now decorate the sloping hillside below Caprice Farm Nursery. Peonies and peony lovers alike, we are lucky indeed to have Al Rogers as a garden guide and mentor.

Ann Lovejoy
Bainbridge Island

Acknowledgments

Here at Caprice, my daughter Robin and son Rick have contributed their peony expertise and shouldered many of my nursery responsibilities, making it possible for me to spend the long hours necessary to write this book.

My editors, Richard Abel and Frances Farrell, have held my hand, opened new visions, and enthusiastically encouraged me through this perilous journey.

This book could not have been written without the dedicated help of friends and peony experts from all over the world, people who have been generous in many ways: with their photographs, with their advice and information, with their skill at translating from original sources, with their willingness to read and criticize portions of the manuscript. Any omissions or errors of fact, however, are my responsibility alone.

Assisting me were Margarete Baber, David Adams, Julie Allan, Roger Anderson, Darrel Apps, David Beattie, Myron Bigger, Galen Burrell, Ainee Busse, Marion Carter, Angelo Cerchione, Chen Junyu, Gordon Davies, Andrew Ellis, Leo Fernig, Stephen Foster, Peggy Goldsmith, Ben Gowen, James Gudsinski, Dorothy and Bruce Hamilton, Ryoji Hashida, Heinz Klose, Kathie Henderson, Robert Herman, Don Hollingsworth, Hong Tao, Barney Hutton, Red Kendicott, Roy Klehm, William Krekler, Chris Laning, Roberta Miller, the New Zealand Peony Growers Group, Michel Rivière, K. Sahin, Paul Sansone, Bill Seidl, Don Smetana, Sharon Streeter, J. Franklin Styer, Jack Styer, Bob Tischler, James Waddick, Gene Wild, and Zhang Yuexian. My thanks to all.

Introduction

Through the ages, peonies have stirred profound emotions. I fell in love with them when I was seven. Every spring my family would visit Cherry Hill Nurseries in nearby West Newbury to walk the endless rows of blooming peonies. This famous Massachusetts nursery was owned by a friend of my father's and was only a few miles away from home. Until then I had been dragged along, but that particular year I found a huge, fragrant white flower speckled with red and fell in love—instantly. The peony was 'Kelway's Glorious', and I excitedly showed it to my parents. They remembered, for that fall on my eighth birthday I received a gift root of 'Kelway's Glorious'. Today, more than sixty years later, my affection for peonies remains undiminished.

In my grandmother's time and through the 1920s, peonies were one of the few perennial flowers grown in colder climates. Their beauty, their ability to hold up after cutting, and their persuasive perfume made them one of the most popular plants of the period. Peonies decorated memorials, graced speakers' stands, flanked commencement platforms, and adorned June weddings. Almost every garden had at least one such enduring plant, and estate gardens featured them by the hundreds.

Gradually, beginning in the 1930s, the introduction of more exotic varieties of flowering shrubs and trees and a wealth of exciting new annuals reduced the relative significance of peonies in the garden and floral indus-

1

try. Once the backbone of the florist's spring and early summer trade because of their ability to endure cold storage, the importance of peonies declined after World War II. The development of rapid transportation methods coupled with the explosion of new flowers displaced the peony as the florist's mainstay. Quick to embrace the novel and unusual, gardeners came to consider peonies old-fashioned.

In a major turnabout, perennials of all kinds are again attracting the interest of the gardening public, and with this burgeoning interest, the peony—after a sixty-year hiatus—is again taking its place in gardens and landscapes. After all, peonies are probably the most versatile of all perennials. They are easy to grow, remarkably long-lived, and their uses are myriad: as cut flowers, as specimen plants in the landscape or in containers, as hedges, or as integral players in perennial beds and borders. They are now valued and grown as much for their attractive season-long foliage as for their floral display.

Their flowers appeal to the heart as well as to our senses of visual beauty and fragrance. They are, indeed, the flower of remembrance and have been for hundreds of years. What a heartwarming feeling it is, for both giver and recipient, special occasion or not, when even as few as six or so blooms are exchanged.

Sad to say, up-to-date information on many aspects of the peony is unavailable, and much of the knowledge contained herein is based on information about the plant that is fragmented at best. In following the trail of some reports back in time, perhaps 100 years or more, I often encountered a string of dutifully repetitive writings that led to a remark that was not always true. I therefore recount the current scientifically supported facts and pass on many valuable insights gathered from the extensive experience of successful commercial growers. Perhaps I can best write from my own experience. Our family runs a mail-order nursery specializing in peonies, and we have grown tens of thousands of these wonderful plants.

To alter the floral characteristics of a plant that is as slow to increase as the peony, nature needs help from keen gardeners. In the case of peonies this help has been supplied by hundreds of peony lovers over the ages. This book introduces many of these people whose efforts continue to have significant impact upon the peony world. Some are members of family nurseries that have prospered for over a century. All share several attributes: a passionate love for the plant, an ability to recognize subtle improvements that may be genetic, and a lifetime dedication. In some cases fortune has smiled. I hope the stories of these successful hybridizers will fascinate the reader as much as they have me.

More than thirty species of peonies have been identified and I discuss them all, focusing on those that are commercially available or those that have been used in creating many of the exciting and relatively new hybrids. As for the ever-expanding universe of cultivars, the American Peony Society (APS), now designated as the International Registrar for Peonies, lists well over 3000, not all of which have been registered. The majority of these are no longer on the market—many indeed never really entered commerce.

Two chapters in this book offer the reader a little direction in the face of such overwhelming numbers. In Chapter 4, I review more than 150 cultivars now available and generally considered first-class. This chapter includes descriptions of many winners of the American Peony Society's coveted Gold Medal as well as the favorites of collectors and growers. And because the time between selection of new superior seedlings and their introduction into commerce is lengthy, I attempt to peer into the future and predict which cultivars may prove of value in years to come; Chapter 7 turns the spotlight on these up-and-comers—and the unjustly neglected.

Many of my readers are, I am sure, well versed in the growing of peonies. Others may just be beginning their acquaintance with this fascinating perennial. For the newcomer, Chapter 5 provides information on culture, from selecting sites to purchasing plants and on to basic care. For those who'd like to start growing peonies commercially, I offer some suggestions in Chapter 8. And though new cultivars come only from seeds, there are several ways to increase cultivars once the new plant is established. Tree peonies are almost entirely propagated by grafting, herbaceous peonies are usually propagated by division, and a few species and certain of their cultivars can be increased by root cuttings. These and other methods of propagation are explained in detail in Chapter 6.

Peonies are extensively grown in temperate climates throughout the world. Brief overviews of their contemporary status in eight key regions are found in Appendix I, followed by a complete listing of all species and cultivars currently in commerce worldwide and the nurseries that make them available. Appendix II is an international source list of these nurseries and others that specialize in peonies, complete with addresses. If the reader would like to locate and purchase a particular species or cultivar, these two appendices are a good beginning.

Finally, a peony is lovely no matter where it is planted, but the effect is magnified—and the gardener's satisfaction is likewise increased—if the plant has been thoughtfully located. In Appendix III, landscape designer Linda Engstrom discusses the overall character and mood of a garden and the principles of design that will achieve them. With three garden plans in tow, she showcases peonies, taking happy advantage of their foliage and recommending appropriate companion plants.

I believe all sincere gardeners, from enthusiastic amateurs to seasoned professionals, are devoted to acquiring as much knowledge and cultural information about their plants as possible. This book has been planned to provide not only the basic fundamentals but detailed information on all aspects of the marvelous plants that make up the genus *Paeonia*.

Chapter 1

The Peculiar Charms and Specialty Uses of Peonies

For many, their days, and indeed their lives, are enhanced by beauty. True of art and music, it is just as true of nature and particularly of flowers. We may avert our eyes from nature that is "red in tooth and claw," but ahh the flowers!

The charms of peonies are manifold. They are one of the most versatile perennials to grow in temperate gardens, and their longevity, willingness to remain in their assigned plot, fragrance, and foliage interest add immeasurably to their appeal. Yet, naturally enough, many are first drawn to peonies by the sheer beauty of their huge masses of vivid blossoms, which appear in a radiant array of red, rose, lavender, and yellow, and every imaginable shade of pink and white. Viewed from a distance, they are seen as waves of color, inevitably drawing the viewer ever closer to admire the individual bloom. Peonies vary from huge, many-petaled blossoms to fine goblets of color, often cradling a heart of gold.

From the spring's first red shoots, slowly unfurling to rich greens, to the deep-toned bronzes and purples of autumn, the robust and various foliage of peonies is a three-season delight. Some species even sport delicate, intricately divided fern- or fennel-like foliage. As if all this were not bounty enough, all types of peony foliage provide great season-long cover for the unattractive foliage of dying early bulbs and perennials.

Just one glimpse of these flowers of remembrance and I am reminded of my grandmother's garden. Then as now, peonies are the essence of the word *perennial,* thriving in the same spot for forty years or more. Indeed, no other perennial is, in all likelihood, as long-lived. If properly cared for, they survive the harshest winters and return to delight us for decades of springs. Well-documented historical accounts of certain garden specimens tell of individual plants that are still going strong after seventy years—a few even longer.

From the earliest of times, fragrances and perfumes have lent a special cachet to people's lives. Not only have they been used for their intrinsic attractiveness but to camouflage the malodorous in eras when few people bathed: perfumes were to people what heavy French sauces were to overly ripe foodstuffs. In modern times, fragrances continue to perform more subtle masking tasks or enhance personal attractiveness. Whether exploding from a strip of paper in a magazine advertisement or wafting from a cut-crystal bottle, many of today's most pleasing scents are floral in origin. Fragrance and flowers, especially as linked to love, chivalry, and a place of retreat, were essential elements in the creation of the mystique of the garden—occidental or oriental. Who has failed when walking through a garden to bend to smell a rose, or to capture one fragrant sprig to carry back into the house?

Peonies are one of a small group of desirable fragrance sources. Not all peony species and cultivars are fragrant, but those that are can be classified by which of five distinct odors they produce. The first, a rose scent, is best typified by such cultivars as 'Festiva Maxima' or 'Mme. de Verneville'. A whiff of honey is frequently given off by those flowers with bright yellow central petals—'Louise Marx', 'Philomele', and 'Top Brass', for example. The tang of lemon is confined to the tree peonies; *Paeonia lutea* and some of its hybrids, such as 'Alice Harding', 'Chromatella', 'Roman Gold', and 'Surprise', are particularly outstanding in this respect. The fourth scent, described variously as sweet or yeasty, is usually found to some degree in suffruticosa tree peonies. While objectionable to some, most find the fragrance delightful.

But not all peony fragrances are attractive. Some can only be characterized as unpleasant, sometimes referred to as soapy, bitter, or even medicinal. This quality is usually associated with pollen-bearing cultivars, the red-flowered single forms of which seem to be the worst offenders. It is also occasionally found in doubles, such as 'Mons. Martin Cahuzac' or 'Victoire de la Marne'. Avoid these bitter-smelling forms as cut flowers, but continue to enjoy them in the garden, where their odor is imperceptible. On the other hand, as a general rule, the full double *Paeonia lactiflora* cultivars, sometimes referred to as Chinese or French peonies, may be counted on to possess in varying degrees a pleasing fragrance, stronger in pinks and whites.

Peonies are landscape flowers supreme. A single plant of either member of the graceful Windflower strain, the striking height of 'Pageant' or 'White Innocence', or almost any tree peony serves well as a specimen in the lawn or in pairs flanking an entranceway. Three plants of 'Coral Charm' make a big, bold splash of color equal to that of any shrub, yet never grow out of bounds. Tiny, fern-leaved *Paeonia tenuifolia* is beautiful both in bloom and for its lasting foliage value in the rock garden.

Tree peonies and the smaller herbaceous forms can be successfully grown in large pots or containers for years, requiring only that their tops and roots be kept in balance. In Asian cultures, potted tree peonies are prominently displayed when in bloom so that they can be contemplated in all their glory for hours on end.

Peonies are among the most drought-resistant perennials. In the wild, many species burst into growth with spring's first moisture and as quietly go dormant as the ground dries. Their cultivars have inherited their parents' ability to withstand drought. Even though the sun bakes the ground, the tubers remain plump and firm, retaining the nutrients needed for the next year's growth. This drought resistance makes them ideal candidates for water-conserving gardens.

Many gardeners in rural areas are plagued by wild deer and rabbits that regularly ravage their gardens. Not so with peonies. One nip, and the animals leave them alone thereafter, an abhorrence presumably due to the bitter taste imparted by the phenol compounds found in the plant's foliage and flowers. This characteristic makes peonies a natural choice to beautify rural gardens where animal damage is a recurring challenge.

Peonies are unsurpassed when cut and brought inside, to enhance the spaces in which we live and gather. Traditionally the heavy, long-stemmed lactiflora doubles have been the preferred cut flowers of the trade, but these as well as the lighter forms make wonderful cut flowers for the home. A short-stemmed tree peony bloom floating in a crystal bowl, a few nodding heads in an Ikebana arrangement, or a boisterous, multicolored bouquet of a dozen or more to grace the entrance hall or dining room table, all give family and friends great pleasure.

The vase life of peonies cut for home decoration can be extended by following a few simple steps. Cut as early in the morning as possible, using a sharp knife or clippers. Take care to leave behind at least two leaves on each remaining stem, and never remove more than one half of the flowers on any given plant. Immediately place the stems in a bucket with several inches of water containing a preservative, such as Floralife. Select flowers that are completely open if the full effect of a bouquet is wanted that very day, or at various stages of opening if the bouquet is intended to last longer. Flowers transport better, however, if picked in bud.

When you are ready to create the arrangement, strip off the leaves that will be under water and recut the stems another inch or so, while they are submerged. This keeps air from entering the stem and blocking the channels for water transport.

Be sure that both the water and the vase used for display are clean. Vase life can be extended by using tepid water and a floral preservative. Several solutions, such as the aforementioned Floralife, are on the market, but a perfectly fine preservative can be made at home. One recipe calls for eight to sixteen ounces of any regular (containing sucrose, not diet), clear (so that it will not color the water!), citrus soft drink, an equal amount of lukewarm tap water, and half a teaspoon of household bleach. A second mixture is comprised of one quart tap water, two tablespoons of *fresh* lemon or lime juice, one tablespoon sugar, and half a tablespoon of household bleach.

The distinctive charm of single peonies should be more widely utilized in flower arrangements. Some object to their shedding pollen, but this does not occur for several days. A shorter vase life perhaps, compared to their more popular double counterparts, but still well worth the effort.

In short, gardeners—whether starting anew or adding to their landscape—will find peonies a smart choice for many reasons. In perennial beds, as specimen plants, or in a cutting garden, the value and charm of the peony is hard to equal.

SPECIALTY USES

Commercially speaking, the peony is usually thought of in connection with the production and sale of roots for garden landscapes, but there are other important uses. The production of peonies as specialty cut flowers generates the greatest income, and the growing market for dried flowers must also be considered. Finally, in China, an ancient tradition continues: acres and acres of peonies are still grown for their healing properties alone.

Cut flowers

Peonies make excellent cut flowers, and a very large commercial market is in place for them. Uncounted numbers of growers all over the temperate world cultivate peonies to meet the demands of the trade. Some grow only a few for their own floral designs. Others sell them at retail, usually along with other flowers, fruits, and vegetables at roadside stands. Some have large operations, where peonies are but one of many different perennials and annuals grown for the wholesale cut flower market. Stems may be sent on to retail florists, to brokers for export, or to the large wholesale markets and auctions. A few growers make cut peonies their major crop; see Chapter 8 for particulars.

The worldwide wholesale peony cut flower trade began in earnest when Amasa Kennicott began to sell blooms to Chicago florists at a penny apiece back in 1884. Demand soon increased the price to 25 cents a dozen. Delighted with this bonanza, Kennicott found a small building that could be sealed up, put a ton of ice in it, and discovered he could successfully store peony buds for a month or more before selling them. This was the start of the still-flourishing Kennicott Brothers Commission house. At about the same time, George Klehm (Carl's uncle) tried to rent cold storage space for his peonies. The owner turned him down, fearing that the moisture would spoil other goods in the cold room. Klehm bribed an employee, who looked the other way while Klehm snuck five buckets of buds into a room filled with lemons. All went well until he was caught trying to remove his flowers. The lemons were unscathed, but Klehm had to pay $5 more to recover his peonies.

Such early undertakings highlight some aspects of the extraordinarily durable postharvest constitution of peonies. Not only can they be picked in the bud stage and easily transported long distances but they are capable of withstanding the rigors of from four to six weeks in cold storage and will then open well when brought out into room temperature. These admirable qualities were the impetus for the development of the flourishing peony cut flower trade. The greatest demand was for doubles, the larger the better, on long stems. Other nurserymen joined Klehm in putting peonies in cold storage, and an industry was launched. Soon Western Cold Storage Company in Chicago had 70,000 square feet devoted to this single flower during the spring. By the 1920s, hundreds of thousands of peonies were reaching wholesale markets in the major cities all over North America. Some, shipped in refrigerated railway cars, would travel 2000 miles or more before reaching their destination.

In the early 1950s, the United States embarked on the construction of its great interstate highway system, which led to much faster ground transportation. This permitted greenhouses located further from metropolitan centers to rush cut flowers of all kinds—not just those that held up well postharvest—to market in refrigerated trucks. The resultant demand for nontraditional flowers radically reduced demand for all traditional cut flowers, peonies included.

Dried flowers

The practice and art of flower drying and arrangement has existed for hundreds of years. In North America, dried flowers were featured in the winter decorations of early residences, and in fact it was their use in the recreated village of Colonial Williamsburg in Virginia that brought dried flowers back to prominence in our century. In response to this increasing demand for dried plant material of all sorts, large numbers of dried peonies are now produced commercially under a variety of exacting conditions.

At home our interest is similarly piqued. Dried peonies are particularly effective in bouquets or wreaths, either by themselves or combined with other flowers. In addition to peony flowers, the leaves of tree peonies, particularly the cut-leaved hybrids, dry well and add a welcome touch of green to dried arrangements. Single buds or individual flowers can be dried in several simple ways. Whatever the flower type and however prepared, dried peony blossoms extend our enjoyment of spring's beautiful peony blooms and are a good antidote to winter's gloom.

The simplest way to dry peonies is to hang them upside down in a warm, dry, dark place. Single flowers in red or dark pink do best using this treatment; the lighter pinks and whites dry to a less desirable parchment-like color.

Flowers should be cut during the day when the foliage is dry. Choose flowers that have just opened, and handle them carefully to avoid bruising. Stems 4–8 inches in length are most desirable. Strip the leaves from the stems, and gather the stems into bunches, up to ten stems per bunch. Bind tightly with rubber bands, placing them as close to the stem ends as possible. Attach curtain hooks or short, bent wires to the rubber bands, and hang the bunches—buds down—on wire or coat hangers suspended in the drying area. The flowers take up to two weeks to dry fully.

A popular method of drying small numbers of opened flowers employs the absorbent material silica gel. Under a microscope, silica gel resembles granulated sugar; each spongelike crystal can hold many times its weight in moisture. One commercially available product, Petalast, contains blue crystals that turn to pink when their moisture-absorbing capacity has been reached. Silica gel may be used over and over; simply sieve the material to remove any bits of broken petals and redry.

Open peony seed pods make an interesting addition to natural dried arrangements. The pods of the lactiflora cultivar 'Rivida' are particularly attractive, as are those of suffruticosa tree peonies. Cut the pods with 2–3 inches of stem after the pods are fully opened. Remove the seeds and allow the woody pods to dry completely.

If kept in an area of low humidity, such as a heated home, dried peonies will remain attractive for months and even years. Dried flowers should be put back in dry storage as soon as spring arrives, however, for open windows lead to higher humidity. Seal them in plastic bags and store in the dark. They can then be brought out again the following fall. *Preserving Flowers* (Moffitt 1989) is an excellent guide to the various methods of home drying.

Peonies and medicine

Magic, myth, and medicine are finely interwoven in peony history. The first written description of the genus *Paeonia* is found in the *Chinese Materia Medica*, published in Quin about 200 B.C. In it, peonies are simply described as medicinal herbs; no existing records from this time speak to their exact use.

In classical times, plants noted for their medicinal specialty use were viewed with awe, believed to be gifts from the gods. The ancient Greeks had the highest regard for peonies for this precise reason. The name of the genus itself, *Paeonia*, is a Latinized rendering of the Greek word *paionia*, which commemorates Paion, physician to the gods and mythological discoverer of the medicinal applications of many herbs. Greek legend tells of the rivalry between Paion, a student who knew all the herbal remedies, and his former teacher. This teacher, Asclepius, was intensely jealous of Paion's success and plotted the murder of his apprentice. But Hades, injured by one of Hercules' arrows, was treated and healed by Paion; grateful for Paion's care, the god transformed the young physician into a plant so that the wrathful Asclepius would not recognize him. This plant is now called *Paeonia officinalis,* and it can still be found growing on the hills and mountainsides of Greece.

The various European vernacular languages adapted the Latin name of the group into their vocabularies: *peony* or *paeony* in English, *pivoine* in French, *päonie* or *päonien* in German, and *paeonia* in Spanish. Little if any attention was paid to defining the various species of this useful plant, however, and all peonies were commonly referred to by the Dioscoridian name of *Paeonia officinalis,* whether reference was to this species or to others, including *P. lactiflora.*

An anonymous 3rd-century Greek poet described the peony as "the Queen of Herbs, a plant with large fleshy roots and an unpleasant taste." The bitter taste was viewed as an indication of its medicinal virtue by the ancient Greek herb-gatherers, or rhizotomists (root cutters). They were not far wrong. As those who have grown peonies in any number know, some roots do indeed emit a pungent odor when cut and are bitter if tasted. Furthermore, severed roots may take as long as two years to rot completely. We now attribute these qualities to the presence of phenol compounds, tannins, antiviral substances, and paeonal, which is a bacteriostatic.

An earlier historical figure of the classical age, the Roman philosopher and naturalist Pliny the Elder (ca. A.D. 23–79), provides us with the first European description of the peony plant and its seeds in his *Natural History.* Already, he tells us, among medicinal plants, "the plant known as Paeonia is the most ancient of all," renowned for its efficacy in curing some twenty ills, including jaundice, gnawing pains of the stomach, and tracheal problems. Pliny's Elizabethan translator Philemon, with a touch more magic than matter, rendered a passage in 1601 thus: "The herbe must be gathered in the night season; for if the Rainbird, Woodpeck or Hicksway, called Piscus Martius, should chance to see it gathered, he would fly in the face and be ready to pick out the eyes of him or her that had it." Such superstitions were, of course, promulgated by the herb-gatherers, who quite enjoyed their monopoly and sought to cloak their arcane practice with an aura of mystery. Many of their patients were so convinced of the plant's magical properties that they grew them as protection against the "evil eye." Culpepper's *Complete Herbal*, published in London during the 17th century, offers more particular prescriptions: "The root, fresh gathered, cures the falling-sickness [and] is effectual for cleansing the womb after childbirth and easing the mother."

It's not surprising that peonies were eventually worked into diets as a preventative. By the Middle Ages peony seeds were a common foodstuff among the poorer classes. They were crushed and used as a seasoning, most often to flavor stews. Wealthier folk bought the whole peony root and baked it to serve as a side dish, especially prized as an accompaniment to roast pork.

Dioscorides included the peony as a medicinal plant in the first *Materia Medica* of the Western world. This magisterial work went through uncounted revisions at the hands of both Christian and Muslim writers, from its initial appearance in the 1st century A.D. until its last edition in the 16th century. For hundreds of years then, in both Europe and Asia, before the nearly universal adoption of the principles of modern Western medicine, peonies figured as ingredients in folk cures.

Both the bark and roots of tree peonies as well as the roots of certain herbaceous species continue to be an integral element of herbal medicines. In particular, extracts of peony plant parts play a major role in traditional Chinese medicine (sometimes abbreviated as TCM), the present medical treatment of choice for more than a billion people worldwide. In agrarian China, where more than half of the households are headed by farmers, some 60 percent of the population continue to rely solely upon traditional Chinese medicine, and many more Chinese citizens depend upon it to some lesser degree. In North America and Europe, the influence of traditional Chinese medicine is growing, and a number of accredited colleges offer degrees in its practice.

The Chinese system employs both acupuncture and herbal remedies, utilizing the roots of *Paeonia lactiflora* (called Radix Paeonae Alba, or bai-shao) and *P. veitchii* (called Radix Paeonae Rubra, or chi-shao), as well as the roots of suffruticosa tree peonies (mu-dan-pi). The roots of *P. emodi* are also occasionally employed.

Bai-shao is used for female disorders, chest pains, and blood or liver disorders. Its roots are cultivated; many are grown in communes outside of Shanghai. Chi-shao is responsibly harvested from roots collected in the wild. It is used in conjunction with other herbs for circulatory problems and is thought to reduce swelling and to allay pain. Mu-dan-pi, whose history as a medicinal traces back at least 500 years, is made of both dried root bark and root cortex. It has bacteriostatic, antipyretic, and anticonvulsant properties and has been shown to inhibit the release of an anaphylactic mediator in allergic reactions (Ellis 1992). Various forms of ancient Chinese herbal remedies that include peonies as an ingredient have names which translate to "Clear-the-Stomach Powder," "Fifth and Sixth Heavenly Stem Pill," and "Clear-the-Liver Decoction."

Further details on this final and most interesting specialty use of peonies can be found in Foster and Chongxi (1992).

Chapter 2

The Modern Peony and Its Hybridizers

Peonies have been described as being "like roses but without thorns and having flowers twice as large." No wonder, then, that the lactiflora cultivars took Europe by storm in 1784 upon their introduction from China, where they had been developed over the centuries as the most revered of ornamental garden flowers (Phillips and Rix 1991). The first tree peony grown in the West was brought to England shortly thereafter, in 1789, by a Mr. Duncan of the British East India Company, who had been retained by Joseph Banks to procure this "new" plant (Haworth-Booth 1963). One of these first tree peonies, a very double variety with magenta flowers, was transported to Kew Gardens near London. A perfect representative of the endurance for which peonies generally would become known, it thrived for more than fifty years before being removed to make way for a new building. At its premature end, it was reported to be 8 feet high and 10 feet wide. At about the same time, Duncan himself planted a double pink tree peony in the family gardens near Arboath (Haw and Lauener 1990). A direct descendant of this plant was successfully moved to the Royal Botanic Garden, Edinburgh, in 1988.

Soon after these original importations, an increasing number of peonies, many of the very heavy, double-petaled lactiflora type, were brought over from China—hence the term Chinese peonies—by collectors and nurseries from various countries in Europe and the United Kingdom. By the early 1800s several English and French nurseries in particular were growing and selling herbaceous peonies, some the product of plant collection expeditions in the eastern Mediterranean, some resulting from the crossing of species native to Europe and the Middle East. The delightful peony had caught the public's fancy—and the hybridizing had begun.

Many of these early cultivars remain in the trade. For instance, the Frenchman Lemon, the first European to produce and market new cultivars from seed-propagated plants, introduced 'Edulis Superba', which is still valued by producers of cut flowers, in 1824. Many of his fellow countryman Crousse's introductions—'Asa Gray', 'Avalanche', and 'Felix Crousse' among them—are still considered standards today, and for landscape use his 'Mons. Jules Elie' is probably the most widely grown pink double of the 20th century. 'Festiva Maxima', a white double still widely grown, is generally thought to have been hybridized by Miellez of France in 1851, though its origin is sometimes credited to an anonymous Belgian. Etienne Mechin and his grandson Auguste Dessert developed a number of enduring cultivars, perhaps the most notable of which is 'Mons. Martin Cahuzac'. Introduced in 1899, it is still one of the deepest red doubles available. Readers interested in learning more about the early history and development of herbaceous and tree peony cultivars are well advised to consult *The Peony* (Harding 1993). It is a fascinating tale, begun long ago in China and Japan and played out on both sides of the Atlantic.

In any case, whether described as French or Chinese, these were the beautiful, enormous double peonies that flooded the U.S. cut flower trade for so many years. Hundreds of acres of lactiflora cultivars were grown to fill the demand. When improved transportation methods opened the market for nontraditional flowers following World War II, commercial peony flower growers reduced acreage and in the process eliminated many of the older varieties. Relatively few of these heirloom cultivars continue to be grown in North America.

The situation in Europe and the United Kingdom is entirely different. *Paeonin*, the 1989 genus monograph by the German Reinhilde Frank, illustrates that many of these oldsters are still highly valued and grown in nurseries including Kelway in England, Klose and von Zeppelin in Germany, and Le Pivoinerie and Pivoines Michel Rivière in France.

And just what is the situation on this side of the Atlantic? With the exception of two rare species possessing little landscape value—*Paeonia brownii* and *P. californica*—peonies are not native to North America. Ornamental peonies were brought to Canada and the United States by the early settlers. Thomas Jefferson made reference to them in his garden notebooks, written in the mid-1700s, and by 1829, William Price (as quoted in Harding 1993), proprietor of the Linnaean Botanic Garden, summed up the climate thus: "No class of flowers has recently attracted more attention in Europe than the peonies. . . . Most of the varieties are extremely splendid and others possess striking peculiarities. Anticipating that a similar taste would be evinced in this country, the proprietor has, by great exertion, obtained every variety possible from Europe and also a number from China."

A similar taste indeed. After the many successes in peony breeding that marked the late 1800s, a lull occurred and the emphasis shifted from Europe to North America. Following the end of the American Civil War in 1865, the promise of free land sent tens of thousands streaming west in covered wagons. As valuable as space was in their crude conveyances, the settlers almost always managed to tuck in a treasured plant or two. Few plants of other genera survived the long and arduous journey, but the "piney toe" (a dormant peony eye with attached root), by contrast, fared quite well. Fortunately, most of these piney toes were eyes and roots of *Paeonia officinalis*, a species that strikes adventitious buds. Such a root can send up new growth, and thus even if the first year's growth is lost, the plant can recover the next year and thrive.

And so the peony conquered another continent—a remarkably successful immigrant. In Oregon, where our nursery is located, a tree peony that was brought across the prairies and mountains from Bethel, Missouri, in 1860 lives on. The plant has even been moved several times since its 1500-mile journey. It is now entrusted to the care of Claire McCarthy of Monmouth, the fifth generation in direct descent from the pioneer who cherished it over the long trail.

The end of the 19th century saw the decline of lavish estate gardens, large-scale settings for which the famed Olmsted brothers and other landscape architects and designers called for peonies by the hundreds. It marked the beginning of the rapid rise of interest in peonies by hybridizers, commercial growers, and home gardeners with more modest plots—which brings us to the time of the modern peony and the people who brought it to us.

Any recounting of the development of modern peonies, here and abroad, must focus on the breakthroughs made by a large number of devoted growers and breeders. Some were professional nursery people, involved with family firms founded more than a century earlier by such venerable old-timers as Archie Brand, James Kelway, John Klehm, and Herman Wild; others began as amateurs and then moved on to peony breeding. If the tremendous expenditure of time is taken into account, few of these operations could be said to be profitable in a way that is counted in dollars, pounds, pfennigs, and yen. Scarcely one seedling in a thousand from most open-pollinated plants would be worth introducing, and yet numerous successes came only at the hands, literally, of these very patient hybridizers and as the result of chance garden crosses as well. Although some of these breeders made significant contributions to the development of hybrids in other genera, many of them spent their entire lives working only with the genus *Paeonia*.

Since most of those party to this burst of activity constituted an informal network, with everything from stock to pollen moving from one place and person to another with remarkable ease, this is a story perhaps best told with an eye toward the people and nurseries involved. Let's proceed alphabetically, then, rather than chronologically, through the history of the intensive breeding operations of the 20th century.

Edward Auten, Jr. (1881–1974) was a Harvard man; upon graduation, he returned to his hometown of Princeville, Illinois, and went into banking —but his passion was gardening. At first he was partial to roses, but he lost most of his specimens to frost in the winter of 1909. Determined to seek out hardier plants, he wisely settled on peonies in 1910.

What began as a hobby soon evolved into a full-time occupation. Auten introduced about 275 peony cultivars over the course of his lifetime, but he was particularly noted for his reds, mostly herbaceous forms such as 'Big Ben' and 'Chocolate Soldier'. His hybrid 'Early Scout' (the result of a cross between *Paeonia tenuifolia* and the lactiflora 'Richard Carvel') was made with pollen sent him by Lyman Glasscock. In 1968, fifty-eight years after peonies first caught his eye, he was awarded the American Peony Society's Saunders Memorial Medal for "his outstanding contributions to garden peonies and hybrids."

Myron Bigger (b. 1902) of Topeka, Kansas, left dairy farming behind to grow cut flowers. He came to peonies by way of two other traditional specialty flower crops, gladioli and daylilies. At its peak, his nursery was growing eight acres of peonies with a harvest of 72,000–84,000 flowers each year. The buds were wrapped and held in cold storage until required by the trade.

Active in the American Peony Society and president from 1958 to 1960, he has been hybridizing and growing peonies for more than sixty years. His 'Kansas', one of the most popular and reliable double reds, received the American Peony Society's Gold Medal in 1957. He is also famous for 'Westerner', the society's Gold Medal winner in 1982 and perhaps the most widely known pink of the Japanese type. His unique and unusual lactifloras 'Orange Lace' (an orangy pink Japanese) and 'Pink Derby' (a pink double of outstanding form and substance) are deserving of equal acclaim.

William Bockstoce (1876–1963), born and raised in Pittsburgh, Pennsylvania, was a building contractor by trade. Though he pursued a wide variety of horticultural interests, peonies were his professed favorite. He developed a dependable technique for getting species that usually flower at different times to bloom simultaneously. Working primarily with crosses between *Paeonia lactiflora* and *P. officinalis*, he sped up the flowering of late-blooming species by controlling the growth of the plants in cold frames. Many of his sixteen introductions remain popular, including the double reds 'Carol', the intensely fragrant 'Diana Parks', and 'Henry Bockstoce'. His most unusual cultivar is 'Bess Bockstoce', known as 'Rose Heart' in Canada, an unusual, fragrant double whose flower opens as a solid rose and changes to a pink center surrounded by a broad band of white. Upon his death, his stock plants and seedlings went to Henry Landis, a Canadian collector who distributed them on a very limited basis.

Oliver Brand (1844–1921) opened the first commercial nursery in the state of Minnesota in 1867, in Faribault, with an assortment of peonies and grafted apple trees. By 1894, he had amassed some 1000 "fancy" peony cultivars as propagating stock. His interest in the plant was more than matched by his son Archie (1871–1953), who began breeding at the turn of the century. From this first batch of seed, planted in 1901, came 'Richard Carvel', a red double that is still widely grown.

Archie Brand attended his first peony show in 1913, traveling by train, streetcar, and foot to St. Paul, Minnesota. He was accompanied by a friend, and together they carried eight boxes of peony buds the final half mile from the end of the trolley line to the exhibition site. Despite the fact that the seedlings were unnamed cultivars, they were the hit of the show.

Myrtle Gentry, a local schoolteacher, was hired to run the Brand Nursery office in 1918 and three years later was made a partner in the nursery. By the 1920s peonies were the leading ornamental crop grown in Minnesota. It is estimated that one third of these were grown in the area around Faribault, in the southeastern part of the state.

Peonies have thrived in the same Brand Nursery soil for more than 125 years now, and the deep, glacial moraine soils there have never needed fertilizing. Rather, peonies were grown as part of a seven-year crop rotation: four years in peonies, followed by a different perennial for two years, and finally, an annual cover crop, grown and plowed under.

At the American Peony Society's 1920 show in Chicago, Brand seedlings proved so popular that seventy-two orders were taken for the roots of one particular cultivar at $50 a root. Some customers were willing to pay $100 each for divisions of certain other Brand introductions. (One hundred dollars in 1920, it should be noted, is the equivalent of nearly $1000 today.)

Early Archie Brand seedlings, all from *Paeonia lactiflora*, are noted for their vigor, clear color, large flower size, and extreme hardiness. A great number are still widely grown today. The salmon-pink 'Hansina Brand' is the only cultivar to win the coveted Grand Champion trophy at three different national exhibitions. The flowers of 'Myrtle Gentry' are widely considered the most fragrant of all peonies. Other Brand peonies still frequently found include 'Krinkled White' and two pink doubles, 'Blanche King' and 'Martha Bulloch'.

The Brands were not interested in selling cut flowers, but their business was perhaps the largest producer of peony roots in the world throughout the 1920s. Departing from the widespread practice of fall planting, Brand planted some peony roots in the spring. These were packed in wooden barrels in the fall and stored over the winter in a sandstone cave owned by a local brewery. Success was attributed to their being planted immediately after removal from cold storage. They often looked poorly the first spring but would form new buds on the roots that emerged the second year.

The Brands had introduced their first seedlings in 1907 and enjoyed glory days through the 1920s. Then the Great Depression hit. Business was so bad that Brand plowed under his entire acreage of seedlings before they bloomed. His last introductions were made in 1943, from plants that had first flowered more than a decade earlier.

The Brands got out of hybridizing but continued on as growers of peonies; when Archie Brand died in 1953, he had thirty-two acres in root production. Three years later Miss Gentry sold the nursery to two local businessmen, the Tischler brothers, Archie and Robert, of whom we shall hear more later.

For our part, what started as a Rogers family hobby collection, **Caprice Farm Nursery** in Sherwood, just south of Portland in western Oregon, was turned into a part-time business by my wife, Dorothy, and me in the late 1970s. Our son and daughter, Rick Rogers and Robin Rogers Blue, are now partners in the family firm, a mail-order nursery specializing in peonies, daylilies, and beardless iris.

Our herbaceous peony collection began with the last stock of Walter Marx, some of whose cultivars we were proud to introduce (see Chapter 6, "Propagation by Seed") and select cultivars from Klehm, Reath, and Tischler. Our herbaceous hybrids came from individual eye divisions (one each!) of Saunders' introductions, purchased from the Goldsmiths.

We augmented tree peonies from Reath's with old suffruticosa plants from Max Reeher's property in Laurel, Oregon. Many of these plants were more than fifty years old at the time of their removal to Caprice Farm, and they had been neglected for years, left to fend for themselves in a field overrun with blackberry brambles and sumac. Even so, some still bravely bloomed, a tribute to their hardiness. A front-end loader was required to move the plants, whose roots were as long as 4 feet or more and whose stems often approached 4 inches in diameter. Surprisingly, many of them "fell apart" on digging. All were divided and planted that fall, and at least 65 percent survived the journey.

Lyman Cousins (1889–1973) of Ontario, Canada, inherited an abiding love of plants from his grandfather, an ardent horticulturist, with whom he worked. A noted artist and lithographer as well, Cousins' interest was first caught by the lines and colors of the genus *Iris*, and he succeeded in hybridizing a winner of the prestigious Dykes Medal of the American Iris Society.

Turning to peonies and work with *Paeonia lactiflora*, he created the still-popular white double, 'Ann Cousins'. Soon, using other species peonies, he wove an intricate network of advanced-generation hybrids, involving complex combinations of *P. lactiflora, P. mlokosewitschii, P. officinalis, P. peregrina,* and *P. wittmanniana.* Thankfully Cousins was a dedicated recordkeeper, and his notebooks, detailing the history of his crosses, were published in volume 196 of the American Peony Society Bulletin. The Cousins notebooks have served as an invaluable guide for subsequent peony breeders.

The Cousins hybrids were first exhibited at the American Peony Society's annual show in 1970, where their extraordinarily luminous new colors, including peach and salmon, earned them the name "inner glow" hybrids and captured the prestigious Saunders Memorial Medal. His stock was acquired by Klehm Nursery, which introduced many of his crosses. The superb glow of 'Etched Salmon' is a good example of his work with color.

Kent Crossley started his New Peony Farm in 1980 with cultivars obtained following the breakup of the main Brand Nursery. Like the Brands' growing fields before him, Crossley's also benefit from the fertile soil of Faribault, Minnesota, often referred to as the peony center of the world. Crossley has a keen eye for peonies and has added stock from other breeders as well. A practicing physician, he not only directs the nursery but is on the faculty of the state's medical school. He served as the president of the American Peony Society from 1989 to 1991.

Nassos Daphnis, a New York City artist, entered into a partnership with the tree peony breeder William Gratwick, keeping the hybridizing program Gratwick had undertaken in 1946 going full tilt. Each spring for a number of years, Daphnis would spend several weeks at Pavilion, Gratwick's estate in western New York State, evaluating new seedlings with Gratwick and hybridizing his extensive collection of tree peonies. Daphnis' new crosses resulted in bold new colors, never before seen in tree peonies.

From these efforts have come more than thirty advanced-generation introductions. Many have won high favor, including 'Boreas' (a dark burgundy-red), 'Gauguin' (yellow with a center and radiating rays of red), 'Leda' (an unusual combination of mauve-pink and plum), 'Tria' (the earliest of the hybrids to bloom, with three canary-yellow blossoms per stem), and 'Zephyrus' (a combination of pink and peach with ruby-red flares).

Toichi Domoto (b. 1902) grew his peonies in Hayward, California, southeast of San Francisco, where the temperatures seldom drop below freezing, even in winter. Domoto's father, a wholesale nurseryman, started importing tree peonies from Japan about 1900. Toichi followed in his father's footsteps and eventually overtook him, becoming interested in hybridizing early on. He began his breeding program with stock plants his father had imported, and by 1937 he had five acres of seedlings.

Forced off the family land by the World War II internment of those of Japanese descent, he started in again after the war on a smaller scale and with a new focus, building what was to become one of the West Coast's leading bonsai nurseries. Though he maintained his interest in peony breeding, it remained only a sideline. The seedling tree peonies he produced were not registered; rather, he sold them to landscapers by color. In 1985 Domoto sold his stock plants to Klehm Nursery, keeping a few in the landscape around his home. Klehm Nursery has since introduced one of his plants as 'Toichi Ruby'.

Orville Fay of Northwood, Illinois, spent his days as a taste and color expert for a large candy manufacturer, but he had a master's eye for flowers. A leading hybridizer of iris and daylilies, his skills earned him a total of five Dykes and Stout Medals, the highest awards given by the American Iris and Hemerocallis Societies, respectively. In addition, he was one of the first plant breeders to treat diploid seedlings with colchicine, thereby converting them to tetraploids and so greatly increasing their breeding potential.

His interest extended to the colorful peony as well. Fay visited nearby Mission Gardens in Techny, Illinois, and received permission from master gardener Brother Charles to gather hybrid peony seed from the mission beds there. After diligently searching every plant in every row, he turned up only four sound seeds. But what a treasure they were. All five of Fay's peony introductions trace to this tiny company, and four of the resulting hybrids remain in great demand. They are the pale yellow 'Prairie Moon' (1959); the deep pink 'Paula Fay' (1968), perhaps the most widely distributed of all the hybrids; the fragrant, coral-pink 'Coral Fay' (1973); and the glistening red 'Blaze' (1973).

Lyman Glasscock (1875–1972), a building contractor in Elmwood, Illinois, spent his leisure hours growing cut flowers for the Memorial Day market. To his great irritation, for it hurt sales, his lactiflora cultivars bloomed too late most years, while the flowers of *Paeonia officinalis* and its cultivars, though open in time, were wanting in quality.

In the spring of 1918, he mounded his dormant plants of *Paeonia officinalis* (including what he knew as *P. officinalis* 'Sunbeam', now considered to be *P. peregrina,* and what he called *P. officinalis* 'Otto Froebel', now *P. peregrina* 'Otto Froebel') with snow and ashes to delay their flowering long enough to allow crossing with the lactiflora cultivars. Working from this genetic pool, he created a number of outstanding hybrids, including 'Burma Ruby' (1951) and 'Golden Glow' (1935)—both winners of the American Peony Society's Gold Medal—and 'Salmon Glow' (1947). He is best remembered, however, for the most popular of all red doubles, 'Red Charm' (1944), another APS Gold Medal winner. One of his rare lactiflora introductions is the incomparable white double, 'Mother's Choice' (1950).

Upon Glasscock's death, his daughter, Elizabeth Falk, took over the garden. She has introduced several advanced-generation hybrids from the remaining seedlings. One worth special mention is the huge rose-red 'Old Faithful', probably the strongest-stemmed double of all herbaceous peonies and almost universally considered the finest herbaceous double hybrid.

William Gratwick (1904–1988) was a lifelong resident of Geneseo, New York. In 1946 he established one of the great tree peony nurseries of the world on his estate, Pavilion. Having acquired most of Saunders' tree peony plants, he too set out to combine the large, well-held flowers, strong stems, and elegant texture of the suffruticosa forms with the broader foliage, vigor, and yellow pigments of *Paeonia lutea*. Though not his intention, many of the resulting cultivars were three parts suffruticosa to one part lutea. He made every possible cross, but most of those he selected had parentage in these proportions.

Gratwick was also interested in selecting superior forms of suffruticosa tree peonies. To this end he obtained seed from the famous Chungai Nurseries in Japan. Four introductions, all singles, came from these seeds. Two of them, 'Companion of Serenity' (a soft pink with ruffles) and 'Guardian of the Monastery' (a swirl of cream, pink, and lavender), are highly prized.

Always the showman, Gratwick did much to promote tree peonies, holding open houses at flowering time and contributing collections of tree peonies to such institutions as the Eastman-Kodak Museum in Rochester, New York. His fruitful partnership with Nassos Daphnis further assured his tree peony legacy. The original stock plants are still growing on the Gratwick estate, under the supervision of Gratwick's daughter, Lee G. Mulligan. Klehm Nursery has first rights to all scions from the old Gratwick plants together with any new hybrids Daphnis decides to introduce.

Alice Harding (Mrs. Edward Harding) lived in New York City but maintained a country estate across the Hudson in New Jersey; she died in 1938, an internationally celebrated horticulturist. Her interest extended to nearly all cultivated garden plants, peonies included. To reward the hybridizers of her day, she generously established two cash awards of $100 each, one for the best herbaceous peony seedling bred in North America and the other for the best herbaceous seedling bred in France. In 1918 the American award was won by E. J. Shaylor for his 'Mrs. Edward Harding', and in 1922 the French award went to Emile Lemoine for 'Alice Harding'. Years later, in 1935, Lemoine introduced another 'Alice Harding', the yellow tree peony used to produce the first intersectional Itoh hybrids.

In 1917 she wrote *The Book of the Peony*, a classic long celebrated for its clear and precise information, followed in 1923 by her *Peonies in the Little Garden*. The best portions of each were recently combined into one volume, *The Peony* (1993). Though many of the cultivars she recommends have fallen out of favor, her literate writing style and charming sidetrips into peony lore make this book, especially as introduced and updated by Roy Klehm, well worth attending to.

Toichi Itoh of Japan made his inspired intersectional leap in the mid-1960s; until then a true, deep yellow–flowered herbaceous peony was nonexistent. He crossed Lemoine's suitably low, yellow, hybrid lutea tree peony 'Alice Harding' with a herbaceous double white lactiflora, 'Kakoden'. It was only after Itoh's death, when the seedlings of this cross first bloomed, that the enormity of his success was realized: he had produced a unique line of herbaceous-appearing plants with the added value of a dwarf growth habit. The four resulting hybrids share the common characteristics of a dominant lemon-yellow petal color and red flares. An American, Louis Smirnow, brought them to the States. 'Yellow Emperor' was introduced in 1974 along with the similar 'Yellow Crown', 'Yellow Dream', and 'Yellow Heaven'.

Another Japanese hybridizer, Yugen Higuchi, subsequently repeated the cross with similar results. As a result of this remarkable breeding effort, the American Peony Society has inaugurated a new and separate category for the intersectional hybrids deriving from this cross: Itoh hybrids.

Kelway and Son is England's premier peony nursery. Founded by James Kelway in 1851, it remained a family operation for three generations and continues today as a large general nursery featuring a number of peony cultivars, most of them Kelway originations. Their annual peony display at the famed Chelsea Flower Show of the Royal Horticultural Society has been one of the centers of attention at the exhibition for years.

Two standard results of Kelway's breeding of *Paeonia lactiflora* available in the international trade are 'Kelway's Glorious' and 'Baroness Schroeder'. These and many other of their introductions, such as 'Kelway's Gorgeous', 'Kelway's Lovely', and 'Kelway's Supreme', remain popular in Great Britain and Europe.

John Klehm, a German immigrant, established what became the Charles Klehm and Son Nursery near Chicago, Illinois, in 1852. The nursery grew evergreen trees exclusively, but John's son Charles Christian became intrigued by peonies after seeing Crousse's 'Mons. Jules Elie' at the Chicago World's Fair in 1899. After the fair, he turned the nursery in the direction of ornamental plants, and Klehm Nursery soon became the first large-scale peony cut flower grower in the country. At its height, Klehm Nursery had 200 acres devoted to peonies grown for both cut flower and root production.

A very active hybridizing program was undertaken as well. The first new cultivars from this breeding program were introduced in the 1950s, among them the enduring pink double, 'Emma Klehm', named for Carl G. Klehm's wife, Emma (née Kirchoff) Klehm. Carl was the third generation of the family to operate the nursery. He continued the selection program as well as the hybridizing program, all the while propagating his father's seedlings.

Carl was responsible for developing the Estate series from *Paeonia lactiflora*, the first peonies to be granted U.S. plant patents. The Estate series cultivars are especially noted for their strong stems and exemplary garden performance. Most produce excellent cut flowers as well, and they are widely grown throughout the temperate world; 'Charlie's White' and 'Raspberry Sundae' are perhaps the best known. The term "Estate" continues to designate the Klehm family introductions.

Carl had a discerning eye and took the lead in identifying and propagating the best peony selections of other hybridizers as well. These include Samuel Wissing's first corals, 'Coral Charm' and 'Coral Supreme'; 'America', the most brilliant of the red singles, from Nathan Rudolph; and the soft pink semi-double, 'Ann Berry Cousins', and the distinguished, edged double, 'Etched Salmon', both bred by Lyman Cousins.

Roy Klehm, grandson of Charles, is the present director of Klehm Nursery. Under his stewardship the nursery has become a leading retail producer of tree and herbaceous peonies, daylilies, hostas, and a wide variety of other perennials.

Heinz Klose and his wife Rosi, both master gardeners, started what is now the largest peony nursery in Germany in 1960, the internationally acclaimed Staudengärtnerei Heinz Klose in Lohfelden. The Kloses have developed an imposing concern specializing in peonies, delphiniums, hellebores, and hostas, all of which are included in their catalog describing some 3000 perennial plants. Specifically, they offer more than 500 peony species and cultivars, including more than twenty lactiflora introductions of Goos and Koenemann.

Their peony hybridizing efforts and expert selections have yielded such noted cultivars as 'Margarete Klose', and their plants regularly receive the highest honors at European shows, where a single display of theirs may feature some 10,000 blooms of seventy cultivars. They ship extensively throughout Europe as well as overseas. In 1993 the nursery was taken over by their son, Heinz-Richard Klose.

William Krekler was born in Ohio in 1900. He studied landscape architecture and was employed for a time by the famous firm of Olmsted Brothers, designing and installing estate gardens on Long Island, New York. After the dissolution of the Olmsted firm he returned to the town of Somerville in his home state; for years he owned and managed Peacock Nurseries in Akron, a concern which specialized in evergreen trees.

Though he never grew peonies for commercial sale, he was a longtime and enthusiastic hybridizer of the genus. In Somerville, he began a program based on planting a bushel of peony seed annually. Large stocks of plants were the result, and Krekler would astutely determine which of the many had a future in his breeding program. Those that did not he would generously donate to individuals and groups around the world, along with an abundance of seed. Every fall for years he mounted a "Free Peonies—U Dig" event. These annual digs were so popular that one year he ran out of the 1000 sheets of planting instructions he had had printed for participants.

He sold his peony plantation to the Charles Klehm and Son Nursery in 1977. In the course of his breeding program he registered more than 400 cultivars, the best of which continue to be propagated and introduced by Klehm Nursery. These include the highly regarded 'Eliza Lundy' (a dwarf version of 'Red Charm'), 'Cora Stubbs' (a raspberry-pink Japanese), 'Nice Gal' (a rose-pink semi-double), 'Camden' (a red single), and 'Martha Reed' (a creamy white double).

Roy Leighton started his commercial peony and lilac nursery in Edmonds, Washington, during this same period. For thirty years he devoted a large acreage to cut flower production. Most notably, he purchased from Silvia Saunders starts of all her father's hybrid introductions. He sold the operation to neighbors Keith and Peggy Goldsmith, whose activities are chronicled in the story on Professor Saunders.

Pierre Lemoine and his son Victor are known around the world for a wide variety of outstanding horticultural achievements in their work with several genera, *Syringa* and *Philadelphus* among them. Their nursery, located in Nancy, France, on a property once worked by the great 19th-century hybridizer Crousse, is responsible for many acclaimed lilac and mock orange introductions as well as peony cultivars.

Pierre's forebear Emile Lemoine was the first to cross two herbaceous peony species, *Paeonia lactiflora* and *P. wittmanniana*. Two of the resulting cultivars, 'Le Printemps' and 'Mai Fleuri', are still available. Many Lemoine hybrid tree peonies—such cultivars as 'Alice Harding', 'Chromatella', and 'Surprise'—resulted from crossing suffruticosa tree peonies with *P. lutea*; though they are not first-class landscape plants, they make fine flowers for cutting when floated in a shallow bowl, and their intoxicating fragrance quickly fills a room. Crossing the heavy, double suffruticosa form with *P. delavayi* yielded 'Sang Lorraine'.

The finest herbaceous peony introductions of the Lemoine nursery include 'Primevere' and 'Sarah Bernhardt'—a distinctly non-Gallic name that hints at the enormous popularity of these plants in the Edwardian gardens of England. Lemoine's lactiflora 'Le Cygne' is considered by many old-time peony collectors to be the most beautifully formed of all peony blossoms and can still be found in many contemporary catalogs. It is not as widely grown as it once was, however, perhaps because of its inconsistency in flowering from year to year in some areas.

Walter Marx (1908–1978) of Boring, Oregon, owned and operated the largest mail-order perennial nursery in the western United States during the 1950s and '60s. This renowned West Coast hybridizer courted East Coast customers by running large advertisements in the Sunday *New York Times*, and on the local front, his spring open houses, which featured both tree and herbaceous peonies, drew thousands. At one time he devoted forty acres to herbaceous peonies for root production; the tree peonies he offered were imported directly from Japan.

He concentrated on growing the most popular lactiflora cultivars of the day as well as some of the early hybrids. As for his breeding efforts, Marx often selected for a pleasing fragrance. He was particularly successful in capturing this trait with the red double 'Mt. St. Helens', and by far the most fragrant single known to me is his white 'Walter Marx'.

Pressure of land development in the Portland suburbs ultimately forced the closing of the nursery. In 1974 we at Caprice Farm Nursery purchased the peonies as well as the beardless iris still being grown on the Marx home property.

Arthur Murawska (1893–1968), born in Chicago, developed a lifelong passion for peonies as a child. Every autumn from the age of ten on, he could be found hanging around the local nursery, seeking any root scraps the dividers would toss his way. He filled his family's lot to brimming and then turned to his neighbors for additional growing space for his plants— such an effort overall that the street he grew up on was known locally as "Peony Row." Though his interest in peonies never diminished, it was not until the early 1960s, when he retired from his position as a locomotive engineer, that Murawska was finally able to devote all his time to his plants.

Most of Murawska's hybridizing work centered on *Paeonia lactiflora*. A sharp-eyed connoisseur of the peony as a garden plant, he was openly critical of the many lactiflora cultivars on the market that produced beautiful flowers but that were of poor habit, plants developed only for the ephemeral glory of the show bench. Murawska's cultivars reflect his insistence upon excellence in the entire plant. His 'Moonstone' is the most dependable blush-pink double available, while 'Princess Margaret' is usually considered the best of the dark pink doubles.

Leroy (Roy) Pehrson (1905–1982), a state highway engineer who lived in Lafayette, Minnesota, occupies an unusual place in the history of peony breeding. He was not active in the American Peony Society, nor did he operate a commercial nursery. What he was was a vigorous recruiter, sponsor, motivator, and coach of dedicated peony hybridizers, and what he did was to create for them *Paeonia*, the indispensable quarterly newsletter.

Pehrson's controlled breeding program, which depended upon advanced-generation hybrids, soon outgrew his limited space. To see his crosses grown out—and out of sheer generosity—he sent seed and unbloomed plants to any grower, amateur or professional, who was prepared to grow them on. One year he asked if he could make some crosses at Brand Nursery, about fifty miles away in Faribault. Robert Tischler, who was then running the place, agreed, only to find upon his return from an out-of-town trip that his display area was nothing but a rolling sea of white bags—no flowers in sight. Pehrson had pollinated and protected each and every open bloom.

Pehrson was intensely interested in creating intersectional hybrids and made wide crosses with a number of different cultivars of tree and herbaceous species with good results, perhaps the first American hybridizer to consistently make successful crosses of such cultivars. Much of his work with herbaceous forms was directed toward yellow-flowered cultivars. His 'Roy's Best Yellow', used extensively in turn as a parent by breeder Chris Laning, was the sensation of its day. Other crosses were based on Saunders' "little reds," 'Good Cheer' and 'Little Dorrit'. Though he enjoyed many triumphs, Pehrson's death cut short his complex breeding program. His works-in-progress were entrusted to Laning and William Seidl, who have continued elements of Pehrson's hybridizing program.

George Peyton (1874–1965) was a longtime budget director of Orange County, Virginia, and an avid amateur horticulturist who continued to make expert rounds in the garden plot well into his ninetieth year. A greatly talented man, he served as president of the American Peony Society for three years and as secretary and editor of the society's Bulletin for fourteen years more.

Always one for firsthand examination, he traveled extensively throughout North America to visit peonies and their growers, and at one time his own garden, a mecca for peony lovers, boasted some 2000 named cultivars. His international standing was such that Queen Elizabeth of England allowed him to name one exceptional peony, hybridized by Arthur Murawska, for her daughter. This is the highly regarded deep pink double, 'Princess Margaret'.

David Reath, a practicing veterinarian, gained unlimited space to advance his interest in peony hybridizing when he inherited the family farm, just outside the northern Michigan city of Vulcan. Reath was intrigued by flowering plants from childhood, first interested in *Iris*, and then *Narcissus* and *Hosta*. Thanks to the encouragement of his mentor, Brother Charles of Mission Gardens in Techny, Illinois, his eye turned to peonies. With the help of Edward Auten, Jr., Orville Fay, and the Saunderses, father and daughter—all of whom supplied him with plants and seed—he greatly expanded his breeding program. As a further boost he obtained the last of her father's plants from Silvia Saunders' nursery and has quite literally, by purchase and name verification, saved many of Saunders' hybrid tree peonies from extinction.

Indeed Reath has been credited with almost single-handedly focusing the interest of North Americans on quality, true-to-name tree peonies. He has introduced a semi-double form of *Paeonia rockii* (widely known as *P. suffruticosa* 'Rock's Variety' or 'Joseph Rock'), and his 'Golden Era', a yellow single hybrid that has proved fertile both ways, is now used extensively for hybridizing. Recent herbaceous cultivars of his breeding destined for fame—all doubles—include 'Pink Pearl' (an airy light pink), 'Rozella' (a glowing rose), and 'White Frost' (a beautifully shaped white).

Pivoines Michel Rivière in Crest, France, began in 1849 as Rutton and Rivière and is currently the largest nursery in Europe exclusively devoted to hybridizing and growing peonies. Michel Rivière—the celebrated author of the French peony book *Le Monde fabuleux des pivoines*—and his son Jean Luc represent the fifth and sixth generations of this esteemed family of peony growers. The focus of their present work is tree peonies.

Hans Sass (1868–1949) and his brother Jacob were prominent iris and peony hybridizers in the 1930s. Working in Washington, Nebraska, they developed a number of enduring and hardy peony cultivars derived from *Paeonia lactiflora*. Two of these introductions are still highly regarded not only for their beauty but also for their reliability: 'Elsa Sass' (a large double white) and 'Sea Shell' (a single pink), both winners of the American Peony Society's Gold Medal.

A. P. Saunders (1869–1953) was a professor of chemistry at Hamilton College in Clinton, New York; he retired from his teaching career in 1939. He is recalled here, however, as the father of the modern hybrid peony and a leader of the American Peony Society; he served as its president and was responsible for establishing and editing in its early years the society's Bulletin. Any number of early peony growers made species crosses, some of which afforded glimpses of things to come, but it was not until Saunders' landmark work that the bewildering number of breeding possibilities inherent in the peony were recognized.

Saunders began to raise seedlings of *Paeonia lactiflora* as early as 1905. By about 1915 he had acquired several more species and undertook his first interspecific crosses. He eventually assembled several specimens of every species then obtainable, choosing plants of the same species from far-flung geographical sources whenever possible. Saunders knew that the distinct forms of a species grown in different regions varied somewhat; he recognized that each bore a unique combination of chromosomes and therefore possessed unique genetic potential.

With such a collection of species at his disposal, Saunders set out to make every possible cross among its members, all accomplished by controlled hand pollination. To this massive breeding program he happily coupled meticulous record keeping, depending upon Dr. A. G. L. Stebbins of the New York Botanical Garden for taxonomic support. Several species came to be redefined as a result of their collaboration.

Saunders' systematic approach to plant hybridizing created dazzling new flower colors and forms in both tree and herbaceous peonies. By the time he completed his breeding program, he had compiled records on more than 15,000 new hybrids. Many of these were advanced-generation crosses, some involving three and four species. The following account is largely based upon John C. Wister's detailed analysis of Saunders' work (Wister 1962).

Saunders' first tree peony crosses used pollen from *Paeonia lutea*, the yellow tree peony of China, derived from a plant supplied by Lemoine in

1913, but he also used pollen from *P. delavayi*, a dark red tree peony. (For a time, all Saunders' tree peony cultivars were incorrectly designated as lutea hybrids.) Pollen from both species was used on pod parents of single or semi-double suffruticosas. From among the resulting plants, Saunders selected for strong-stemmed flowers in a wonderful array of colors, ranging from deep reds, scarlets, and apricots to ambers, golds, and lemon-yellows. In 1928 the sensation of the American Peony Society's annual show, held in Boston that year, was Saunders' first tree peony introduction, the brilliant yellow 'Argosy'.

Similar crosses had been made previously by both Lemoine and hybridizer Louis Henry in France, but they used the big, double suffruticosa tree peony form as pod parent. Fragrant yellow doubles, some edged with red, were the result, but the beautiful flowers were so large and heavy that their stems could not support them. Some of these hybrids, such as 'Alice Harding', 'Chromatella', 'Souvenir de Maxime Cornu', and 'Surprise', can still be found.

For many years Saunders had the advantage of a knowledgeable helper, William Gratwick. The latter did much of the tree peony grafting required to increase stocks of Saunders' crosses. When the nursery was dispersed, the tree peony plants produced in this hybridizing program were turned over to Gratwick and moved to his estate. They included two very rare, fertile, second-generation hybrids, which, while not sufficiently distinguished to introduce, formed the basis for Gratwick's later advanced-generation hybridizing program.

Saunders' first herbaceous cross was *Paeonia lactiflora* and *P. officinalis*, which yielded a series of single reds, distinguished when introduced in Boston in 1928 but now mostly superseded. In a variation on the theme, *P. lactiflora* crossed with a white *P. officinalis* produced the rare double 'Camellia', whose white flowers are suffused with a delicate pink flush.

Saunders then turned to what he knew as *Paeonia lobata*, now considered *P. peregrina*. The most promising representative of this species, in Saunders' opinion, was a plant that he received in 1928 from British plantsman Amos Perry. Expecting a very low fertility rate, he made 134 crosses using *P. peregrina* pollen on *P. lactiflora*, bagging each flower as soon as the cross was made. That fall he had more than 2000 seeds, seventy-nine of them from a single flower of 'Primevere' alone. He later noted, "This is entirely unheard of in the annals of my crossings. No species cross has ever given me such results."

This is the cross that ensured Saunders' legacy. From these seeds more than 1200 plantlets germinated, giving him a huge gene pool from which to select. Plants started blooming in 1933, and as Saunders later remarked, "Every plant turned out to be either a splendid red with many scarlet or cerise shades new to herbaceous peonies, or a vivid pink in salmon, coral, flamingo, or cherry." No color appeared undesirable and none turned to mauve as the flowers aged, as happens with some *Paeonia lactiflora* cultivars. Rather, they faded off into equally attractive shades of peach, ivory, or white.

About forty plants (3 percent) from this lactiflora-peregrina cross were introduced over the years and the majority remain unmatched. 'Cecelia', a goblet-shaped cherry-red single with fringed petal edges, is not found in current catalogs but may be available in smaller lots from various specialist nurseries and is worth seeking out. 'Cytherea', perhaps the most famous of the group, is a widely available semi-double rose hybrid, turning to pink and peach. Others still in the trade include 'Constance Spry' (a deep bright red semi-double); 'Ellen Cowley' (a bright cherry-red semi-double); 'Grace Root' (a clear salmon-pink single); 'Great Lady' (a single or semi-double of a deep luminous pink); 'Laura Magnuson' (a clear bright rose semi-double); 'Lovely Rose' (a creamy rose-pink semi-double); 'Lustrous' (an intense scarlet semi-double); 'Red Red Rose' (a rose-red semi-double); 'Rose Garland' (a rose-colored single); 'Rosy Cheek' (a rose-colored semi-double); and 'Skylark' (a bright rose-pink single).

Using other forms of *Paeonia peregrina*, particularly 'Otto Froebel' (a rosy salmon), he produced 'Birthday' (a unique taffeta-textured pink), 'Hope' (a bright cherry to salmon-pink), 'Honor' (a bright pink with pale flares), and 'Legion of Honor' (a brilliant scarlet).

Occasionally several seedlings of a cross were so similar that Saunders grouped the plants together and labeled them a strain. Such a close relationship, the Windflower strain, developed in two different lines using *Paeonia emodi* as the pollen parent. With *P. beresowskii* he named the best of the offspring 'Late Windflower'. With *P. veitchii* the best was named 'Early Windflower'. Neither the plants nor the flowers of either hybrid can be easily distinguished from the other. Both are very early bloomers; 'Late Windflower' appears about one week after the early form. Each bears a multitude of small, nodding, pure white single flowers, topping plants with wonderfully fine cut-leaved foliage, and both are much used by landscape designers.

Crossing *Paeonia emodi* and *P. lactiflora* rewarded Saunders with 'White Innocence', the tallest herbaceous peony at 5 feet. Its single white flowers have an unusual green center.

Crossing *Paeonia lactiflora* and *P. macrophylla* produced plants much lower in height than the previous cross, but with huge, shiny leaves, traits inherited from the pollen parent, *P. macrophylla*. These, as is true of all crosses involving *P. macrophylla* (which Saunders, following Stern, knew as *P. wittmanniana* var. *macrophylla*), are very early bloomers. About 1000 plants were generated in this cross. From the first generation came 'Audrey' (a pale pink near-double with noticeable fragrance) and 'Chalice' and 'Seraphim' (both white singles).

Generally all first-generation hybrid crosses (F1s) are sterile, but as they mature some occasionally set a seed or two. As Saunders noted, "In these F2s [second-generation hybrids] a surprising and welcome change occurs, for the natural fertility is in large part restored. So it is with the *Paeonia wittmanniana* var. *macrophylla* hybrids, the F2s have strong viable pollen and are regular and abundant seed setters." 'Archangel', 'Garden Peace', and 'Requiem'—all distinctive white singles—are representative of this second-generation cross of *P. lactiflora* and *P. macrophylla*. Triple crosses involving the above second-generation hybrids with *P. officinalis* produced 'Pageant', a robust, tall, rosy pink single with a huge boss of gold in its center.

Saunders also worked with *Paeonia mascula* subsp. *coriacea* (which he knew as *P. coriacea*), the most southerly growing of all the herbaceous peonies. Native to Spain and Morocco, its offspring appear to be tender in northerly climates. Saunders' cross of *P. lactiflora* and *P. mascula* subsp. *coriacea* yielded very few seeds, but the offspring were all an unusual shade of lavender-rose. The best were grouped together and introduced as the Lavender strain in 1939. Like the parent, these beautiful lavender-pink singles required more southerly climates to flourish, a very desirable characteristic. Several growers, ourselves included, are presently trying to develop a stock of 'Lavender' sufficient to offer to the public; though a lot may be too small to warrant catalog space or public notice, a nursery may very well have a few members of the Lavender strain tucked away. Keep your eyes open, and don't be afraid to make inquiries!

The best of the Saunders cultivars resulting from a cross of *Paeonia mlokosewitschii* and *P. tenuifolia* is the second-generation hybrid 'Nosegay', a vigorous, very early, pale pink single on a bush noted for its narrow cut-leaved foliage. 'Daystar', a third-generation cross, is the earliest herbaceous peony to bloom. It is a dwarf with large leaves and pale yellow single blossoms.

One of Saunders' most interesting crosses was *Paeonia officinalis* and *P. peregrina*. The first notable outcome was the intensely red-flowered 'Scarlet Tanager', followed by the dwarfs 'Good Cheer' and 'Little Dorrit', which "little reds"—though somewhat difficult to grow—have been extensively used in creating several new advanced-generation hybrids.

As Saunders extended his hybridizing program he began to combine genes of three and then four species. 'Campagna', one of the choicest resulting cultivars, is a very early, white-flowered form resulting from *Paeonia lactiflora*, *P. macrophylla*, and *P. officinalis*. Using pollen of second-generation *P. lactiflora*, *P. mlokosewitschii*, and *P. tenuifolia* crosses produced 'Roselette' (a pink-flowered cultivar) and 'Rushlight' (in creamy ivory), both popular singles. Quadruple hybrids, referred to as "quads" in Saunders' notebooks, were obtained by using *P. lactiflora* as pod parent and pollen from plants incorporating *P. macrophylla*, *P. mlokosewitschii*, and *P. peregrina*. Many cultivars of this genetic potpourri remain in the trade. One is 'Sunlight', a very early, low-growing plant that clumps up quickly into a dense bush. Before opening fully, its ivory-yellow flowers have a decidedly pink cast. Another, 'Firelight', is 40 inches tall. Its flowers are of a creamy rose, set off by distinctive darker pink flares.

Silvia Saunders eventually took over her father's nursery and was awarded the Distinguished Service Medal by the Garden Club of America for her work in popularizing hybrid peonies. While the large commercial peony growers of the day recognized her father's genius, few committed themselves to growing his introductions. Most judged—rightly at the time—that the public was interested only in the show put on by the larger double lactifloras.

Many of Saunders' herbaceous hybrid cultivars were rescued from commercial limbo by two people. The first was David Reath of Vulcan, Michigan, who purchased the original parent stock when Silvia Saunders sold out. The other was Roy Leighton of Edmonds, Washington. He acquired specimens of all the Saunders' introductions and in turn sold his collection to Keith and Peggy Goldsmith, who owned a neighboring nursery.

Thanks to the Goldsmiths' efforts, the plants were made known throughout the Pacific Northwest. After operating their nursery for thirty years, the Goldsmiths passed their very select stock on to us at Caprice

Farm and to Alfred Mantagna and Dwight Waitman, who used these prized plants to start their A & D Nursery in Snohomish, Washington, in 1978. Theirs was a relatively small operation, catering to customers from the metropolitan Seattle area. They sold the nursery in 1988, and it now operates officially as A & D Peony and Perennial Nursery. The new owners are Don Smetana, the retired creative director of a Seattle advertising firm, and Keith Able, a horticulturist and landscaper. They have expanded the plantings and established a display garden. Here and elsewhere, the Saunders' cultivars are finally receiving the recognition they deserve and are in great demand by gardeners worldwide. How times have changed!

Louis Smirnow (1896–1989) of Brookville, New York, did much to popularize tree peonies among gardeners. As a retired corporate executive, he published an annual catalog with hundreds of color illustrations of outstanding, hard-to-find herbaceous and tree peonies. Having little land of his own, he depended upon others to grow the plants he cataloged.

Smirnow was a world traveler, visiting China, Japan, and Korea, in part to search out new peonies. In Japan he discovered representatives of the "impossible" intersectional cross achieved by Toichi Itoh, the one which brought together the genes of both the herbaceous and the tree peony. Smirnow was the first to see their commercial possibilities and so purchased the entire stock for distribution in the United States.

The American Peony Society was a longtime beneficiary of Smirnow's leadership; he was active in the society both as president and as director. In the mid-1980s, his mail-order business was taken over briefly by his son and daughter-in-law, Robert and Dorothy Smirnow, who then sold it to Australian interests.

Frederick C. Stern (1884–1967) of Suffolk, England, was a soldier, big-game hunter, and amateur steeplechase jockey. In their spare time, he and his wife took on a different sort of challenge, transforming the yawning gape of an abandoned chalk-pit into a remarkable garden dedicated to rare plants originating in Asia. But Stern's enduring contribution to world horticulture is his encyclopedic study of peony species, *A Study of the Genus Paeonia*, published by the Royal Horticultural Society in 1946. It is the culmination of work begun after World War I, when Stern first began to collect wild peony plants and their seed. This handsome and beautifully illustrated book, long out of print, is now a collector's item.

J. Franklyn Styer was another leading peony grower who did much to popularize the peony. He inherited his father's cut flower operation, which supplied florists on the East Coast of the United States with peonies from the 1920s onward. Demand increased to such a point that four shrewdly situated farms were required to satisfy the market: harvesting began at the southernmost farm in Virginia and ended with one in upper New York State, thus spacing commercial production over a five-week period. The cultivars he hybridized were used to satisfy his own production needs and were not marketed.

Styer had a strong interest in plant physiology and supported research on peony dormancy at his alma mater, Pennsylvania State University. After fifty years in the peony cut flower business, he sold the company to an employee, Sandra Evanikek, and retired.

Robert Tischler and his brother Archie purchased the Brand Nursery from Myrtle Gentry in 1956. Robert continued the operation, even after his brother's death, until 1976, when he sold the business and most of the land to Farmers Seed and Nursery Company. Tischler retained rights to all unnamed seedlings, however, and started in again, on a smaller scale, as Tischler Peony Garden, Faribault, Minnesota. A tragic airplane crash killed all three of the new owner's top executives and left Farmers Seed and Nursery Company in turmoil. In 1980 the Brand name and some of the remaining peonies were sold to a company employee, Gerald Lund, of Saint Cloud, Minnesota.

The advancement of peonies has depended mightily upon the keen aesthetic judgment of dedicated "experts." Well, most of the time. Consider the history of one of Tischler's introductions, the peony 'Douglas Brand'.

Douglas Brand, Archie Brand's nephew, was a close observer of peonies; he could name many cultivars simply by examining their foliage or roots. One day he and Tischler walked the rows selecting seedlings for future introduction accompanied by Douglas' eight-year-old son, John. The men took a quick look at one in the long line of hopefuls, and both agreed this particular seedling was not worthwhile. The boy begged them to keep it, however, and they did—simply to humor him.

Today 'Douglas Brand' is considered the top red exhibition peony by most fanciers. A glistening red double whose flowers often approach 10 inches in diameter, it was among the first of Robert Tischler's seedlings to be introduced. And all because a determined boy spoke up.

Tischler has introduced other exquisite cultivars, many of them with smaller flowers on lower bushes, bred with today's smaller landscapes in mind. Two of these compact pinks are 'Bouquet Perfect' and 'Heidi'. Here at Caprice Farm Nursery, these two are virtually always the most popular lactiflora cultivars with our open-house visitors.

He also specializes in growing the fernleaf peony, *Paeonia tenuifolia*. Tischler carved out this niche for himself by purchasing clumps of *P. tenuifolia* wherever he could find them and now has one of the world's largest collections of this choice species.

It is almost poetic that, even as they forge ahead, the Tischlers live in a house built on the foundation of the old Brand homestead, and peonies still grow on the adjoining land as they have for more than a century.

Herman Wild, a German immigrant, found his piece of American paradise sooner than he expected, as a member of a wagon train, headed west. When he and the other pioneers reached the northern edge of the Ozark Mountains, he was so taken by the beauty of the wildflower meadows and the land's fruitful appearance that he left the party then and there. It was in this fertile land in the very southwest corner of Missouri, now called Sarcoxie, that he staked his claim and established the Wild Nursery in 1868.

The farm passed from Herman to his son James. James paid the princely sum of $45 for a lot of peony roots at his eight-year-old son Gilbert's request and allowed the boy to plant them behind the house. Three years later Gilbert included a crate of peony flower buds in a carload of strawberries going to the Omaha market. They sold for 3 cents each and the peony business was off and running.

Under Gilbert's direction, the nursery continued to grow. His son Allen became involved, and together they started a bare-root operation, growing iris and daylilies as well as both bare-root and cut flower peonies. Allen's wife, Haidee, took charge of bunching and packing the cut flowers. It was a typical family operation.

Gilbert and Allen started a peony hybridizing program in 1925, eventually introducing about forty new cultivars. They also introduced and marketed a large number of excellent cultivars hybridized by other breeders, among them Auten, Cooper, Minks, Nicholls, and White. By 1948 the Wild Nursery had become a major Midwest tourist attraction. More than 14,000 carloads of people toured the fields on a single Sunday in May. Nearly a million cut flowers per year were sent to clients—a crop that required eighteen refrigerated railway cars to transport. Shipments were dispatched to every corner of the country from San Francisco to New York.

By the mid-1950s the Wilds had nearly 1000 cultivars under cultivation on their 135 acres, but disaster struck in 1957 when a harsh late freeze took a large portion of their plantings. Following this loss, the nursery discontinued the cut flower business and concentrated on root production. Another natural disaster occurred in 1971, when more than 100 inches of rain fell during the growing period. The fields could not be worked, and many of the family's finest cultivars were lost to fungus and root rot.

Gene Wild and her brother James, who obtained a degree in horticulture from the University of Missouri, were the fourth consecutive generation of Wilds to operate the nursery. Though daylilies were their primary focus, peonies continued to play a part in the business.

The association of the Wild family with the nursery ended on 1 June 1991, when the heirs sold to Greg Jones and John Huitsong. Happily, the peony operation will be continued by the new owners.

John C. Wister (1887–1982) had a tremendous influence on many aspects of American and European horticulture. Graduating in landscape architecture from Harvard, he became the longtime director of what is now the Scott Arboretum of Swarthmore College, near Philadelphia. This remarkable garden contains a great number of tree peonies among other noteworthy collections, thanks to Wister's regard for the plants.

In 1968 the American Peony Society awarded him the Saunders Memorial Medal for his role as editor of and contributor to *The Peonies* (Wister 1962), which continues to be a highly regarded reference for peony hybridizers. Wister was a member of some fifty horticultural societies and received, in addition to recognition from the American Peony Society, the highest honors bestowed by the American Daffodil Society, the American Rhododendron Society, and the International Lilac Society. He also received the first Liberty Hyde Bailey Award presented by the American Horticultural Council. His wife, Gertrude S. Wister, who contributed greatly to his peony book, summed up his life best: "He was an ardent missionary for garden plants."

Now let us focus on the first plant society devoted to peonies, the American Peony Society. This group, mentioned so often in the stories we have just heard, brought some much-needed organization to the explosion of enthusiasm—and cultivars—and linked in common cause many of the people who created and popularized the modern peony.

It was not unusual at the turn of the century to find that nurserymen had labeled many of their plants incorrectly, and peony growers were no exception. They did so not just out of ignorance but in many cases as a deliberate marketing ploy, aiming to sell indifferent forms under the names of more desirable cultivars. In addition, the descriptions in the catalogs of even the best growers were typically inaccurate and misleading, all of which circumstances conspired to make it nearly impossible to purchase peonies that were true to name. Brand Nursery, for example, purchased 'Edulis Superba' under twenty-two different names during a one-year period. Seeking to counter this unethical practice, an earnest band of commercial peony growers met in Detroit, Michigan, in 1903 and incorporated in New York State the following year as the American Peony Society.

One of the new society's first actions was to appoint a committee, chaired by John Craig of Cornell University, to deal with the problem of confused nomenclature. He in turn persuaded Cornell to allocate space in the university's experimental fields so that all cultivars then in commerce could be grown and evaluated. Ten nurseries in the United States and five nurseries in Europe sent plants to Cornell for this purpose. The result was a collection of more than 700 species and cultivars.

E. J. Coit, a doctoral candidate in horticulture, supervised the project. Each plant was carefully examined during its bloom season for seven consecutive years, from 1906 to 1912, and the records were then compared to its original description. Coit, aided by members of the society's committee, then achieved the society's goal by establishing valid names for 750 cultivars. The results were published in the Cornell Bulletin, numbers 259, 278, and 306. Some of the test plants were incorporated into Cornell's display garden; the balance were sold with the proceeds benefiting the society.

The American Peony Society grew rapidly, from thirty-seven members in 1904 to 700 in 1927. Membership is again on the rise and now numbers nearly 1200, including professional growers and collectors. Annual meetings take place at various spots in the United States and Canada—usually somewhere in the Midwest, where most of the display gardens and leading nurseries are located—and are scheduled to coincide with the anticipated bloom season of the host city.

One of the principal events of each year's meeting, and one that looms large to the entrants, is the floral exhibition and show, which provides a competitive setting for displaying new seedlings of merit and improved forms of older cultivars. Entries are judged by a select committee appointed by the society and various citations and prizes are awarded.

These annual events were especially elaborate affairs during the 1920s. The 1923 show, held at the Minnesota State Fairgrounds, opened with a parade featuring floats decorated with 50,000 peony blossoms. One exhibition class during this decade of big shows called for one bloom each of 100 different cultivars—surely an extraordinary sensory extravaganza for the public not to mention a logistical feat for the stagers. Many exhibitors brought a dozen or more buds of each cultivar they intended to enter so that at the last minute they could select the best bloom to go on the judging table. In 1941 the exceedingly competitive Harry F. Little brought more than 6000 buds so that he might select the best two for entering in a single class. At another show, Edward Auten's seedling display covered an area of more than 290 square feet.

Throughout the 1920s the American Peony Society employed a system that rated all cultivars on a scale of 5.0 to 10.0, with a 10.0 signifying perfection and a 5.0 evidently indicating only that the cultivar lived and flowered. While in general the ratings indicated relative value, so much criticism resulted that the system was discarded, since the bloom quality of some cultivars is highly variable. Though the one or two blossoms exhibited might be exceptional, the preponderance of the flowers on the same plant might be of lower quality. Reflective of true quality or not, a low rating was ruinous; any cultivar receiving a rating below 8.0 immediately lost virtually all market value. For example, 'Mme. de Verneville', which had enjoyed decades of favor until then, received a 7.9 rating—probably downgraded for small blossoms—and nearly disappeared from the trade; it is now considered one of the finest wholesale cut flower varieties.

At the height of the peony's popularity in North America, the society published *The Manual of the American Peony Society* (Boyd 1928). A contributed volume with chapters written by various experts, this book served as the standard reference for more than thirty years. During the Depression of the 1930s and on through World War II, with interest in peonies both as cut flowers and as plants in the landscape steadily declining, membership in the society fell in parallel, leaving only a small coterie of hard-core enthusiasts to support the society's various horticultural projects.

In the mid-1950s, Mr. and Mrs. Byron Gist with the help of Mr. and Mrs. Allen Wild and Gene Wild took on one such project, the monumental task of compiling a list of all cultivars that had ever been included in any catalog. The end result was a master list of 3400 names, together with whatever information could be found concerning color, flower type, hybridizer, and year of introduction. This massive database was edited by Greta Kessenich, who saw it through to its 1976 publication by the American Peony Society as *History of the Peonies and Their Originations.*

But this was not the greatest contribution Greta Kessenich has made to the peony. Together with a handful of like-minded members of the American Peony Society, she promoted a resurgence of interest in, enthusiasm for, and dedication to the genus *Paeonia.* She assumed in 1972 the multiple roles of secretary and treasurer of the society and editor and director of its Bulletin. Under her leadership, not only has a revival of interest in this remarkable genus been accomplished but the traditional activities of the society have been reinvigorated.

The American Peony Society is presently the largest and most influential peony society in the world. As such it was designated by the International Society for Horticultural Science's Commission for Registration as the International Registration Authority for peonies under the provisions set out in the *International Code of Nomenclature for Cultivated Plants* (1980). Readers interested in learning more about the group and its continuing services are encouraged to write

American Peony Society
250 Interlachen Road
Hopkins, Minnesota 55343 U.S.A.

Chapter 3

Species

The peony family, Paeoniaceae, is one of the world's most ancient flowering plant groups and was once included in the Ranunculaceae, which family has evolved and spread over a wide range in the Northern Hemisphere. Peonies, the genus *Paeonia*, are native to Morocco and Spain across the mountainous regions of Europe and the Mediterranean, through the Caucasus to central Asia, and on into China and Japan and even the western United States. Despite their wide distribution, peony plants are rarely common or numerous in the wild.

Geological evidence tells us that peonies have been in existence for more than 100,000 years, and indeed their seeds—the means by which the genus became so thoroughly if not densely dispersed throughout the temperate zones—are quite typical of primitive plants. The tiny embryo is surrounded by a large mass of endosperm and coated with a shell-like covering. This hard seed coat allows the embryo to remain viable for several years until conditions are suitable for germination.

The genus *Paeonia*, though made up of a relatively small number of species, is very complex taxonomically. Peonies are not only extremely variable under natural conditions but through the many centuries of cultivar selection, their variability has vastly increased. This diversity accounts, at least in part, for the bewildering array of species classifications and reclassifications by various authors.

Chromosome counts done to date show that species may be either diploid (10 chromosomes, $2n = 10$) or tetraploid (20 chromosomes, $2n = 20$), with the ploidy correlating to geographical distribution. The diploid species are pre-glacial relics pushed southward by the advancing ice sheet of the Pleistocene period; many of these species took refuge in warmer areas such as the Mediterranean islands. Interestingly, all tree peonies are diploid.

Tetraploids, on the other hand, have persisted and spread thanks to the greater amount of genetic material provided by their doubled number of chromosomes. The mere possession of double the genetic material allows for many more favorable combinations of genes, thus giving their offspring a relatively wider range of tolerance to diverse ecological conditions.

With respect to growth and habit, the genus *Paeonia* falls into two distinct groups. The first group is made up of the shrubby or tree peonies, long known as Moutan. Because their native habitat is confined to the most remote and inaccessible regions of the mountains of China, only recently have the species been located in the wild and described by botanists.

Many members of the other group, the herbaceous perennial species, have on the other hand been readily accessible to European gardeners and botanists for years. In the last three centuries, and in tandem with the emerging science of botany, exploration of the European and Middle Eastern mountains and woods has provided a growing list of species beyond those identified by Linnaeus around 1760.

With the exception of the popular herbaceous species—*Paeonia lactiflora*, *P. officinalis*, and *P. tenuifolia*—one can hardly find species peonies in general landscape use in North America, whereas a number of species are used in European gardens. Yet many peony species are remarkably worthy garden plants in their own right. Many bloom early, thus prolonging the flowering season. Those of small stature make superb additions to the rock garden. And due to the relatively wide range of conditions to which the various peony species are native, they are climatically suited to everything from cool and moist to mild and dry.

Perhaps the most compelling reason for growing peony species in the garden stems from ecological considerations. Many populations of wild peonies are at risk in their native lands. In the Mediterranean region particularly, touristic development and intensive agriculture have destroyed most of the habitat of several peony species, and they are now well on their way to extinction. Preservation of these species will depend on careful garden cultivation, coupled with efforts to restore at least some pockets of wild populations wherever possible.

The final reason for growing species is a most practical horticultural one: Species still remain the best genetic source for creating new hybrids. Unlikely though it may seem, yet-unseen cultivars, from species selections as well as from crosses between species, may well differ from and prove more attractive than even the hundreds of cultivars presently in cultivation. Some may even extend the range of easy-to-grow cultivars to warmer regions.

British peony specialist Frederick C. Stern set the pattern for the modern classification and terminology of peonies in his landmark work, *A Study of the Genus Paeonia* (1946). Since the publication of this primary study, a number of developments have led botanists to modify Stern's work. Several new species have been discovered and described, including one named for Stern. The principal difficulty, however—and one which has caused the greatest confusion—is the recent publication of several different systems of classification, each proposing numerous name changes.

Even though practicing gardeners often become impatient with scientists and their taxonomic shifts, it is well to keep in touch with them, if only to ensure consistency and continuity of naming. Throughout this book and especially in the species descriptions that follow, I have made every effort to incorporate recent discoveries and name changes so that readers can associate the plants they grow under older names with the names employed in the newer systems of classifications. This is vitally important for hybridizers, who must know which species are closely related to one another.

For some species the reports are meager, and in some cases, considerable doubt exists as to whether or not a species is correctly identified. Under the circumstances, it is difficult to consistently make specific soil and climate recommendations.

TREE PEONIES

Section *Moutan*: Subsection *Vaginatae*

Stern grouped the woody peonies, his section *Moutan*, into two subsections. The first, subsection *Vaginatae*, contained *Paeonia suffruticosa* Andrews and a variety *spontanea* Rehder. It was not until 1913, however, that

Reginald Farrer reported sighting *P. suffruticosa* in the wild. Sometime after 1925, Joseph F. Rock sent back to the Arnold Arboretum in the United States seed from what he believed was a wild form of this species, in spite of the fact that he gathered it from a plant tended in a lamasery garden in Zhoni, Gansu Province. Plants from this seed have been quite widely cultivated and sold in the United States, Great Britain, and New Zealand under the name *P. suffruticosa* 'Rock's Variety' or 'Joseph Rock', both now known as *P. rockii*.

In recent years Chinese botanists have undertaken extensive field studies aimed at locating wild populations of tree peonies and at distinguishing and analyzing the various forms of the species which have until now been loosely subsumed under the name *Paeonia suffruticosa*. The leading figure in this effort is Hong Tao of the Chinese Academy of Forestry in Beijing, People's Republic of China. Italy's Gian Lupo Osti has been associated with much of this work as well.

As a result of their explorations and botanical investigations, a different classification system for tree peonies, published in China's Bulletin of Botanical Research, was proposed by Hong and his Chinese associates in 1992. Hong's principal and most radical thesis is that the numerous plants previously designated as *Paeonia suffruticosa* are in fact cultivars developed in China (and later in Japan) over a period of centuries and were derived from various crosses between four wild species newly described by him and his associates. In particular, Hong believes that one of these species, *P. ostii*, is the wild woody peony from which many of the tree peony cultivars originated. He therefore identifies what we would call suffruticosas as "Osti's peony cultivar group" and notes that members of this group are particularly well adapted to the warmer subtropical climate of southern China.

Hong and his associates conclude that the term "suffruticosa" should be used to encompass what is in fact only a large group of cultivars. The four species they describe all contributed to a greater or lesser extent, in their judgment, to the gene pool of this "suffruticosa" cultivar group. Most of the presently grown garden forms of tree peonies appear to be members of this group.

Because the Chinese work was based upon extensive and detailed examinations of a large number of plants in their native habitat, I believe these studies supersede even the recent classification system of Haw and Lauener (1990) as well as that of Stern and others.

The four species in Hong's new classification will take some time to become common in cultivation, as material for propagation is only slowly becoming available. A few will be divisions of wild plants; most will have been raised from seed in specialized nurseries and botanic gardens.

The four species described by Hong and his associates are as follows:

Paeonia jishanensis Hong and Zhao
Named for the district in Shaanxi Province where it was found, this is a smaller shrub, 4 feet in height, with somewhat ovate and lobed leaflets. The ten-petaled flowers are white and sometimes slightly pink at the base. The filaments, disc, and style are purplish red. Diploid (10 chromosomes).

Paeonia ostii Hong and Zhang
Named for the Italian specialist, "Osti's peony" is the endangered and very precious wild woody peony species endemic in China, found in the provinces of Gansu, Shaanxi, and Anhui. It grows to 5 feet and has lanceolate leaflets; the terminal leaflet occasionally has three lobes. The flower, which lacks basal blotches or flares, is entirely white, or white tinged with pink. The filaments, disc, and style are purplish red. Diploid (10 chromosomes).

Paeonia rockii (Haw and Lauener) Hong and J. Li
The same plant that is familiar to many under the name *Paeonia suffruticosa* 'Rock's Variety' or *P. suffruticosa* 'Joseph Rock'. The shrub, often 5–6 feet tall, has deeply divided leaflets and large white flowers, with a purple blotch on the base of each petal. The filaments, disc, and style are white. Diploid (10 chromosomes). (Plate 104)

Paeonia yananensis Hong and M. Li
An extremely rare plant, named for the district in Shaanxi Province in which it was found. It stands at just 16 inches and has few leaflets. The petals are white or pale purplish rose with a dark red basal blotch. The filaments, disc, and style are reddish purple. Diploid (10 chromosomes).

Section *Moutan*: Subsection *Delavayanae*

Stern's second subsection of tree peonies, subsection *Delavayanae*, includes several species discovered in the mountains of southwestern China toward the end of the 19th century. In it, he identified and defined the following species:

Paeonia delavayi Franchet

Found in North Yunnan in the Lijiang range. This relatively bare-stemmed shrub can reach a height of up to 5.5 feet. The leaflets appear in clusters of three; those at the end of the stem stand clear of the rest. The hidden flowers are smaller than those of the suffruticosa group, with characteristic blackish red or maroon petals, the darkest in the genus. The thick, fleshy lobes, which form a disc at the base of the carpels, are another distinguishing feature. Though the species has no genuine garden merit, it is the source of the dark maroon colors in today's tree peony hybrids. Plants raised from collected seed routinely differ somewhat in habit of growth, shade of color (some are quite attractive reds), and size. Hardy to U.S. Department of Agriculture hardiness zone 5, though it seldom blooms in climates colder than zones 7 or 8. Diploid (10 chromosomes).

Paeonia lutea Delavay ex Franchet var. *lutea*

This is a native of Yunnan Province, most abundant in the mountains above Dali. It differs from the previous species in the color of its flowers, which are a clear lemon-yellow. It varies greatly in size over the range where it has been found, from 3 feet to more than 6 feet in height. The small flowers, 2–3 inches in diameter, are usually hidden by the foliage. Once again, the species has no real landscape value, but its appealing lemonlike fragrance is often passed on to its hybrid offspring. Hardy to zone 5, though it seldom blooms in climates colder than zones 7 or 8; even then, it is sparsely floriferous at best. Diploid (10 chromosomes).

Paeonia lutea var. *ludlowii* F. C. Stern and Taylor

A native of the higher elevations of Tibet, found in southeast Xizang near the Tsango gorges. It was first discovered about 1936. Flowers are yellow; both flowers and leaves are larger and more prominent than those of *Paeonia lutea* and *P. delavayi*. Seedlings display considerable variation in size. It makes a splendid large bush, attaining a height of up to 8 feet, and its huge, exotic-looking leaves, green in maturity, make it a valuable plant in the landscape. It is a rank grower and is often covered with flowers. Despite its mountain origin, it often freezes completely to the ground and then sprouts again in spring, in bronzy tones, from crown buds, and it blooms profusely in New Zealand. Usually very few sets of multiple flower buds are produced for such a large plant. There are few reports of successful hybridizing with this species as a parent. Diploid (10 chromosomes).

Paeonia potaninii Komarov

Found in northwest Yunnan and west Sichuan Provinces. This is a smaller plant than *Paeonia lutea* in most respects, with deeply divided, fine leaflets and rather small red flowers. In cultivation, white- and yellow-flowered forms have appeared; the yellow form was described in 1943 as variety *trollioides* (Stapf ex W. T. Stearn) W. T. Stearn. Diploid (10 chromosomes).

All these species have been used by Western hybridizers in this century to produce tree peonies yielding hitherto unknown colors. Even the recalcitrant *Paeonia potaninii* has recently been crossed successfully. This species increases well by stolons—a trait not usually found in tree peonies—which accelerates the number of plants produced. One modern hybridizer whose specialty is intersectional hybrids saw its potential and explored further; see the discussion of Roger Anderson's work in Chapter 7.

Paralleling the revision of Stern's *Paeonia suffruticosa* section by the Chinese botanists, Osti reports he has found evidence in the wild suggesting that *P. delavayi*, *P. lutea*, and *P. potaninii* are all forms of a single species marked by considerable variation. Since his proposition has not yet been published, however, it has not had the benefit of widespread scrutiny.

HERBACEOUS PEONIES

Stern placed the species of herbaceous peonies into two sections. The first, section *Onaepia*, is a group made up of the only two North American species. The second, section *Paeon*, is used to group thirty or so species native to the Old World. The section *Paeon* is in turn divided into two subsections: *Foliolatae* and *Dissectifoliae*. As the names imply, the form and structure of the foliage provided Stern with the basis for his classification. Readers interested in learning more about identifying species through leaf form are referred to *A Study of the Genus Paeonia* (Stern 1946).

As we've said, a number of events have forced revisions of Stern's work since his classification system was published in 1946. Several new species native to Greece and Turkey as well as Tibet and China have been identified, named, and described. There are also tantalizing but sketchy reports of a handful of new species in the Caucasus. Such developments have forced taxonomists to reexamine the relationships among the earlier established species along with those of the more recently identified species. Most critically, these more exhaustive investigations are being conducted at a time when the concept of wide species morphological variability has come to be generally accepted among botanists. Acknowledgment of this widespread natural phenomenon of biodiversity in turn justifies the reduction of the number of species in all genera by taxonomists. As a result, a broad spectrum of species in the plant world have been "downgraded," reclassified as subspecies and even varieties.

The most obvious examples in the genus *Paeonia* are *P. mascula* and *P. officinalis*, the two species most widely distributed across Europe, designated in the early herbals as the "male" and "female" peonies. The authoritative *Flora Europaea* (Cullen and Heywood 1964) treats each of these as complexes, embracing a considerable number of subspecies previously regarded as species.

A useful summary of the accumulating changes in the taxonomy and nomenclature of peonies was prepared a few years ago by the English botanical bibliographer Ray Cooper, who undertook a complete analysis of the situation in his *Survey of the Paeonia Species in the Light of Recent Literature* (1988). Cooper's account of peony species literature was published in abbreviated form by Rivière in 1992 under the title "Notes on the Peony Species." This paper is Cooper's personal contribution to the efforts of both the National Council for the Conservation of Plants and Gardens in Great Britain and the Species Peonies International Network (SPIN), an international group of gardeners who are growing and studying the species of *Paeonia*, the two groups who jointly commissioned his work. For more on both organizations, see Appendix I.

In the following descriptions of the herbaceous peony species, I have retained Stern's system of sections and subsections, modified by an overlay of Cooper's more recent conclusions based upon geography and taxonomic niceties—in particular the seven groupings he calls for within the two subsections of Stern's section *Paeon*. This seemed to me to be the wisest and most logical organizing principle.

Section *Onaepia*: The North American species

Paeonia brownii Douglas ex Hooker
Usually found in isolated high desert and mountain areas in the Pacific Northwest, particularly in Idaho, southern Oregon, and eastern Washington, but also in California, Nevada, Utah, and Wyoming. The small (.75–1.25 inches in diameter) but heavy, cup-shaped flowers, whose maroon, yellow, and green petals never expand, are borne atop dark green foliage, facing downward. Five to seven biternate leaflets are carried on very short stalks. The plant reaches a variable 10–17 inches in height. In the wild it spends a long dormant winter under snow followed by a transient wet spring that enables it to grow, flower, and ripen seed. The subsequent long, hot, dry summer bakes it into dormancy again. There are very few reports of successful cultivation under garden conditions, and none whatever of hybrid offspring. Diploid (10 chromosomes). (Plate 94)

Paeonia californica Nuttall ex Torrey and Gray
Found only in restricted areas of central and southern California, at low elevations. Somewhat taller than *Paeonia brownii* and with larger leaves. Leaflets are papery, with top surfaces darker than the undersides. The lax stems, up to 34 inches in length, carry up to four flowers per stem. Flowers are similar in shape and size to those of *P. brownii*, but of a uniform purplish brown on the outside of the petals. The plant begins its growth cycle with the autumn rains and dies back in the spring with the onset of droughty conditions. Its roots are designed to conserve moisture, and thus this species does well in sandy, well-drained soils under semi-arid conditions. Dormancy requirements are not known. A few specialists have had very limited success in growing the species, but not in hybridizing it. Diploid (10 chromosomes). (Plate 95)

Section *Paeon*: Subsection *Foliolatae*

In proposing the subsection *Foliolatae*, Stern sought to distinguish those plants whose lower leaves, elliptic or ovate in shape, are cut to the axis into nine to sixteen leaflets. Cooper's further groupings within the subsection, based upon geography and taxonomic characteristics, are also noted.

• Cooper's "officinalis complex"

Paeonia officinalis has been in cultivation for centuries; a double red and a white were described as early as 1636. Through the development of selected sports, a large number of cultivars have been derived from the species, displaying a wide range of color (white, pink, and deep red) and form (both single and double). Plant habit is equally diverse.

This ready expression of morphological variation coupled with the recent taxonomic tendency to reduce the number of plant species by accepting a range of type within a single species has led to the reclassification of a number of closely related forms. These have been brought together into what is now called the "officinalis complex."

Members of this group have roots in the form of fusiform tubers, attached to their crowns by thin strings. All are strong growers under a wide variety of cultural conditions:

Paeonia officinalis Linnaeus subsp. *officinalis*
This is the species from which the *Paeonia officinalis* complex takes its name. It occurs in southern France, Switzerland, and northern Italy, east to Hungary and south to Albania. The stems are 14–24 inches in length and the lower leaves are biternate, with numerous narrowly elliptic leaflets. Flowers are usually pink, but a color range from white to red has been reported for various populations at various stations. Tetraploid (20 chromosomes). (Plate 102)

Paeonia officinalis subsp. *banatica* (Rochel) Soó
This subspecies is found in Hungary, Croatia, and Romania. Because it possesses characteristics of both *Paeonia mascula* and of *P. officinalis* subsp. *officinalis,* the plant has provoked much disagreement among botanists trying to settle upon a precise taxonomic position for it. The stems are 14–20 inches in length. The middle leaflets are incised into segments, with the lateral leaflets entire and either broad or ovate. The rose-red flowers are 3–5 inches across. Tetraploid (20 chromosomes).

Paeonia officinalis subsp. *microcarpa*
Previously known as *Paeonia humilis* Retzius, this form grows in southwest Europe. The stems are 10–16 inches in length, and the leaflets are divided into thirty or more elliptic and sharply pointed segments. The red flowers are 3.5–5.5 inches in diameter. It is easily grown and makes an excellent garden subject. Tetraploid (20 chromosomes).

Leaf form, *Paeonia officinalis.*

Paeonia officinalis subsp. *villosa* (Huth) Cullen and Heywood
Previously called *Paeonia humilis* var. *villosa,* this form is closely re-
lated in all ways to subspecies *microcarpa*. It is found in the south of
France and nearby Italy. Tetraploid (20 chromosomes).

Viewed as a whole, these four subspecies form a geographical replacement complex extending from Portugal to the Balkan Republics (former
Yugoslavia) and Romania. Intermediate forms frequently occur in areas in
which these taxa overlap one another. There seems to be no justification,
therefore, for following Stern in regarding them as different in status—
hence the creation of the *Paeonia officinalis* complex.

Two other plants native to the Mediterranean islands—though not
classed as subspecies of *Paeonia officinalis*—are also placed by Cooper in
the *P. officinalis* complex as they are closely related to *P. officinalis*:

Paeonia clusii F. C. Stern and W. T. Stearn subsp. *clusii*
This species is endemic to Crete. The pink or purplish stems are 8–12
inches in length. The lower leaves are biternate, with leaflets dissected
into more than thirty segments, which are themselves lobed or toothed,

making a total of forty to eighty leaflets. The flowers are white, rarely flushed pink, and 3–4 inches across. Tetraploid (20 chromosomes).

Paeonia clusii subsp. *rhodia* (W. T. Stearn) Tzanoudakis
This form closely resembles *Paeonia clusii* subsp. *clusii* but is a slightly larger plant. Diploid (10 chromosomes).

The last of the *Paeonia officinalis* group is an "odd man out," a peony known only in gardens. It was purportedly brought to Great Britain from Russia in the early 19th century but has never been found in the wild:

Paeonia mollis Anderson
This species reaches a height of 18 inches. Its lower leaves are biternate. All the leaflets are incised into a total of approximately twenty-five narrowly elliptic divisions, some of which are deeply lobed. The flowers, which can be either red or white, are about 3 inches across. Tetraploid (20 chromosomes).

• Cooper's "white and yellow peonies from the region of the Caucasus Mountains"

Paeonia macrophylla (Albov) Lomakin
This member of the clan—treated by Stern as a variety of *Paeonia wittmanniana* rather than as a separate species—is native to the western Caucasus and is distinguished by its elliptic to lanceolate leaflets. These are dark green and grow to a large size (10 × 6 inches). The flowers are white, tinged with yellow. Its hybrid offspring inherit its large leaves and early flowering period. Tetraploid (20 chromosomes).

Paeonia mlokosewitschii Lomakin
This mouthful of a binomial is frequently and usefully shortened to "mloko." A very showy plant, about 3 feet high, it is found in the southeast Caucasus in the valley of Lagodeki on sunny slopes and in hornbeam-oak forests. The foliage consists of oval or ovate leaflets of dark green. The flower, 4 inches across, is a clear, glowing yellow, the only true yellow among the herbaceous peony species. It blooms very early. Judged a weak grower by some, it nevertheless does well in many areas, including the heavy clay soils of the Pacific Northwest. Diploid (10 chromosomes). (Plate 101)

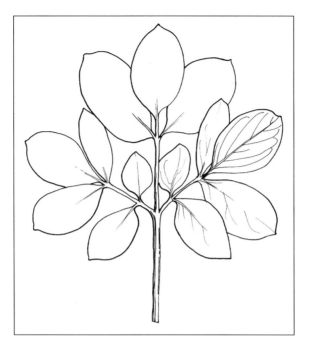

Leaf form, *Paeonia mlokosewitschii.*

Paeonia wittmanniana Hartwig ex Lindley

A plant closely related to *Paeonia mlokosewitschii*, especially with regard to size and season of bloom, but with leaves of a lighter green and
with leaflets more elliptic than those of *P. mlokosewitschii*. It is found
in alpine valleys and on rocky slopes. Its flowers are yellowish to white.
It has been known to withstand the winters of upper New York State
(zone 4). Tetraploid (20 chromosomes).

In addition to these firmly established species, local botanists in the
Caucasus distinguish other plants that may prove to be true species, or—
since many peony species cross easily and widely—may prove to be only
natural hybrids. Some of these problematic forms have already passed into
cultivation by way of zealous amateurs who sought and received seed from
botanic gardens in the Caucasian region. Of these questionable species,
the only two known to be growing in the West are the white-flowered *Paeonia steveniana* and *P. chameleon*, whose petals change from pink to white
with age.

• Cooper's "south-European and Mediterranean peonies"

The southern European/Mediterranean region is the native habitat of what is now recognized as an extraordinarily diverse group of plants centered upon *Paeonia mascula*. As a consequence this group is now identified as the *P. mascula* complex. Most of these species and their subspecies are tetraploid.

Paeonia mascula (Linnaeus) Miller subsp. *mascula*
This plant grows in southern Italy, Sicily, and to the east in Greece and Asia Minor. It forms large clumps with thick, fleshy roots. Occasional stands of wild plants further to the north mark the sites of vanished monastery gardens, from which the plant may have escaped. A quite variable plant, about 24 inches high. The lower leaves are biternate, and the nine to twenty-one elliptic or ovate leaflets are dark green on top. The flowers are about 5 inches across and rose-red in color, though purplish red and white forms have also been reported. Tetraploid (20 chromosomes). (Plate 98)

Two distinct forms of *Paeonia mascula* are found in North Africa. One was formerly named *P. coriacea* Boissier var. *coriacea* and the other *P. coriacea* var. *atlantica* (Cosson) F. C. Stern. They are now both classified as subspecies of *P. mascula*:

Paeonia mascula subsp. *atlantica* (Cosson) Maire
This form is found in Algeria in forests at the 4500- to 6500-foot elevation. It is very similar to subspecies *coriacea* described below, differentiated by the hairiness on the back of the leaves. Tetraploid (20 chromosomes).

Paeonia mascula subsp. *coriacea* (Boissier) Malagarriga
This subspecies, the most southerly growing of all the herbaceous peonies, is found in the Atlas Mountains of Morocco as well as in southern Spain. It reaches a height of 22 inches. The lower leaves of its leathery foliage are biternate, with from nine to fourteen elliptic leaflets. The light pink flowers are about 4 inches in diameter. Tetraploid (20 chromosomes).

Other members of the *Paeonia mascula* complex—subspecies and near relatives of *P. mascula*—are as follows:

Paeonia mascula subsp. *arietina* (Anderson) Cullen and Heywood
A native of Eastern Europe and Asia Minor, this subspecies reaches a height of 18–25 inches. Its leaves are biternate, with twelve to sixteen narrowly elliptic leaflets. The flowers are 4 inches across, red in the wild but sometimes varying from pink to carmine in cultivated plants. Chromosome number unknown. (Plate 99)

Paeonia mascula subsp. *hellenica* Tzanoudakis
In a 1978 research report, the Greek botanist D. M. Tzanoudakis identified two new peonies in Greece, this white-flowered plant, which he treated along with two local varieties as a subspecies of *Paeonia mascula*, and a new, dark red species, *P. parnassica*, described below. Both are still rare in cultivation. *Paeonia mascula* subsp. *hellenica* reaches a height of 12–24 inches. The lower leaves are biternate, with nine to twenty-one broadly ovate leaflets. The white flowers are 4–5 inches across, with five to seven petals. Chromosome number unknown.

Paeonia mascula subsp. *russii* (Bivoni-Bernardi) Cullen and Heywood
The largest population of this close relative of *Paeonia cambessedesii* is found on Sicily, but smaller populations grow on other Mediterranean islands as well as in southern Italy and Greece. Its habitat varies from subalpine meadows to scrub and mountain steppes. The plant reaches a height of 18 inches and bears pink flowers, 4 inches in diameter. Both stems and leaves are purplish; the lower leaves are biternate, with ovate leaflets. Some report it to have creeping rhizomes. Tetraploid (20 chromosomes).

Paeonia mascula subsp. *triternata* (Boissier) W. T. Stearn and Davis
This plant, found in the Crimea as well as southeast Europe and Turkey, is another that was long regarded as a species, under the name *Paeonia daurica* Andrews, but that is now classed as a subspecies of *P. mascula*. It grows to 24 inches in height and bears rose-colored flowers, up to 4 inches in diameter. The lower leaves are thick and biternate, with nine to eleven leaflets, ovate or orbicular in shape. The leaflets have undulating margins—a unique characteristic among peony species. Chromosome number unknown. (Plate 100)

Paeonia parnassica Tzanoudakis
This is the other new species identified by Tzanoudakis and another close relative of *Paeonia mascula*. It is endemic to the mountains of south-central Greece, growing to 26 inches high. The flowers are of a deep red; the lower leaves are biternate, with nine to thirteen leaflets. Chromosome number unknown.

The four remaining peony species closely related to *Paeonia mascula*—all clearly identified and long established—are found at the western end of the Mediterranean:

Paeonia broteroi Boissier and Reuter
This species is now viewed as a close relative of *Paeonia mascula* but not a subspecies thereof. It is endemic to Spain and Portugal. The plant reaches a height of 16 inches. Leaves are biternate, and the leaflets are elliptic and shining green. The rose-colored flowers are about 4 inches across. Diploid (10 chromosomes).

Paeonia cambessedesii Willkomm
This plant is endemic to the Balearic Islands of the Mediterranean—Majorca in particular—but perhaps not for long since it is an endangered species. It grows to 18 inches high. The leaves, which appear at regular intervals along the red-tinged stem, are biternate, and the leaflets have raised veins suffused with purple. The flowers are up to 4 inches across and of a deep rose. For both its flower and foliage, this is one of the most beautiful of peonies, but alas, most difficult to grow. It appears to need a mild climate and very sharp drainage. Indeed, the man it was named for—a Spaniard, one Sr. Cambessedes—reputedly obtained his specimen plants by shooting them off steep cliffs with a shotgun. Probably not hardy below zone 7, and then only in protected places. Since it is a copious seeder, it offers the potential of hybrids easier than the species to manage. Diploid (10 chromosomes). (Plate 96)

Paeonia kesrouanensis Thiébault
A native of Syria, growing to 24 inches. Its leaves are very like its close relative *Paeonia mascula*, with fourteen leaflets in all. The leaf veins are purplish and the pink flowers are 4 inches across. Chromosome number unknown.

Paeonia turcica Davis and Cullen

This is another newcomer, first described in 1965 and also considered a close relative of *Paeonia mascula*. It grows sparsely in southwest Anatolia and is very similar to the Syrian species, *P. kesrouanensis*. Chromosome number unknown.

Yet to be dealt with in the *Paeonia mascula* complex is a difficult oddity. It is a peony that has never been found in the wild but was first recorded in the Cambridge Botanic Garden in 1890. Since then it has become fairly widely grown and must be considered a species since it comes true from seed:

Paeonia bakeri Lynch

Grows to 24 inches high. The lower leaves biternate and the leaflets oval. The magenta-red flower is more than 4 inches across. It looks like a robust form of *Paeonia mascula* subsp. *arietina*. Chromosome number unknown.

• Cooper's "Asian members"

The number of species in this group is limited, in part because the flora of Asia has not been as fully explored as that of Europe and the Middle East. Further complicating the question of the number of *Paeonia* species in the Far East is the fact that the plants collected have not been as meticulously studied as their European relatives.

Paeonia emodi Wallich ex Royle

Native to the Himalayas, far removed from the ancestral home of *Paeonia lactiflora*, this species nevertheless closely resembles *P. lactiflora* with respect to foliage and the production of two to four white flowers per stem. Approaches a height of 3 feet. Saunders used this species with *P. lactiflora* to produce his towering 'White Innocence'. Diploid (10 chromosomes). (Plate 97)

Paeonia japonica (Makino) Miyabe and Takeda

This species is found in the northern islands of Japan. It is smaller than *Paeonia obovata*, which it closely resembles, and produces only white flowers. Almost unknown in Western landscapes save in botanic and collectors' gardens, it has not been successfully used in hybridizing. Diploid (10 chromosomes).

Paeonia lactiflora Pallas

This is the most widely grown peony of all the Asian species. Native to a wide area, ranging from Siberia and Mongolia to northern China, it reaches a height of 24 inches. It has light green stems flushed with red. The lower leaves are biternate, the leaflets entire or lobed and elliptic in shape. Generally the flowers are white, though red flowers have occasionally been seen in the wild. Flowers are borne several to the stem and are 3–4 inches in diameter and sweetly scented. This species has rigid roots that thicken at the crown. For many years it was called *Paeonia albiflora* Pallas or *P. chinensis* hort. Described for a second time in 1788 by Pallas, who had forgotten he had already given it a different name many years before, the proper name was at last accepted. Brought to the Occident about 1800, it was widely and immediately beloved and was used to produce thousands of cultivars and hybrids; indeed, it is the ancestor of the majority of garden peonies. Very hardy. Diploid (10 chromosomes).

Paeonia mairei Léveille

This species is found at high elevations in the south-central provinces of China. The rose-colored flowers are about 4 inches across, the stems are about 20 inches in length, and the lower leaves are biternate, with elliptic leaves. Known only from herbarium specimens, it has not been used for breeding. Chromosome number unknown.

Paeonia obovata Maximowicz

This species is native to Siberia, Manchuria, China, and Japan and is found in mountain woods and scrub. Its flowers are white to rose-purple, carried on stems some 16–24 inches in length. The white form is often sold under the name of *Paeonia obovata* var. *alba*. The lower leaves are biternate, with obovate leaflets. An unusual feature of this species is the marked increase in the size of its leaves between the time of flowering and the ripening of seed. Diploid (10 chromosomes).

Section *Paeon*: Subsection *Dissectifoliae*

In contrast to subsection *Foliolatae*, the lower leaves of plants in Stern's subsection *Dissectifoliae* are distinguished by being very much divided into twenty-five or more leaflets, which are lobed or toothed in shape. Cooper's further divisions within the subsection, based upon geography and taxonomic characteristics, are maintained.

• Cooper's "peregrina group"

The plants in this group, though scarce in the wild, are found over a wide range from southern Italy through the Balkans to the Turkish coast. Several forms have been reported from botanic stations in Romania and Bulgaria. There seems good reason to accept the findings of variant forms from outlying areas, but since none are well characterized or in cultivation, Cooper and others have placed the species and these variants in a complex named for the key species:

Paeonia peregrina Miller
The key species is well established as the form that grows in Greece—once known in England as the "single red peony of Constantinople." Formerly known as *Paeonia decora* and *P. lobata*, or by the cultivar names 'Sunbeam' and 'Fire King'. This plant grows to 20 inches high with much-divided, biternate lower leaves. Its foliage is easily recognized—somewhat broader and coarser than those of the other members of the subsection *Dissectifoliae*. The deep red flower is cup-shaped and 3–5 inches across. Perhaps the most spectacular member of the peony tribe, this plant makes a good garden subject and is one of the latest of the species to bloom. Several forms of this species were used by various breeders under the names *P. officinalis* 'Fire King', *P. officinalis* 'Otto Froebel', and *P. officinalis* 'Sunbeam'. Saunders especially relied upon them heavily; they formed the backbone of his hybridizing efforts. Tetraploid (20 chromosomes). (Plate 103)

• Cooper's "tenuifolia group"

Paeonia tenuifolia Linnaeus
This is the well-known and popular fernleaf peony, first described by Linnaeus in 1759. It is distributed from Transylvania to the Caucasus. The stems are 10–24 inches in length. The leaves are dense, and the flowers appear to rest atop the leaves. Lower leaves are biternate but are completely dissected and lobed into many narrow segments. The flowers are 2.5–3 inches across and of a deep crimson. Variant characteris-

tics have emerged in garden cultivation, including pink or red flowers in both single and double forms. A splendid specimen plant of exquisite habit. Diploid (10 chromosomes). (Plate 105)

In addition to the species by which this group is known, botanists in the Caucasian republics have described several other plants as distinct species or as subspecies of *Paeonia tenuifolia*. These forms have not been well studied in the West, nor has material from the wild been available for cultivation. For this reason, it remains more or less uncertain which members of this group will eventually receive species status. There appear to be forms of *P. tenuifolia* with somewhat broader segments or leaflets (*P. tenuifolia* subsp. *biebersteiniana*), with much shorter stems some 4–8 inches in length (*P. lithophila*), and with longer segments of leaflets (*P. carthalinica*). There are also several natural hybrids between *P. tenuifolia* and *P. mascula* subsp. *triternata* (*P. ×majko*, for example). These names are worth recording in the event that some of these plants become available to gardeners.

• Cooper's "anomala group"

Paeonia anomala Linnaeus var. *anomala*
Though named by Linnaeus, the species is believed to have been discovered in the mid-1700s by Gmelin. It is characterized by its leaves, which are dissected into a number of segments that are again divided. This species occupies a vast stretch of habitat, reaching from the Urals in Russia south to the Pamir Mountains in Central Asia and to Siberia. The stems are up to 20 inches in length. The lower leaves are biternate but very much divided into narrow segments, some of which are deeply lobed. The crimson flowers are 3–3.5 inches across, with ovate petals. The true species is seldom found in cultivation. Diploid (10 chromosomes). (Plate 93)

Paeonia anomala var. *intermedia* (Meyer and Ledebour) Fedtschenko
Stern used this name to identify a variant form of the species, one that is much more readily available. It is called *Paeonia hybrida* var. *intermedia* by some Russian botanists. This form seems to occupy an even wider range than does the key species, from the Kola Peninsula in northern Russia to the Altai, in addition to the range of *P. anomala*. The flowers are purple to red. This is probably the same plant offered

by nurseries under various other names including *P. intermedia* and *P. ural.* Several other subspecies or varieties of *P. anomala* have been described by botanists in Central Asia, but again no plant material has reached Western plantsmen and therefore no definitive description or name can be offered. Diploid (10 chromosomes).

Paeonia beresowskii Komarov

This is a plant from the same region as that in which *Paeonia veitchii* is found. It was named by a Russian botanist several years after the introduction of *P. veitchii.* Stern treated it as *P. veitchii*, but Wister and other American specialists believe that it is a distinct species despite superficial similarities between the two plants. They differ in their flowering period and in the traits of their hybrid offspring. Diploid (10 chromosomes).

Paeonia sinjiangensis Pan

First described in 1979, it is found in the province of Xinjiang. It appears to be intermediate between *Paeonia anomala* and *P. veitchii*, but has only one flower per stem. Plants have not yet appeared in Western gardens. Chromosome number unknown.

Paeonia sterniana Fletcher

Most appropriately named to honor F. C. Stern, this species was discovered in southeast Tibet at the 9500-foot elevation and brought to the West in 1947, from seeds and plants collected by Ludlow and Elliott. It reaches a height of 36 inches. The leaves are alternate and biternate, the many leaflets segmented, narrow, and elliptic. The solitary flowers are to 3 inches across; the petals are white, thin, and papery. Though at one time it was found in a few gardens in Great Britain, the plant now appears to be extremely rare in cultivation. Chromosome number unknown.

Paeonia veitchii Lynch var. *veitchii*

This species, a peony very similar to *Paeonia anomala*, also poses various problems of identification. It grows fairly widely in China at high elevations. It is 8–20 inches high with biternate lower leaves and deeply incised leaflets, which are dark green on the top. There are usually two or more flowers per stem in various shades of pink or magenta. Diploid (10 chromosomes). (Plate 106)

Paeonia veitchii var. *woodwardii* (Stapf and Cox) F. C. Stern

Found near Zhoni in Gansu in open yak-grazing country at 9000–11,000 feet. This is a smaller plant; it stands at just 12 inches and bears several pink to rose-pink flowers per stem. A delightful garden plant and easy to grow in any soil. Diploid (10 chromosomes).

Do not let the present inadequacy of cultural information deter you from trying at least one or two of these delightful peonies in your garden. While some are very specific as to their cultural needs, many are well worth trying. Simply remember that the location of a species in the wild is a good indication of the condition that it likes and should do well in. Obviously those from the Mediterranean areas are better adapted to gentler climes, while those native to northern areas of the world or higher elevations are more likely to thrive in more rugged, colder climates. Acquiring species peonies is perhaps the greatest difficulty you'll encounter. Collectors should look for some of the more difficult-to-find species listed in Appendix I and try their hand at them.

Chapter 4

Recommended Cultivars

If only a handful of species peonies are being grown in the gardens of the world, the blame may be placed on the glorious distraction of the more than 1300 cultivars that are presently available commercially worldwide, as Appendix I will attest. Many are scarce—offered by only one source—and time has passed others by. In any case, it is a difficult and possibly presumptuous task to select a relative few to recommend highly, and yet such listings, made with the help of commercial growers all over the world—one of recommended herbaceous cultivars and the other of recommended tree peony cultivars—will make up the bulk of this chapter. These are peonies that have proven themselves; all do well under a wide variety of climatic and cultural conditions. A number have been recognized as superior by peony enthusiasts and commercial growers of roots and cut flowers from around the world.

But gardeners as a group will not only have different gardening requirements but varying definitions of beauty as well. For this reason, you may want to try several of the cultivars included here—or for that matter, try others I haven't singled out. We can agree on some terms, however, before I begin describing my favorites.

In their catalog descriptions, most nurserymen use one scale for identifying time of bloom when referring to the old-fashioned lactiflora cultivars and another scale entirely for species and hybrids. This has only confused gardeners. For purposes of comparison among all cultivars referred to in this chapter, I have chosen a different system, based on the flower season designations proposed by Silvia Saunders and reported by Don Hollingsworth in volume 251 of the American Peony Society Bulletin.

The specific seasons of bloom I shall use, along with some representative plants, are as follows:

> Very Early: Early herbaceous hybrids, such as Saunders' 'Claire de Lune' and 'Sunlight'.
>
> Early: *Paeonia tenuifolia* and herbaceous hybrids, such as 'Early Windflower', 'Paula Fay', and 'Red Glory', as well as most suffruticosa tree peonies.
>
> Early Midseason: Herbaceous hybrids, such as 'America', 'Cytherea', and 'Salmon Glow', as well as most hybrid tree peonies.
>
> Midseason: Late herbaceous hybrids, such as 'Red Charm', and early lactiflora cultivars, such as 'Charlie's White', 'Miss America', and the Itoh, or intersectional, hybrids.
>
> Late: The bulk of the lactiflora cultivars, such as 'Gardenia', 'Gay Paree', and 'Sea Shell'.
>
> Very Late: Late lactiflora cultivars, such as 'Elsa Sass' and 'Vivid Rose'.

In a typical weather year, each season of bloom will last approximately five to ten days; thus the total blooming window for peonies, from the earliest plants to the latest, is between forty-five and sixty days. This lengthy bloom period, it should be pointed out in passing, makes it possible for the gardener fond of peonies to have plants in bloom for as long as many of the other highly regarded flowering shrubs.

Obviously, climatic conditions influence blooming time. In areas such as the U.S. Department of Agriculture's hardiness zone 8, where our nursery is located, the season usually runs from mid-April through early June. In colder areas, such as Minnesota (zones 3 and 4), the season usually runs from mid-May through the end of June and occasionally into early July. Whatever the anticipated bloom season, cold, wet weather delays its start, while a warm spring or an early heat wave accelerates blooming. But despite these climatic variations, the bloom sequence is quite predictable for mature plants, that is to say those that have been in the ground three or more years.

Differing climatic conditions affect peony plant growth in various ways. In unusually cool, wet springs the early hybrid cultivars bloom approximately on schedule, but those that usually flower in midseason may be up to two weeks behind schedule. The late forms will be similarly delayed. Further, many cultivars will grow taller than usual, producing stems perhaps 8 inches or more beyond the norm.

If on the other hand the spring weather is warmer than usual, flowering time will be advanced. The bloom season will start up to three weeks early, depending on location; cultivars of all kinds respond in the same way. A sudden heat wave may compress the entire bloom season. In general, overly hot weather leads to shorter-lived flowers.

Warmth, or the lack of it, will also affect color. For example, when the weather has been cool, the base color of 'Raspberry Sundae' will be a deeper pink, and the red overlay may be completely absent on some flowers. Given a cold, wet spring, white lactiflora cultivars may open showing tones of pink, which can last for several days.

Another category we can standardize is flower size. Peony flowers may range from 3 inches to more than 12 inches in diameter. Careful attention to culture and vigilant disbudding (removal of any small side buds) will yield the largest bloom possible. For purposes of comparison among the recommended cultivars, I have characterized the size of bloom as follows:

Small: 3–5 inches in diameter
Medium: 5–7 inches in diameter
Large: 7–9 inches in diameter
Very Large: more than 9 inches in diameter

Finally, this glossary of flower form terms, derived from those currently employed in peony shows, will be the reader's guide to the morphological terminology of the following plant descriptions:

Single: A fertile center (pollen-bearing stamens and seed-bearing carpels) surrounded by five or more petals in a single layers.
Semi-double: A fertile center surrounded by several layers of petals.
Japanese: A center of heavier, colored staminodes (sterile stamens) surrounded by five or more petals. Wider petaloids often push up through the staminodes.

Anemone: A center nearly filled with petaloids. This is a stage between Japanese and double; some catalogs place such plants in
the Japanese class, others describe them as doubles.
Double: A usually sterile bloom, with both the stamens and carpels
of the center transformed into petaloids.

Different arrangements of petals lead to doubles being further described as
globular, bomb, or rose form. In the following descriptions, I do not always
distinguish between these various double forms. Keep in mind, too, that
under some conditions, flowers of different form may appear on the same
plant. This instability often occurs in young plants but can be a consequence of weather and cultural conditions as well.

One last note: The vast majority of peonies grow to a height of 30–36
inches; I have not specified a height for plants that can be expected to attain this typical size.

HERBACEOUS PEONIES

'A. B. Franklin' (Franklin 1928). Awarded the APS Gold Medal in 1933. A
large but compact double white, with soft rose and ivory hues. This reliable
bloomer usually requires staking. Late.

'Alice Harding' (Lemoine 1922). A double whose pale pink outer petals
surround a creamy white center. Strong stems support the large, fragrant
flowers, which are further set off by the excellent foliage. Very popular in
Europe, but not considered reliable in North America. Late. (Plate 3)

'America' (Rudolph 1976). Awarded the APS Gold Medal in 1992. A large
single hybrid of a brilliant scarlet, a hue with great carrying power in the
landscape. An improvement on its parent, 'Burma Ruby'. Early Midseason.
(Plate 4)

'Barrington Belle' (C. G. Klehm 1971). This lactiflora may have flowers of
either Japanese or anemone form, or a combination of both. The rose-red
guard petals surround a broad central tuft of rose-pink to red staminodes.
The large blooms are carried on sturdy stems. Midseason.

'Bonanza' (Franklin 1947). A color-fast, luminous, dark red double containing hints of cherry and mahogany. Its large flowers are displayed on a strong, upright bush. Midseason.

'Bowl of Cream' (C. G. Klehm 1963). Awarded the APS Gold Medal in 1981. A pure white double of rose-form, with hidden stamens. Flowers are often very large, and the plant is a robust grower with bright green foliage. Late. (Plate 16)

'Bride's Dream' (Krekler 1965). A medium-sized flower of Japanese form, with pure white petals surrounding very narrow white petaloids. Late.

'Bu-Te' (Wassenberg 1954). Awarded the APS Gold Medal in 1975. Large, white, cup-shaped flowers of Japanese form are held on 42-inch stems above a dense, round bush. Late. (Plate 17)

'Burma Ruby' (Glasscock 1951). Awarded the APS Gold Medal in 1985. A bright red hybrid, its single flowers are held above a nicely shaped bush. The large flowers last well when cut. Early. (Plate 18)

'Carolina Moon' (Auten 1940). A large white double with yellow tints, it has not yet received the recognition it deserves. Late. (Plate 20)

'Charlie's White' (C. G. Klehm 1951). Famous Klehm introduction, rated "tops" by most cut flower growers because of its ability to hold up in cold storage. This double white is a good all-around peony whose large, fragrant flower is at its best when first open. The deep green foliage remains attractive through the summer. Midseason.

'Chocolate Soldier' (Auten 1939). A unique hybrid, the result of a cross between *Paeonia lactiflora* and *P. officinalis*. While usually of Japanese form, the same bush may produce both single and double flowers as well. Some of the large blooms are solid dark red, others may be flushed with yellow. Dense, dark green foliage. Midseason.

'Cincinnati' (Krekler 1962). Large double flowers of crabapple pink, each petal tipped with silver. The golden accents on central stamens provide contrast. Late. (Plate 21)

'Claire de Lune' (White–Wild 1954). Perhaps the finest of the single ivory-yellow hybrids and the only plant that grew from White's thousands of crosses of 'Mons. Jules Elie' and *Paeonia mlokosewitschii*. The medium-sized flower has well-rounded, cup-shaped petals, set off by deep, almost orange anthers. Thin but straight and stiff stems, 28–32 inches in length. The plant forms a wide clump, to 4 feet, with time. Very Early.

'Coral Charm' (Wissing 1964). Awarded the APS Gold Medal in 1986. A glowing coral to peach semi-double peony. Very large flowers cover a wide, vigorous bush. Listed at 36 inches, but often taller. The result of inbreeding *Paeonia lactiflora* 'Minnie Shaylor' with hybrid lines. Early. (Plate 23)

'Coral 'n Gold' (Cousins–R. Klehm 1981). A large, dazzling coral single or semi-double hybrid with cup-shaped petals. It is becoming quite popular. Early.

'Coral Sunset' (Wissing–C. G. Klehm 1981). A semi-double hybrid, the result of a cross between *Paeonia lactiflora* and *P. peregrina* 'Otto Froebel'. The large flower is of an intense coral with overtones of rose. Roy Klehm, the introducer of the new Coral strain, thinks the color of this cultivar is the best of the series. Early. (Plate 24)

'Cytherea' (Saunders 1953). Awarded the APS Gold Medal in 1980. A low plant, 26–30 inches in height, with dense foliage. This semi-double hybrid (a cross between *Paeonia lactiflora* and *P. peregrina*) is covered with large, cup-shaped, rose-pink flowers. Excellent, long-lasting cut flower for home or commerce. Sometimes spreads via underground roots. Early Midseason. (Plate 27)

'Diana Parks' (Bockstoce 1942). A brilliant carmine-red double, the result of a cross between *Paeonia lactiflora* and *P. officinalis*. One of the most fragrant of all red peonies, the blooms of this hybrid are borne on 42-inch stems that are strong but sometimes crooked. The large flowers hold well when cut. Early Midseason.

'Do Tell' (Auten 1946). A Japanese form with a very unusual color combination: the outer petals are orchid-pink and the contrasting scoop of center staminodes are of a much darker rose-pink to red and a lighter blush. The large flowers are held above a strong plant with crisp foliage. Late. (Plate 29)

'Dolorodell' (Lins 1942). Awarded the APS Gold Medal in 1984. A vivid medium-pink double, with large blooms. Strong-stemmed and cloaked in heavy foliage to the ground. Late.

'Doris Cooper' (Cooper 1946). Awarded the APS Gold Medal in 1949. Large double flowers of a light salmon-pink, fading to white. The bush produces ample stems. Very Late.

'Douglas Brand' (Tischler 1972). A brilliant watermelon-red double whose blooms, when the plant is disbudded, often reach 10 inches in diameter. Unusually heavy stems hold the very large blossoms upright. Considered by many collectors to be the most desirable double red. Highly recommended. Late. (Plate 30)

'Duchesse de Nemours' (Calot 1856). An old standard much used in the cut flower trade. A cup-shaped white double whose central petals are a light yellow deepening to pale green. Large, fragrant flowers on a sprawling bush. Midseason.

'Early Scout' (Auten 1952). A very dark red single hybrid with the dense, ferny foliage of its parent, *Paeonia tenuifolia*, and small blooms. The plant reaches a height of 18–24 inches. It seems to do better in the northerly latitudes. Very Early. (Plate 31)

'Early Windflower' (Saunders 1939). The result of a cross between *Paeonia emodi* and *P. veitchii*. A large but graceful, light, and airy plant with small, nodding, single white flowers and light green, cut-leaved foliage. Plant and flowers are nearly indistinguishable from 'Late Windflower', which blooms a week to ten days later. Both are wonderful specimen plants whose foliage adds interest throughout the seasons. Early. (Plate 32)

'Edulis Superba' (Lemon 1824). A fragrant, rosy pink double, somewhat rough in form. The plant flowers profusely and the medium-sized blooms store well, which has ensured its popularity with cut flower growers since its introduction. Lax stems, some 34–38 inches in length. Midseason. (Plate 33)

'Eliza Lundy' (Krekler 1975). There is some confusion as to whether this is a hybrid form of or a selection from *Paeonia officinalis*. A deep red double whose medium-sized blossoms very closely resemble 'Red Charm' except for their smaller size. Arching stems make a low bush, some 24 inches high, spreading to 36 inches across. Foliage goes dormant early. Early.

'Elsa Sass' (Sass 1930). Awarded the APS Gold Medal in 1943. A superb double, 25–32 inches high, whose white outer petals surround a center of pale pink and yellow tones. Dark green, broad-leaved foliage. A reliable bearer of heavy crops of large flowers and satisfactory for any use. Very Late.

'Emma Klehm' (C. G. Klehm 1951). A large, glowing, very dark pink double on a low bush, 24–28 inches in height, with foliage to the ground. Very Late. (Plate 34)

'Etched Salmon' (Cousins–R. Klehm 1981). A charming hybrid double in a soft salmon-pink to coral whose petals have a delicately etched edge. The medium to large flowers are carried on a strong bush with impeccable plant habits. Early Midseason. (Plate 35)

'Eventide' (Glasscock 1945). A hybrid, the result of a cross between *Paeonia lactiflora* and *P. peregrina*. A cup-shaped coral to pink single with crinkled texture, its large flowers are borne on a 38-inch plant. Strong grower. Early. (Plate 36)

'Fairbanks' (Auten 1945). A medium-sized blush of Japanese form. The vigorous plant produces stems 36–38 inches in length. Very Late.

'Felix Crousse' (Crousse 1881). Brilliant carmine-red blooms, touched with silver. A medium to large double, it has long had the reputation of being a good cut flower for commercial use, though later introductions, including the next, have improved upon both its form and color. Late. (Plate 38)

'Felix Supreme' (Kriek 1955). An improved 'Felix Crousse'. The double red blooms are large and abundant and the plants are vigorous. It is suitable for the home garden or commercial cut flower production. Late.

'Festiva Maxima' (Miellez 1851). The most popular old white. A globular double with crimson flecks, its name means "gayest" and "greatest." Large, fragrant blooms on a plant with dark green foliage. Midseason.

'Firelight' (Saunders 1950). A very popular single, one of Saunders' quadruple hybrids. The flat, large to very large blooms are of a rose color with darker pink flares, borne on 24-inch stems. The plant reaches a height of 40 inches. Early.

'Flame' (Glasscock 1939). A hot pink single with orange tones, the result of a cross between *Paeonia lactiflora* and *P. peregrina*. The stocky plants, with strong, straight stems, perform well in partial shade. Its medium-sized flowers hold well when cut. Early. (Plate 41)

'Gardenia' (Lins 1955). This very desirable cultivar, shaped like the flower for which it is named, has large double blooms ranging in color from blush to white. The flowers are carried on vigorous, stocky, 34-inch stems. Late. (Plate 43)

'Gay Paree' (Auten 1933). A flamboyant, medium-sized flower of Japanese form whose cerise-pink petals surround a center of creamy white. Pink petaloids frequently come up through the center, producing a tufted effect. A vigorous grower with 30-inch stems. Late. (Plate 45)

'Gene Wild' (Cooper 1956). An open double of delicate light to medium pink. The large petals of good substance are sometimes tipped with red and hide the stamens. Strong stems. Late. (Plate 46)

'Glowing Candles' (Wild 1966). A medium to large flower of Japanese form, with delicate, pale pink outer petals. Petaloids often arise from the chamois-colored center. Side buds prolong the bloom period of this plant, which grows well from northern Canada down to Oregon. Late.

'Golden Glow' (Glasscock 1935). Awarded the APS Gold Medal in 1946, the first hybrid to be thus recognized. A hot pink single with orange tints, the center of its large flower is a mass of glowing yellow stamens. While it is a strong grower and fast increaser, the flower is short-lived and stems tend to be lax. Early. (Plate 48)

'Hansina Brand' (Brand 1925). Awarded the APS Gold Medal in 1946. A large high-domed double whose light pink petals deepen to salmon-pink at the base. Acclaimed for its qualities on the show bench as well as in the garden. The strong bush produces abundant flowers each year, but the quality is undependable. Late.

'Henry Bockstoce' (Bockstoce 1955). A large dark red double, an advanced-generation hybrid of a cross between *Paeonia lactiflora* and *P. officinalis*. The center of each blossom is shaped like a rosebud. It flowers abundantly. Early.

'Henry St. Clair' (Brand 1941). This brilliant red double sometimes produces a few buried stamens deep in its large bomb form. An excellent long-lasting cut flower with strong stems, it should be more widely known. Mid-season. (Plate 54)

'Honey Gold' (C. G. Klehm). A double whose broad, creamy white guard petals surround a center of palest yellow. Its large flowers are borne on 30-inch stems. A good cut flower, with a light, sweet fragrance. Late. (Plate 56)

'Irwin Altman' (Kelsey 1940). A distinctive and luminous double with symmetrically arranged, clear light red petals. This dependable cultivar frequently bears large blooms on first-year plants. Very fragrant. Late. (Plate 59)

'Isani-Gidui' (ex Japan pre-1928). The standard Japanese form of earlier years. Medium to large white flowers are borne on bending stems and exude a medicinal odor. Late. (Plate 60)

'Jan van Leeuwen' (van Leeuwen 1928). A white flower of Japanese form. Its medium-sized blooms are smaller than those of 'Isani-Gidui' but are carried on stronger stems. Very Late. (Plate 61)

'Kansas' (Bigger 1940). Awarded the APS Gold Medal in 1957. A red double of varying intensity, it can be counted upon, year after year, to produce an abundance of large flowers on a vigorous, healthy bush. It is an excellent cut flower, and with its highly held blooms makes a choice garden subject as well. One of the few red doubles that does well in southerly climates. Midseason. (Plate 63)

'Kelway's Glorious' (Kelway 1909). A very large, saucer-shaped white double with a creamy center. It forms a shapely bush with dark green foliage and its flowers are quite fragrant. No less esteemed a peony authority than George Peyton rated this cultivar the best peony grown. Late.

'Krinkled White' (Brand 1928). A large white single with taffeta-textured petals and white-topped green pistils showing through the yellow center. Blooms are held on slender stems. This very popular cultivar withstands drought and holds up well when cut. Late. (Plate 65)

'L'Etincelante' (Dessert 1905). A medium-sized, cup-shaped pink single whose petals are bordered with silver. A vigorous plant, its roots are prized for grafting. Very Late. (Plate 66)

'Laddie' (Glasscock 1941). A dwarf hybrid, only 12 inches high, with single red flowers and cut-leaved foliage that discloses its *Paeonia tenuifolia* heritage. It is a better grower than its species parent or 'Early Scout' in the South. Its low profile and small flowers make it wonderful in the rock garden, but room must be provided for its large root system. Very Early.

'Lady Alexandra Duff' (Kelway 1902). A blush-pink double whose flowers are borne in clusters. With its abundance of small blooms and graceful foliage, it lends a note of cottage-style informality to the garden. Late. (Plate 67)

'Late Windflower' (Saunders 1939). The result of a cross between *Paeonia beresowskii* and *P. emodi*. It has everything in common with 'Early Windflower' except that its leaves are perhaps even more finely cut and its small single white blooms appear a week to ten days later. Early.

'Le Jour' (Shaylor 1915). A large, rather loose, white single. Produces an abundance of splayed blooms on strong, straight stems with only a few side buds. Excellent when cut for the home. Midseason. (Plate 69)

'Lillian Wild' (Wild 1930). Double blush flowers that soon turn to white. Bloom size increases as the plant matures, so the flowers on older plants are often very large. Late. (Plate 71)

'Longfellow' (Brand 1907). A bright red double whose large flowers are borne on 24-inch stems. The blooms are sometimes irregular in shape and not abundant, but the plant endures in the market because of its unfading, clear color both in the garden and as a cut flower. Late.

'Lottie Dawson Rea' (Rea 1939). A large and well-built white double with a light pink center. The foliage is dark green. Flowers generously and dependably. Late.

'Lotus Queen' (Murawska 1947). A Japanese form with pure white guard petals and finely cut, yellow staminodes. A medium-sized flower, cup-shaped and slightly fragrant. Late.

'Louis van Houtte' (Calot 1867). An old-time double, the medium to large cherry-red flowers bloom on 36-inch stems. It is usually grown for cut flower production. Late.

'Lowell Thomas' (Rosenfield 1934). A medium-sized, dark red double or semi-double with stamens showing. A low-growing, dependable bloomer, it reaches a height of only 24 inches. Late. (Plate 74)

'Ludovica' (Saunders 1941). A translucent, rose-colored hybrid, the result of a cross between *Paeonia lactiflora* and *P. peregrina*. The large semi-double flowers have four rows of cup-shaped petals. A very low, bushy plant, well-suited for the perennial border or as a hedge. Early.

'Mandarin's Coat' (Marx–Rogers 1978). A symmetrical, medium-sized Japanese whose rose-colored petals surround a sparkling gold center. Only 24 inches high. Though relatively new, it has proven itself from Minnesota to Oregon. Late. (Plate 77)

'Martha Bulloch' (Brand 1907). A flat double pink, this dependable cultivar produces an abundance of large blooms. The foliage is narrow. Late.

'Mary E. Nicholls' (Nicholls 1941). A pure white double of a desirable rose form. It bears large, very fragrant flowers in great quantity and produces numerous side buds. Worthwhile. Late.

'Minnie Shaylor' (Shaylor 1919). A large semi-double white, similar to 'Miss America' but a faster increaser. Midseason to Late.

'Minuet' (Franklin 1931). A medium-sized pink double. It stores well and its very long, 40-inch stems make it a desirable cut flower. Late. (Plate 80)

'Miss America' (Mann–van Steen 1936). A two-time APS Gold Medal winner, in 1956 and 1971, and the standard for white semi-doubles. Though somewhat slow to increase in some areas, it makes a dependable bush up to 4 feet in diameter and produces numerous large flowers. Good in the garden as well as for cut flowers. It is the earliest of the lactifloras, and so does well in more southerly areas. Midseason. (Plate 81)

'Mme. de Verneville' (Crousse 1885). A white double whose center crown of petals is accented with crimson. Its fragrant, medium-sized blooms excel as cut flowers: they hold up very well in cold storage and the plant itself is extremely floriferous. One of the fastest-increasing plants. Late.

'Mons. Jules Elie' (Crousse 1888). This large, fragrant rose-pink double has been the most popular pink in North America for decades and is widely grown. A very desirable cut flower on a freely blooming bush of light green foliage. Midseason. (Plate 82)

'Moonstone' (Murawska 1943). Awarded the APS Gold Medal in 1959. A blush double, with white outer petals surrounding the pale pink inner ones, it is a thoroughly finished-looking flower that excels everywhere. The large blooms are durable and numerous. Midseason to Late. (Plate 83)

'Mother's Choice' (Glasscock 1950). A large, compact, pure white double whose blooms are held on 30-inch stems. The bush is wide-leaved and dependable. Even small first-year flowers are true to form. Late. (Plate 84)

'Mr. Ed' (C. G. Klehm 1980). A blush double that sometimes sports pink flowers on the same bush. The large blooms are fragrant and have proven to be good cut flowers. Late.

'Mrs. Franklin D. Roosevelt' (Franklin 1932). Awarded the APS Gold Medal in 1948. A refined, pure light pink double, the large heavy blooms are cup-shaped, with overlapping petals. It is noticeably fragrant and satisfactory for any use. Late. (Plate 85)

'Mrs. J. V. Edlund' (Edlund 1929). Awarded the APS Gold Medal in 1933. A large, fragrant, pure white double, it is one of the early Gold Medal winners whose popularity has faded. Very Late.

'Mrs. Livingston Farrand' (Nicholls 1935). A clear, pure salmon-pink double. The glossy flowers may vary from medium to very large in size on the same bush. The long stems, 38–40 inches in length, often sprawl on the ground. Very Late. (Plate 86)

'Myrtle Gentry' (Brand 1925). When first open, the double flower is a flushed salmon-pink blush but soon turns a waxy white. The very large blooms are held above a dense bush on 24-inch stems. Some contend it is the most fragrant of all peonies. Very Late. (Plate 87)

'Nice Gal' (Krekler 1965). A symmetrically formed semi-double of frosted rose-pink. Its large flowers are carried atop the dense green foliage, which is only 22 inches high. Late. (Plate 88)

'Nick Shaylor' (Allison 1931). An early APS Gold Medal winner, honored for a second time with the APS Gold Medal in 1972. A large, blush-pink double that soon changes to white, its petals are thick and loose on the outer edges and more closely packed in the center. The 28-inch stems droop under the heavy load of flowers. Late. (Plate 89)

'Norma Volz' (Volz 1962). Awarded the APS Gold Medal in 1987. A large, full, double blush with pink and yellow tints. Though it shows well, growers in some sections find it often produces few flowers. Late. (Plate 90)

'Old Faithful' (Glasscock–Falk 1964). This is my personal favorite in red doubles, a dark red to rose-red, entirely free of purple undertones. Its strong stems never fall, even under the worst of conditions. The foliage is an attractive dark green and the very large flowers face upward, making it a wonderful specimen plant. An advanced-generation hybrid of unknown parentage, it is the latest hybrid to bloom. Late. (Plate 92)

'Paladin' (Saunders 1950). A medium-sized, semi-double hybrid (*Paeonia lactiflora* and *P. peregrina*) of a distinctive, glowing carmine-red. Loose form. The buds are shaped like long, pointed rose-buds and are borne over the low, 24-inch, mound-shaped bush. Performs better some years than others. Very highly rated by some. Early Midseason.

'Paul M. Wild' (Wild 1964). This large, velvety red double resists fading. It is 38 inches tall, with excellent garden habits. Late. (Plate 108)

'Paula Fay' (Fay 1968). Awarded the APS Gold Medal in 1988. A vivid pink semi-double, this hybrid (a 'Bravura' seedling) sports five rows of petals in its medium-sized blooms. Always dependable and good for any purpose, including cut flower production. Early. (Plate 109)

'Pico' (Freeborn 1934). A large single white with a dense center of yellow. Strong, loose-leaved stems. Midseason.

'Pillow Talk' (C. G. Klehm 1973). A large, light pink double of rose form. It is a strong grower with glossy green foliage. The plant reaches a height of 26–32 inches. Late. (Plate 110)

'Postilion' (Saunders 1941). A hybrid, the result of a cross between *Paeonia lactiflora* and *P. officinalis*. Perhaps Saunders' best-known red. Very large semi-double flowers on strong stems. Early.

'Prairie Moon' (Fay 1959). This outstanding hybrid (the result of a cross between 'Archangel' and 'Laura Magnuson') ranges in color from pale yellow to ivory or cream. It is of variable form, usually a semi-double or single, particularly on young plants, but sometimes occurs as a loose double. Dependably flowering with large blooms. A strong grower, it is excellent for any purpose. Early to Midseason. (Plate 112)

'Princess Margaret' (Murawska 1960). A large, fragrant, cup-shaped double of a rich, dark pink-rose, free of blue tones. Great as an exhibition flower as well as a garden specimen. Late. (Plate 113)

'Raspberry Sundae' (C. G. Klehm 1968). This cultivar bears large blooms ranging in color from blush to cream with varying amounts of raspberry-pink splashed atop the flowers. A distinctive flower with a mild, sweet fragrance. Late. (Plate 114)

'Red Charm' (Glasscock 1944). Awarded the APS Gold Medal in 1956. A very large, waxy, dark red hybrid, the result of a cross between *Paeonia lactiflora* and *P. officinalis*. Each of its flowers develops into a high, rounded mound. Every gardener should have this plant—it would be difficult to find a better peony. Midseason. (Plate 115)

'Red Comet' (Auten 1956). A seedling of 'Radiant Red', this is an intense, dark red double on strong stems. The large blooms, dependably produced, are as good for cutting as they are in the garden. It should be better known. Midseason.

'Red Glory' (Auten 1937). A hybrid, the result of a cross between *Paeonia lactiflora* and *P. officinalis*. The very large semi-double blooms are borne on a massive bush, which often spreads to 4 feet. The first of the intense red peonies to flower, it needs staking but is well worth the effort. Early. (Plate 116)

'Requiem' (Saunders 1941). One of the most widely grown of Saunders' hybrids, the result of a cross between *Paeonia lactiflora* and *P. macrophylla*. A waxy white single, its medium-sized flowers are borne on the 38-inch stems of a dense plant with large leaves. Midseason. (Plate 119)

'Rosedale' (Auten 1936). A compact plant, 25–30 inches in height, which produces numerous medium-sized, clear rose-red flowers of either double or semi-double form. A hybrid of *Paeonia lactiflora* and *P. officinalis*. Excellent as a cut flower where the trade will accept a shorter stem. Highly regarded in Europe, New Zealand, and North America. Late. (Plate 121)

'Roselette' (Saunders 1950). A large, clear pink single whose petals have a crinkled texture. It is a second-generation hybrid descended from *Paeonia lactiflora*, *P. mlokosewitschii*, and *P. tenuifolia* crosses. An average number of strong stems rise well above the dense bush. Stores well after cutting. Early. (Plate 122)

Paeonia officinalis 'Rubra'. Probably the most widely grown red double of pioneer days and one of the two most widely available cultivars of species peonies in North America; the other is *Paeonia tenuifolia* 'Rubra Plena', which follows. It became the custom to decorate the graves of Civil War veterans with these red blooms, which is why the plant is still referred to as the Memorial Day peony, and indeed its medium-sized flowers appear very early in the season. A good grower with sprawling stems, 24–28 inches in length. Valuable as a cut flower for the early market. White and pink forms of the species are occasionally found but do not seem to grow as well as the red forms. Very Early.

Paeonia tenuifolia 'Rubra Plena'. Also known as the fernleaf peony. A dark red double whose small flowers are nestled atop finely divided, ferny foliage. The bloom is fleeting and the foliage goes dormant in early summer. It is a dwarf plant, usually 8 inches high when young, though height will vary with climate and age. Widely used in rock gardens, where room must be made for its large root system, unusual in such a small plant. It seems to prefer the cold; in warmer climates with wet winters, it often languishes. A single form is sometimes available. Early.

'Rushlight' (Saunders 1950). A single in tones of warm ivory and cream. A second-generation hybrid, descended from *Paeonia lactiflora*, *P. mlokosewitschii*, and *P. tenuifolia* crosses, its large flower is prized by those who grow it. Early. (Plate 123)

'Salmon Glow' (Glasscock 1947). A flat single that opens salmon and changes to a lavender-tinged pink. This very vigorous hybrid grows well and dependably produces an above-average number of medium-sized flowers. Stems often lax. Early Midseason.

'Sanctus' (Saunders 1952–1955). Either a second- or third-generation hybrid of a cross between *Paeonia lactiflora* and *P. officinalis*. A single white whose medium-sized flowers are borne on a dense, large-leaved bush, held just above the foliage by 24-inch stems. A favorite early white of many. Early.

'Sarah Bernhardt' (Lemoine 1906). A dark rose-pink double. The stems are lax and require support if they are to hold the large flowers. This dependable bloomer has been a standard in the cut flower trade for years. Very Late. (Plate 124)

'Scarlet O'Hara' (Glasscock–Falk 1956). A very large red single, the result of a cross between *Paeonia lactiflora* and *P. officinalis*. The plant reaches a height of 38 inches and has long slender roots, up to 4 feet in length, that are ideal for grafting. While other reds may be more distinctive, the robust growth habit of this hybrid permits it to thrive under less-than-ideal conditions. Midseason. (Plate 125)

'Sea Shell' (Sass 1937). Awarded the APS Gold Medal in 1990. A long-blooming, strong-growing plant, it produces an abundance of large, fragrant flowers of a soft, warm, satiny pink. Excellent for exhibition or general garden use, this standard pink single is still hard to beat. (A few blooms in a vase with baby's breath make a wonderful arrangement!) Late. (Plate 126)

'Shawnee Chief' (Bigger 1940). A dark red double whose medium-sized flowers are borne on strong stems and hold up well in storage when cut. The glossy green foliage remains attractive well into the fall. It is a stronger grower than either 'Felix Crousse' or 'Philippe Rivoire'. Midseason. (Plate 127)

'Shirley Temple' (origin unknown). A large, fragrant double, a pale rose-pink blush in color, soon turning to white. Very desirable as a cut flower. Most popular in Europe. Midseason. (Plate 129)

'Snow Mountain' (Bigger 1946). This large double unfolds pink-blush and gradually builds into a high mountain of snow-white petals. It always opens well. Late. (Plate 131)

'Stardust' (Glasscock–Falk 1964). A shining white single lactiflora with large, neatly cupped blooms held on strong stems. Though not itself a hybrid (it is a grandchild of 'Le Cygne'), it is the progenitor of the majority of Glasscock's hybrid creations. It seems to do best in northerly climates. Late. (Plate 132)

'Starlight' (Saunders 1949). Another of Saunders' quadruple hybrids. A medium-sized single with creamy ivory to pale amber petals, it is very like 'Claire de Lune', but blooms a week earlier. Very Early.

'Sunlight' (Saunders 1950). Small, delicate, pale yellow single flowers with pink tints are borne on a dwarf bush only 18 inches high. A quadruple hybrid. Very Early.

'Sword Dance' (Auten 1933). An outstanding red of Japanese form. The medium-sized flower is brilliant and showy, with petaloids arising in the center. Stands heat well. Late. (Plate 133)

'Top Brass' (C. G. Klehm 1968). This dependable large double, white when viewed from a distance, has white guard petals surrounding a high center of ivory, light pink, and yellow. The blooms, upon closer inspection, will reward one with a honey scent. The plant reaches a height of 28 inches. Late. (Plate 134)

'Vivid Rose' (C. G. Klehm 1952). Large, well-formed, dark pink doubles carried on stems 24–28 inches in length. Very fragrant and a vigorous grower. The buds keep well in storage and always open well. Very Late. (Plate 137)

'Walter Mains' (Mains 1957). Awarded the APS Gold Medal in 1974. A hybrid, the result of a cross between *Paeonia lactiflora* and *P. officinalis*, the petals of this large Japanese red are edged in gold. A strong grower. Early.

'Westerner' (Bigger 1942). Awarded the APS Gold Medal in 1982. A sturdy Japanese form whose light pink petals form a bowl filled with long, yellow staminodes. The large flowers are held high on sturdy stems rising from a vigorous bush. Late.

'White Cap' (Winchell 1956). Awarded the APS Gold Medal in 1991. A unique, eye-catching combination of ivory and pale pink staminodes set off by raspberry guard petals. The medium-sized blooms of Japanese form are held high above the foliage. Late.

'White Innocence' (Saunders 1947). Tallest of all herbaceous hybrid peonies at 5 feet. The stamens of the very unusual, small, white single flowers have been transformed to greenish white pistil-like forms. The mature plant is spectacular when used as a specimen or at the back of the border. Midseason. (Plate 140)

'Wilford Johnson' (Brand 1966). Double, pinkish rose flowers held aloft by strong, 28-inch stems. The large blooms rest uniformly on top of the dense foliage producing a sheet of color. It excels as a hedge plant or in the perennial border. Late.

TREE PEONIES

In contrast to the herbaceous peonies, the cultivars of tree peonies derive from a very few species. Unless otherwise specified, all cultivars are suffruticosas, and all hybrids are presumed to be crosses between suffruticosa tree peonies and *Paeonia lutea*. The spelling of Japanese names conforms to those given in *A Book of Tree and Herbaceous Peonies in Modern Japan* (Hashida 1990). Hybrids are usually 3–4 feet tall, and again, I have noted only the exceptions to that rule in the descriptions that follow.

'Age of Gold' (Saunders 1948). Awarded the APS Gold Medal in 1973. A semi-double hybrid, its medium-sized, creamy yellow flowers deepen to gold. Red flares. Foliage to the ground. Early Midseason. (Plate 2)

'Alice Harding' (Lemoine 1935). A dwarf hybrid, 16–20 inches tall, with foliage to the ground. This large, fragrant, lemon-yellow semi-double, with rich red flares, is a parent of all the first Itoh hybrids. Early Midseason.

'Banquet' (Saunders 1941). A first-generation hybrid seedling, selfed. Large, semi-double flowers of strawberry-red with touches of gold on the undersides of the petals. The cut-leaved foliage stands out in the landscape. Early Midseason. (Plate 7)

'Black Panther' (Saunders 1948). A mahogany-red semi-double hybrid, with large flowers and cut-leaved foliage. Early Midseason. (Plate 2)

'Black Pirate' (Saunders 1948). A hybrid with single or semi-double flowers of a very dark red with even darker flares. The large blooms have a very glossy finish and are held high above the foliage. Early Midseason.

'Boreas' (Daphnis). A first-generation hybrid seedling, selfed, with rich, nonfading, burgundy-red flowers. Twisted petals give the semi-double blooms an airy appearance despite their very large size. Early Midseason. (Plate 14)

'Chinese Dragon' (Saunders 1948). Awarded the APS Gold Medal in 1983. A single or semi-double with crimson flowers highlighted by dark red flares. The blooms of this hybrid tree peony are often very large, and its deep green foliage is touched with a hint of bronze. Early Midseason.

'Companion of Serenity' (Gratwick 1959). A light pink single, deepening near the center. Its delicate flowers are large to very large and ruffled. Early. (Plate 22)

'Gauguin' (Daphnis). A hybrid, its single flower is an unusual combination of yellow petals with a bold red center and veins. The amount of red often varies from blossom to blossom and from plant to plant. Neat, dark green foliage and large blooms. Early. (Plate 44)

'Gessekai' (ex Japan). One of the first tree peonies to bloom. Produces very large double or semi-double flowers of purest white. Early. (Plate 47)

'Godaishu' (ex Japan). Semi-double white with very large blooms held high above the foliage. An old favorite. Early.

'Gold Sovereign' (Saunders 1949). A flat, bright gold rosette with a golden boss of stamens. The large semi-double blooms of this hybrid are carried on a vigorous 5-foot plant. Highly recommended for more southerly areas. Early Midseason.

'Guardian of the Monastery' (Gratwick 1959). Single flowers of a soft lavender-pink with red flares. A vigorous tree peony with very large blooms. Early. (Plate 50)

'Hanakisoi' (ex Japan 1926). A vivid, medium pink that serves as the standard by which other pinks are judged. The very large semi-double flowers are carried on stiff stems. One of the last of the suffruticosas to bloom. Midseason. (Plate 51)

'Hesperus' (Saunders 1948). An exotic hybrid of "old rose" pink with yellow undertones and purple flares. Large single flowers with taffeta-textured petals. Early Midseason.

'High Noon' (Saunders 1952). Awarded the APS Gold Medal in 1989. This columnar-shaped hybrid tree peony reaches a height of 5–6 feet. Its large, fragrant, semi-double flowers are lemon-yellow, set off by raspberry flares. Frequent fall rebloom. Early Midseason. (Plate 55)

'Kamata-nishiki' (ex Japan 1893). A rich, dark purple semi-double whose buds are shaped like tea roses. The very large flowers are carried on a bush that grows 4–5 feet tall. Early. (Plate 62)

'Leda' (Daphnis). A hybrid, the result of a cross between 'Kokamon' and a second-generation hybrid seedling. A fragrant, ruffled semi-double of mauve-pink, highlighted with flares, veins, and streaks of dark plum. The large to very large flowers are held high above the glossy, deep green, broad-leaved foliage. Early to Early Midseason. (Plate 70)

'Madame Andre de Villers' (A. Rivière 1955). A full double in rose-red. Very large flowers and fine plant habits. Choice. Early. (Plate 76)

'Marchioness' (Saunders 1942). A large single hybrid of pearly mauve to yellow, suffused with rose. Prominent raspberry flares. An unusually striking combination. Early Midseason. (Plate 78)

'Renkaku' (ex Japan 1931). A semi-double white. The plant grows more broad than tall, to a width of 5 feet, producing an abundance of very large flowers, even on young plants. Early. (Plate 118)

'Renown' (Saunders 1949). Silvia Saunders' favorite of all her father's tree peony hybrids. The large single flowers, somewhat irregularly shaped, are a bright but light copper-red with yellow undertones. Occasional late summer rebloom. Early Midseason.

'Shintenchi' (ex Japan pre-1931). A very large, semi-double flower that opens a cameo pink and slowly changes to white. Petals are heavily ruffled with small, darker pink flares. Both plant and flower are of a heavy texture. Early. (Plate 128)

'Taiyo' (ex Japan pre-1931). A bright ruby-red semi-double. The very large blooms are borne on a vigorous bush, which can attain a height of 4–5 feet. Early.

'Themis' (Daphnis). A semi-double hybrid of an unusual shade of light pink, deepening to red at base. The large flowers show hints of blue. Early Midseason.

'Tria' (Daphnis). Three blossoms per stem. The clear, canary yellow flowers, medium to large in size, unfold in sequence. The petals of this single hybrid have a crinkled texture. Early. (Plate 135)

'Vesuvian' (Saunders 1948). A very low hybrid that makes a perfect mound of foliage some 2 feet high. Large double flowers of black-red with dramatic purple undertones. Early Midseason. (Plate 136)

'Yachiyo-tsubaki' (ex Japan pre-1931). A semi-double coral-pink whose very large flowers are silky smooth and tailored. Vigorous and dependable, it is one of my favorite tree peonies. Early.

'Yae Zakura' (ex Japan pre-1931). Pure pink semi-doubles carried on a vigorous bush. A very large bloom, but refined all the same. Early. (Plate 142)

'Zephyrus' (Daphnis). Very large blooms, some 10 inches across. These semi-double hybrid flowers are an unusual combination of pearly pink and peach with ruby-red flares. Healthy, broad, deep green foliage. Early Midseason.

Chapter 5
Culture

Peonies are among the least demanding of all perennials. A chapter on peony culture could almost be this brief: Successful peony growing requires little more than good drainage and a climate with weather cold enough to satisfy dormancy requirements—with a bit of fertile soil thrown into the mix for good measure. Peonies need moisture in the spring, but little thereafter. If they are kept weed-free and protected against the remarkably few pests and diseases to which they are susceptible, the only thing left to do will be to stake the long-stemmed, top-heavy doubles, protect them from the wind, and enjoy the view.

Where can peonies be grown successfully? In many more areas than is commonly believed. They are produced commercially as far north as Finland and central Saskatchewan, Canada, down to the higher elevations of southern California. In the Southern Hemisphere, they grow well in New Zealand and can even be found, happily thriving, in some microclimates near Melbourne, Australia, and on the island of Tasmania.

Growth cycle

Whatever the hemisphere, peony tubers start sending out their feeder roots in the fall, developing an extensive network of root hairs before the ground is frozen; they begin growing again when the ground thaws.

Though the activity is unseen, peonies continue to grow below ground weeks after their leaves die back in the fall and before they appear again in the spring. The function of a peony tuber is analogous to that of a bulb: the early spring growth is supported by nutrients stored in the tuber the previous year.

Above ground, growth is first evident with the emergence of the elongating stem of a crown bud. Its sharp point pushes through the soil surface and then splits, permitting a leafy shoot to grow. This first visible sign of growth is usually related to time of bloom. Cultivars such as 'Daystar' and 'Early Windflower' are early bloomers as well as the first to emerge. Late-blooming lactiflora cultivars such as 'Vivid Rose' and 'Walter E. Wipsom' are among the last to emerge. In areas with mild winters and early springs, this procession of emergence from the early to the late bloomers may span three weeks or more, starting sometime in late winter or early spring. Where winters are bitter and spring comes late and with a rush, growth starts later and the period of emergence and bloom is compressed.

Early growth in peonies comes in a fascinating burst of color. The new shoots range from delicate pinks to glistening reds, and the tender leaves that follow unfurl in bronzes, reds, and greens. Changes can be seen almost daily throughout the spring as the leaves and stems of the various cultivars gradually assume their verdant hues, while the stems and leaf veins of some cultivars, such as 'Picotee', will remain red throughout the season, in handsome contrast to the deep green foliage. Unlike tree peonies, both herbaceous peonies and Itoh hybrids die to the ground each fall.

Dormancy and cultivar selection

A winter chilling is absolutely necessary for peonies to prosper and flower. The dormancy requirement, like that of apples and other fruit trees, is satisfied when the soil temperature remains in a specific low range over a sufficiently long period. This is a signal to the crown—the nerve center of the plant as it were, the part of the plant between stems and roots—to start growth and flowering when the soil warms in the spring.

Temperature levels and lengths of dormancy may be different for each species and cultivar, but specific ranges have not yet been determined. For the present, the dormancy requirement is met either by a long spell of cool weather or a few hours of cold most days over an even longer period. Caprice Farm Nursery is located in the U.S. Department of Agriculture's hardiness zone 8, which is a zone warmer than some peony experts recommend as optimal. Many of our winters never see temperatures drop below 25°F, and yet most species and cultivars grow extremely well here. Repeated reports of satisfactory peony flowering have also come from microclimates in the United States as far south as northern Alabama, southern California, and Texas—all zone 9 regions.

Dormancy requirements necessary to force the potted peony cultivars widely used for cut flower production were reported by Byrne and Halevy in 1986. Working in Davis, California, they subjected 'Festiva Maxima' to various regimens of artificial cooling. Flower bud dormancy was broken by four weeks at 46°F. Lengthening the storage time to six weeks or reducing the temperature to just above freezing increased the total number of shoots that emerged.

Experienced growers have long advocated from 480 to 900 hours of natural or controlled cooling to break the dormancy of most herbaceous peonies. In my experience, a minimum of 480 hours at temperatures from just above freezing to 46°F is sufficient for most species and cultivars. Undoubtedly, slightly higher temperatures over a longer period of time would also do. Another rule of thumb that seems to work: If you can grow apples, you can grow peonies. A good rough guide, but do not attempt to grow a peony beside an apple cultivar specifically bred for semitropical areas!

As for species peonies, gardeners should consider their native habitats, which indicate the climates and soil features to which the plants are best adapted and hint at suitable dormancy requirements. *Paeonia lactiflora*, native to Siberia and northern China, and its many cultivars require the longest winter dormancy—often as much as 900 hours to do their best. Cultivars developed from species native to warmer climates present less demanding dormancy requirements. *Paeonia mascula* subsp. *russii*, native to Sicily, is an example. 'Picotee', the only known cultivar selected from this subspecies, is a vigorous grower in the zones 7 and 8, yet may languish in zones 6 and lower. Even so, reports from Detroit, Michigan (zone 6), say it does well in that location.

There are other surprises. *Paeonia mlokosewitschii* hails from the chilly Caucasus and should do well in northerly areas, and yet this species is known to flourish in the milder areas of England as well as along the West Coast of the United States. Conflicting reports exist as to its vigor further north. Saunders wrote, "It should be in the garden of everyone who cares for lovely plants. . . . With me, in a stiff clay and a very severe climate, it flourishes like a weed. . . . But some of my correspondents in various parts of the United States find it an uncertain grower, and M. Lemoine writes me that it does poorly with him in Nancy [France]."

Fanciers and growers along the West Coast of North America and in the south of England have had difficulties with some lactiflora cultivars bred in the upper Midwest (zones 3, 4, and 5). For example, the double reds 'Mary Brand' and 'Richard Carvel' never put on for us in zone 8 the flower display that is typical in their colder home territory of Faribault, Minnesota. Robert Tischler's newer introductions, such as 'Bouquet Perfect' and 'Heidi', seem to have overcome this problem. They perform exceedingly well in northerly locations yet also thrive in milder climates.

Tree peonies do well in slightly more southerly or warmer areas. Toichi Domoto of Hayward, California (zone 10), was one of the foremost growers of these exciting plants for years, as we learned in Chapter 2. Coastal areas like his with many foggy winter days seem to satisfy dormancy requirements even though freezes seldom occur. While tree peonies grow well and can flower below zone 5, the buds often freeze. To succeed in the colder zones, the entire plant must be well insulated during the winter.

If your climate is marginally too warm for peony growing, you might consider creating a suitable microclimate. Begin by choosing a site protected from harsh afternoon sun. The east and north sides of a building or an area that enjoys dappled shade would both be advantageous. Avoid planting near surfaces that reflect heat, such as a white wall. Use mulches to keep the soil cool during the summer, and be sure to pull these mulches away as soon as the weather turns cold. This will give the tuber the best chance of being adequately chilled.

The growing range can also be extended southward through the careful selection of cultivars. Early-blooming hybrids, which contain genes from species originating in warmer climes, are ideal for areas marked by warm springs. The very earliest of them flower up to three weeks before the earliest lactifloras, and thus their flowers are opened before the really hot weather sets in. And delightfully long-lasting flowers they are, too, in light and airy forms: singles, semi-doubles, and Japanese. Many of the best of these early-blooming hybrids are identified in Chapter 4; the descriptions provided there will suggest a number of cultivars capable of marching southward. Avoid heavy doubles, which are invariably related to the chill-loving *Paeonia lactiflora*, the last of the species to bloom. The ever-intensifying heat of the new season may cook the buds before they open.

Purchasing and planting

Keep in mind that a peony is a long-term investment; if properly cared for, a plant will bring you pleasure for forty years or more. The savvy gardener plans ahead, therefore, by requesting the catalogs of several specialist peony nurseries, which offer not only a wider choice of plants but often better grown plants as well. Select the plants most suitable to your situation, and order them for fall delivery. It is best to plant peonies in the fall; this allows the plants to make the most of the favorable autumn and early winter days to adapt to their new surroundings and to add root structure. Nevertheless, gardeners should take advantage of the opportunity if local nurseries offer healthy-looking potted plants of desired cultivars in the spring.

If you plan to purchase your plants from a retail nursery, take heed, for retail nurseries have the habit of potting up their peonies in the fall. Root growth initiated in the fall is insufficient to form a solid root ball, and when a plant thus treated is removed from its pot, the root ball often shatters. To minimize plant damage, prepare the planting site and amend the backfill before attempting to remove your plant from its pot. When the hole is dug and the soil prepared, carefully remove the peony from its pot and plant immediately. If the pot is made of fiber, cut the sides down to the bottom in several places and nearly around the bottom as well. Then plant, tattered pot and all.

Select planting sites that receive at least six hours of sunlight a day, that are well away from competing tree or shrub roots, and that are at least 2 feet away from a wall or a paved driveway or walkway. If planting near a roof overhang, place the plants beyond the roofline so rain can reach them. Plants being grown primarily for cut flowers could be planted to edge the vegetable garden or with perennial asparagus or rhubarb, which have similar soil requirements.

A permanent, long-term perennial needs the best start possible. My father, an avid gardener, had this advice for me: "Always dig a dollar hole to put a ten-cent plant in." Since I was the one digging the holes and removing all the rocks from our New England soil, it was advice I thoroughly detested at the time. Today I treasure it and I continue to urge its wisdom, for it remains as valid and as important as ever.

The planting hole for a peony in fertile soil should be at least 15 inches deep and 30 inches wide. A smaller planting hole may suffice for the first two or three years' growth, but it will not be adequate beyond that time. Remember the time-tested adage: The first year the peony sleeps, the second year it creeps, and the third year it leaps. The planting hole must be sufficiently large to accommodate that third-year leap and the growth of the years beyond.

Obviously, the better the soil, the more vigorous the peonies will be. If your soil is questionable, have it tested. The cost of such a test, equal to that of a choice peony root, is a sound investment. When preparing a new bed for several peonies, till or spade the soil as deeply as possible. Add fertilizer as indicated by the soil test and till again. If the soil has not been tested, add nitrogen (N), phosphorus (P), and potassium (K) as recommended on a package of general garden fertilizer; see the section on fertilization, next up in this chapter, for specifics. If possible, let the bed—prepared and fertilized—lie fallow for several weeks. Just before planting, weed and till once more.

Upgrading poor soil for planting just a few peonies is not difficult. In particular, the soil in built-up areas may need some help. Such spots are notorious for having had the topsoil buried during preparation for construction and the ensuing labors. At typical planting depths, the soil is usually made up of poor subsoil and building debris, covered, at best, with a thin skin of topsoil.

Here is the remedy. Dig large holes, at least 24 inches in diameter and at least 18 inches deep. If some good topsoil can be salvaged, set it aside and discard the subsoil. Next, mix well-aged compost with the topsoil to make the backfill mixture. Do not use fresh manure, which burns tender new roots, or sawdust or bark dust; they rob the soil of nitrogen. If planting in heavy clay, do not add sand—the mixture may end up like concrete. Rather, mix in compost or peat moss to loosen and amend the clay.

Peonies tolerate a wide pH range, though slightly acidic to near neutral soil (pH 6.0–7.0) is the usual recommendation. I have grown peonies that produced satisfactory though not optimum growth in soil that tested as low as pH 5.6, so suffice it to say that peonies can be grown with acid-loving plants such as azaleas and rhododendrons in a soil of pH 5.6–6.9. A row of pastel-colored peonies placed in front of a towering hedge of dark-flowered rhodies is a breathtaking sight.

If the new peony root appears dry, soak it overnight before planting. Plant eyes up and roots down. Peonies sometimes fail to bloom if the top

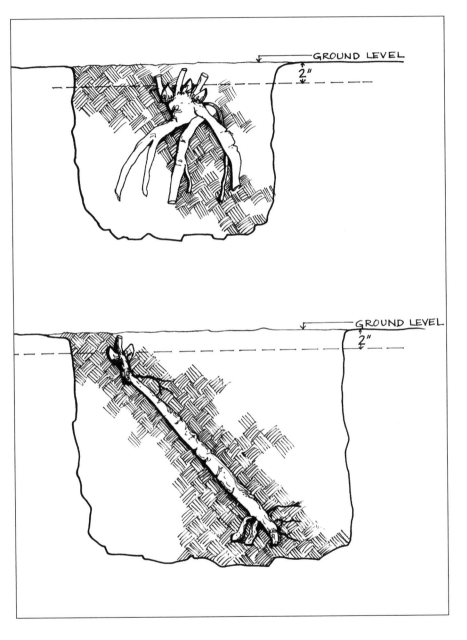

Planting lactiflora roots.

eyes wind up more than 2 inches below ground level after the soil has set-tled—why we do not know. It is better to plant the top eye too near the sur-face than too far below; if an eye is mechanically injured or is damaged by cold from being too shallowly planted, another will take its place. All the same, it is a good idea to conclude planting by marking the locations of the new plants with small stakes. This will help forestall damage to the eyes be-fore plants break ground in the early spring.

To prevent the tuber from sinking below 2 inches from ground level, fill the hole with amended soil, firm it slightly, then pour in 8–12 quarts of water. The water compacts the soil, preventing the plant or tuber from set-tling. Set the tuber to the correct depth, add enough soil to backfill to soil level, slightly mound the hole, and water again.

In southerly areas characterized by limited winter cold (zone 9), plant with the top eye at or just below the surface. This placement assures that the crown will be subjected to the lowest possible temperatures to break dormancy, since the temperatures in the top few inches of soil are strongly influenced by the air temperature.

To assure dormancy requirements, bare-root peonies should be planted in the fall. To encourage the best feeder root growth, the longer the time between planting and the onset of freezing temperatures the better. For northern climates, September or early October planting is best. In more moderate areas, zones 7–8, where hard freezes do not occur until later, planting can be done up to mid-November and even into December. If a hard freeze is expected before the order for new peonies arrives, don't worry. Prepare the sites as suggested. Remove the planting soil to a frost-free area and heavily mulch the planting holes. When the plants arrive, re-move the mulch. Position each plant in its hole, using the unfrozen soil to fill in around it, and water. Finally, mound mulch back over the new plant-ings.

Remember that newly planted peonies should not be allowed to dry out, and it therefore may be necessary—especially if the peonies were planted early in the fall—to water occasionally to keep the soil moist. After the ground freezes hard, cover new plants with several inches of a loose mulch (evergreen boughs, cornstalks, or straw) or mound loose dirt over the site. Mulching prevents soil-heaving, the cycle of freezing and thawing that can lift a plant to the surface.

Fertilization

Peonies are greedy feeders and so require a regular nutrition program. Soils in a limited number of sites are so intrinsically rich that they do not require additional fertilizer. In Chapter 2, we heard about Minnesota's glacial moraine, where peonies thrive in fields that have never once been fertilized in over a century of continuous peony production. Such cases are quite exceptional. Most soils will need constant nutrient replacement.

As with most root crops, the primary nutrients required by peonies are phosphorus (P) and potassium (K). If a common granular fertilizer (N–P–K) is used, the ratio of nitrogen (N) should never be higher than those of the other two major ingredients: mixes such as 5–10–10, 10–10–10, or 12–12–12 all work well. Lawn fertilizers, with their high amounts of nitrogen, should be avoided. Heavy nitrogen feeding produces lush foliage but poor flower and root growth.

Natural nutritional materials—raw bone meal (I dislike the steamed form because many nutrients are lost in the process), wood ashes, compost, sterilized steer manure, and well-rotted animal manures—are all good. Do not use any animal manures until they are thoroughly rotted and the heat attendant thereto is exhausted. Poultry and rabbit manures are both too rich in nitrogen to be utilized as the sole nutrient source. Home compost, sewage sludge (often available in metropolitan areas) composted with sawdust, or composted yard debris make excellent soil amendments, adding humus and trace elements as well as small amounts of the major nutrient elements.

Because all natural nutrient amendments must be broken down to their elemental chemical constituents in the soil before they are available to plants, they should be applied in the fall or winter after the peony foliage has been removed. Place fertilizers well away from the eyes, or you will risk damaging the next year's growth. During the fall and winter, the soluble nutrients are spread around and carried by rain and melted snow down to the growing roots.

After planting, no further nutrients need be added until the second fall. This application should be light—about two ounces per plant of a balanced chemical fertilizer. By the third year and thereafter, both tree and herbaceous peonies need twice-yearly applications of four ounces of fertilizer, the first in late fall or winter while the plants are dormant, and the second at flowering time.

Watering

Peonies are quite drought resistant. Most of their growth cycle is completed by the time the plants have bloomed in the spring. They can withstand drought during the summer, but if springs are dry, an inch of water per week is needed for good bloom. First-year growth will be improved if peonies are watered during their first summer.

If an irrigation system is to be employed, select a drip system if possible. This avoids wetting foliage and therefore reduces the likelihood of fungal infections. The sage advice of Dr. David Adams of the Oregon Extension Service is worth remembering: The best fungicide in the world is a dry leaf. Overwatering is not a problem as long as the soil is well drained. Standing water is fatal.

Staking

The longer stems of many cultivars with heavy double flowers will bow down, often to the ground, by the time the massive flowers have fully opened. Rainy or windy conditions only aggravate this tendency. One solution, of course, is to avoid planting these old-fashioned, oft-scented beauties —but this is a draconian resort at best!

You can grow these rewarding cultivars and avoid the problem altogether—with very little trouble or expense—by routinely staking the plants each spring. Often a single pass of heavy-duty garden twine around the plant, about a foot from the top, gives sufficient support, provided the foliage is tied up snugly. Alternatively, two lines—the first 8–12 inches from the top and a second another 12 inches below the first—can be used. Even better support is provided if the twine is then tied to a 2-by-2-inch stake placed behind the plant and securely anchored in the soil. Another possibility is to insert four to six lighter weight, green bamboo stakes around the outer edge of the plant. When green jute twine is wound around the green bamboo and green foliage, the stem support is almost invisible.

Metal plant supports are available in garden shops, but unfortunately these are flimsily constructed and not large enough to contain a mature peony. What's worse, the lower ends of so-called tomato rings are so close together that they may damage the crown when stuck down over the plant. Much better are the old-fashioned heavy-duty two-ring peony supports that are sometimes available. Made of 9-gauge galvanized wire, they are 30 inches high, with a top ring approximately 18 inches in diameter and a bottom ring 14 inches in diameter. These rings provide full support to the plant and can be stored over the winter and reused for a number of years.

Pruning

Older stems of tree peonies often become brittle. In most cases they simply snap under their own weight, but occasionally they are helped along by a passing wheelbarrow or a marauding dog. Branches that sweep out horizontally are especially prone to breakage. The hybrid 'Chinese Dragon' seems particularly given to this habit of growth. If a branch is broken, what remains of it should be cut back, either to the next set of leaves or down to ground level.

If your aim is to have larger—rather than more—flowers, prune brittle old stems by cutting them off at the base in the fall every two or three years. Such pruning encourages new growth from the crown. Some gardeners prune their tree peonies by removing cross branches and any new stems coming from the base, leaving perhaps three strong stems at the outer edge of the plant. A variation of this approach is to remove one third of the oldest stems of mature plants each fall. This pruning program results in larger flowers on the younger wood in the next year.

Diseases and pests

Both herbaceous and tree peonies are for the most part disease-free. There are, however, a few diseases that can under certain circumstances be troublesome. Most are caused by fungi, which typically attack one or more parts of the plant.

Botrytis bud blight is caused by the fungi *Botrytis paeoniae* and *B. cinerea*. These common fungi are microscopic plants that lack chlorophyll and connective tissue. They occur worldwide on a wide range of hosts in many genera of plants and are most active when the temperature is low and the humidity is high. Germination time is short, and their white spores can be carried long distances by wind. They overwinter in a dormant state, called sclerotia, in dead foliage, becoming active again when it warms up in the spring. Previously reported to exist only in the soft tissues of bud, leaf, and stem, botrytis blight has now been found, under certain conditions, within root tissues. *Botrytis paeoniae* is the usual culprit in North America; *Botrytis cinerea* is more prevalent in China.

Stems and buds afflicted with botrytis blight suddenly wilt, often just before the plant would be expected to flower. The affected area quickly turns brown and dries up. Except on small first-year plants, the fungus seldom affects all the stems on a plant.

In general this disease can be prevented by employing good sanitary practices. All stalks of herbaceous peonies should be cut to the ground each fall and the cuttings either immediately burned, or bagged and hauled away. Do not compost them. Treat any fallen leaves or debris in the same way. If peonies are planted in a mixed perennial bed, treat all plants that display similar symptoms in the same fashion.

Good air circulation is an important ally in the fight to prevent botrytis since fungus spores require a film of water on the leaves for germination. Plant peonies well apart and away from buildings, fences, and other plants that would interfere with air circulation. Full exposure to the sun is helpful. If it becomes necessary to water peonies while they are actively growing, do so early in the day so the foliage will be dry by nightfall.

Botrytis is seldom seen in warm and relatively dry springs. If on the other hand the spring is cold and wet, vigilance is essential. Check plants every day or two, and if a wilted stem is found, cut off the affected part. Be sure to cut well below the affected area, just above a lower leaf node. Be careful not to let the diseased tissue touch any other part of the plant. Carry a disposable bag to put the diseased stems in, and disinfect clippers after each cut by dipping them in rubbing alcohol or wiping with an alcohol-saturated cloth. These precautions usually provide all the control necessary.

If the disease appears one year and the next spring's weather is rainy, initiate a protective spray program. The classic Bordeaux spray is effective against *Botrytis* and since it remains a standard spray material for home fruit orchards, it is readily available in garden stores. The major drawback of this fungicide—a combination of copper sulfate and lime mixed in water—is that it stains. Take care that the spray does not drift onto surrounding painted or concrete surfaces, as the green stain it leaves is very difficult to remove.

Apply Bordeaux spray at least twenty-four hours prior to watering or a forecasted rain. Plants will need at least three applications, one every week to twelve days or so. The first application should coincide with the emergence of new growth, just as the shoots begin to break the surface. This application should cover both the shoots and the surrounding ground area. The second and third applications should wet the entire plant including the undersides of the leaves as well as the ground underneath. These sprays are protective and work by killing the fungus spores before they can grow into the plant tissue. If not diluted by rain or irrigation, each application will be effective for about fourteen days.

A planting that includes the early hybrids as well as the later lactiflora cultivars may need an additional application in the spring since the plants will push through the soil at different times. Another protective spray in the fall, applied over the entire planted area after the foliage has been removed, is also helpful if the problem has been severe.

Research done at Rutgers University in the 1940s indicated that the severity of peony blight is affected by three factors, singly or in combination: the presence of root nematodes, dry spells or low temperatures early in the spring, and a lack of potassium in plant tissues resulting from inadequate potassium levels in the soils. Thus, eliminating nematodes, watering during dry spells, and adequate fertilization are all smart preventative steps and will help strengthen the plant, making it more resistant to this disease.

Another fungal disease variously called leaf blotch, measles, or red stem spot (caused by *Cladosporium paeoniae*) may affect peonies, particularly in the midsection of North America. The first signs of this infection are dark purple spots on the surfaces of the upper leaves. Young stems may have elongated reddish brown streaks, and small reddish spots may also appear on the flower petals. Since both *Botrytis* and *Cladosporium* are fungi, the same protective spray program will control both.

New products to control fungi are always appearing, and so it is a good idea to consult a garden expert from time to time to learn what is available—and approved. Benlate, for instance, was long considered a good fungicide for peonies, but unfortunately, registration for use of this tried-and-true fungicide on ornamental plants has been withdrawn. Another proven material to control fungal diseases, though it is not always available, is Captan (also sold as Orthocide). Fellow grower Roy Klehm recommends using it three times during the spring growing season, the first application at full strength and the second two applications at half strength (Harding 1993).

Rootknot nematodes (*Meloidogyne* spp.), soil-dwelling microscopic parasites, are quite destructive of peonies. Affected plants develop dwarfed, spindly shoots that typically die within a season or two. The longer roots of infected plants are usually very irregular and gnarled in shape, and the small, fibrous feeder roots are dotted with galls (rounded swellings) the size of small peas. The centers of these nematode galls are yellowish and alive with nematode larvae.

Once established, nematodes are a persistent pest. It is difficult to control them without the use of powerful chemicals, which are not available to the home gardener, so examine newly purchased roots carefully. If any evidence of infection is evident, do not plant them. Notify the supplier and request a replacement or a refund. If there is even a suspicion that a plant in the garden is affected, dig it up and destroy it; it is simply not worth the risk. Then dispose of the surrounding soil.

The garden symphylan (*Scutigerella immaculata*) is another soil-dweller that can be a problem. This pest, which can be up to a quarter of an inch long, is a white, soft-bodied insect with six to twelve pairs of legs and vibrating antennae. It moves up and down through the soil, retreating to lower depths with low temperatures or drought.

Symphylans emerge from eggs, found in clusters of four to twenty-five at various soil depths. The eggs are generally laid in early spring and again in the fall. The nymphs and adults are active in spring (April and May) and late summer (August and September). Symphylans take from fifty to sixty days to grow from egg to adult stage. Both nymphs and adults damage plants by eating the growing tips of new root hairs, the only means of acquiring nutrients available to most plants. This pest is particularly destructive of spring-planted roots. Fall root-hair growth is less affected since cooler soil temperatures drive most of the symphylans below the peony root growth zone.

Garden symphylans are usually found in fine-textured, heavy clay soils, high in organic matter, or in ground that has been recently converted from livestock pasture or woodland. To determine their presence, take several soil samples from the top 8 inches of soil and spread the dirt out in a very thin layer on a dark surface. Upon careful examination, the white adults can be seen with the naked eye.

To control symphylans, spray the tilled soil with Lindane or a similar sterilizing agent, or work in a soil sterilant, such as Basimid. Follow the label directions precisely. Do nothing with this sterilized soil for three weeks, to allow the chemicals to completely dissipate. To check the level of dissipation, sow a few radish seed, which are particularly susceptible to even the lowest levels of pesticides. Successful germination will prove that the soil is safe to use. If germination is poor, wait a week and test again.

Another method of controlling symphylans is to leave the bed fallow for a year. Till frequently enough to keep weeds and grasses down, leaving nothing for the symphylans to eat. This greatly reduces their population. If the pest is present in established peony beds, Lindane, which will not damage plants, can be sprayed over the entire area in accordance with the label instructions. Water heavily immediately after spraying.

Other problems have been reported, although rarely. One is the bacterium *Septoria paeoniae*, which causes leaf spotting and stem cankers. This infection can be controlled by the same rigorous sanitary practices suggested for fungal diseases. Another rarity, mosaic disease—presumably viral—may cause concentric rings of alternating light and dark green on the leaves. Affected plants are dwarfed and since there is no cure, they should be dug out and disposed of. Diagnoses of these uncommon diseases should be referred to agricultural pathologists.

Finally, flea beetles have been reported as a problem by some cut flower growers (see Chapter 8). These insects damage flowers during their formation by chewing the edges of the bud. They are at their peak during long periods of warm weather; if found, they may be sprayed with pyrethrum or rotenone.

Chapter 6
Propagation

Propagation by seed

In the wild, both herbaceous and tree peonies have survived over the eons by reproducing from seed. Species peonies, all originally singles, are self-fertile, meaning the pollen produced by the stamens of the flower can fertilize other flowers from the same plant, leading to the production of viable seed. In other words, seeds from species plants isolated from other peony species readily and reliably reproduce the species.

Commercial production of species peonies by seed propagation is very successful. Propagating cultivars from seed, however, is a different story, and breeders who sow the seeds of intentional crosses in the hope of creating improved cultivars face an even more difficult situation. First, because they are cultivars and usually carry a complex mix of widely varying genetic material, the progeny almost never resemble their parents. Furthermore, unlike the species, not all cultivars are capable of producing seed. For example, plants producing full double flowers lack either or both stamens and pistils; in such forms, these reproductive parts of the flower have metamorphosed to petals or petaloids. The Japanese forms often develop carpels, but the stamens have metamorphosed to non–pollen-bearing staminodes. There are occasional exceptions to this rule, and a normally sterile plant may develop viable pollen or a pistil. Cultivars that produce single or semi-double flowers usually have both stamens and pistil and so can develop seed. As a consequence, propagators must turn to such forms for breeding purposes.

Saving and sowing seeds from herbaceous peony plants other than species cannot be recommended, except perhaps to the most dedicated hybridizer. It takes five or six years from seed harvest to the time of mature bloom, and even after this investment of time, something new and exciting may occur in only one plant in a thousand. Clearly, the expense and space required for cultivation becomes prohibitive. Our experience with a seed-propagation program begun by the accomplished hybridizer Walter Marx illustrates these difficulties.

As we learned in Chapter 2, Marx ran a leading perennial nursery in the late 1950s and '60s. In that era almost all peony cultivars available commercially were derived from *Paeonia lactiflora*. One year on a whim, Marx harvested all the seeds in a forty-acre field of named peony cultivars. The resulting bushel of seed was planted out in rows 3 inches apart and grown on for several years. The most promising plants were identified, then divided and replanted. Further selection and replanting from these original seedlings was repeated several times. When Caprice Farm Nursery purchased the Marx peonies in 1978, we found that the stock included thirteen unnamed peony seedlings, which Marx had concluded were worthy to be named, registered, and introduced—the useful outcome of all this effort. It took us additional time to propagate enough plants to introduce these cultivars, among them 'Cream Puff', 'Fire Opal', 'Louise Marx', 'Mt. St. Helens', and 'Walter Marx'. Twenty years had elapsed between the time Marx planted the seed and Caprice Farm Nursery could put the first plants on the market.

Suffruticosa tree peony cultivars, on the other hand, often produce a copious crop of seeds, which may yield some pretty singles worthy of planting out in the landscape. Still, significant space and time must be allotted to the project. The rare seed on hybrid tree peony plants should always be saved, since the chances of something choice and different developing are very good indeed. Remember the treasures introduced by Daphnis!

Mature tree peony seeds are purplish red; herbaceous seeds are brown. The optimum time to gather seeds is when the pods crack open and the seeds are sticky. Dip the harvested seeds in a 10-percent solution of bleach and then rinse in clean water to eliminate fungi and bacteria. Discard any seeds that are shriveled or soft. The remaining sound seeds can then be handled in one of two ways.

The first option is to plant the seeds outside immediately in a prepared bed. The gardener who chooses this method can expect a certain percentage of germination the following spring, with the balance appearing the second spring. If planting is delayed, initial germination may likewise be delayed, by two years. Seedlings require at least one cycle of warm–cold–warm before putting out their first leaves.

The second option is to hold the seeds over the winter in plastic bags, together with a mixture of moist perlite, sand, or peat moss. Seal the tops of the bags to retain moisture and store in a warm, shaded place to initiate the requisite temperature cycle. Check the bags frequently for white rootlets, the first sign of germination. When these rootlets are 2–4 inches long, transfer the bags to a refrigerator kept at 45–48°F for three or four months. When the ground warms in the spring, plant the seeds with roots in finely tilled soil, rich in organic matter. Choose a spot that can be irrigated if necessary. Good soil drainage is essential.

In either case, cover the seedbed with a loose mulch of evergreen boughs, straw, or cornstalks after the soil freezes to prevent soil-heave during the winter. Remove this mulch when it warms up in the spring. The following fall—after growing two years—the plants can be dug and lined out in rows, spaced 12–16 inches or more between plants.

Peonies tend to change their appearance during the maturation process. The first bloom may not always typify the final form. Over two to three years, flower form may change from single to semi-double or even to the Japanese form, with stamens changing to staminodes, before finally emerging as a full double. Others retain their initial form.

Readers interested in hybridizing should consult three books: *The Peonies* (Wister 1962), *The American Hybrid Peony* (Kessenich and Hollingsworth 1990), and *Notes on Some Systemic Relationships in the Genus Paeonia* (Stebbins 1939). I strongly urge those who are interested in the relative ability/propensity of a particular species to cross-pollinate with another to consult this last work, which offers observations based, in good part, on the detailed records of the crosses made by Saunders. In addition the informal newsletter *Paeonia*, begun by Roy Pehrson in 1970 and edited by Donald R. Smith, serves a network of people interested in peony hybridizing. This newsletter not only provides the latest hybridizing information but also conducts a seed distribution program, which offers seeds from advanced crosses to all members.

Propagation by division

For roughly 2000 years, from the time of the earliest attempts at propagation, cultivated herbaceous peonies have been increased by division, and division remains without question the method of choice for propagating herbaceous peonies. In simple terms, division means cutting the plant crown into two or more pieces, each having one or more eyes—either on top or embedded in the crown tissue—and each with a number of attached roots. This asexual method insures that the new plant is an exact replica of the parent plant. A division of 'Festiva Maxima', the end result of perhaps forty successive divisions over the years, yields the same plant as the one hybridized by Miellez in 1851. The chance of a mutation along the way is negligible.

The crown of a herbaceous peony is the very essence of the plant, controlling the growth of both roots and new shoots. Both the crown and the roots are protected against bacteria and fungi by their production of phenol compounds. These built-in protectants are the reason severed roots may remain in the ground for many months, and occasionally years, without decaying. Eyes are conical and shiny in appearance and vary in size. Some are very small, less than a quarter of an inch long, particularly if the plant is dug before fall. Some cultivars, such as 'Magnolia Flower', develop eyes an inch long or more. The color of the eyes varies from white to red.

Herbaceous plants are usually dug for dividing after they have been in the ground three or four years, at which time they have developed numerous eyes, perhaps as many as ten to twenty. We at Caprice Farm Nursery experience about 180 frost-free growing days a year, and we dig and divide most of our cultivars three years after planting. Growers and gardeners in northern climes typically allow four years before division of herbaceous peonies is attempted.

When a crown division and associated roots are planted, the bigger eyes enlarge to emerge in the spring as new shoots. If this first set of stems is lost, through disease or mechanical damage, the crown initiates growth from the remaining eyes. When such a loss occurs early in the season and the division is quite substantial, new growth occurs that same spring. When the loss occurs later in the season, or if the plant is weak, growth is delayed until the second spring.

Herbaceous peony roots come in several sizes in commerce. Peony experts consider the standard field-grown division with three to five eyes optimal. Plants of this size have a substantial root mass, and if given adequate

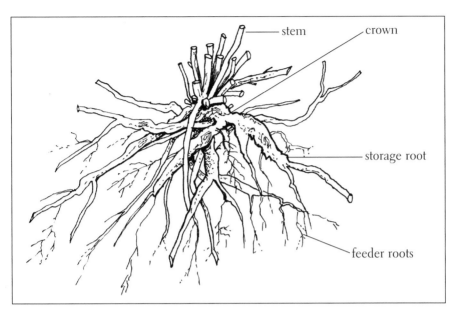

Four-year-old herbaceous plant.

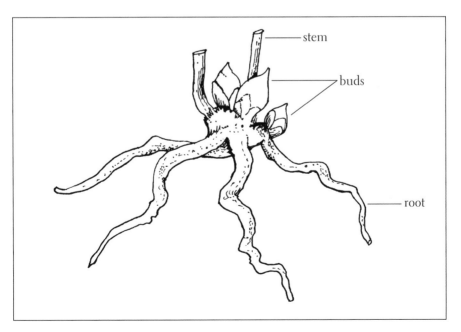

Stylized three-eye herbaceous division.

care after planting in the fall, they make a good plant the first year. A vigorous division often flowers in the first year, but every such standard division should certainly flower by the second.

There are two schools of thought as to the amount of root that must be included in a standard division. I believe each division should include at least one large root, 8 inches long, or its equivalent in several smaller ones. It seems to me that the more substantial the division, the greater the food reserves, and so the greater the ability to cope with disease or injury. Others feel that divisions with shorter roots force the plant to put out new roots more quickly.

Some growers plant little one- to two-eye divisions in crowded beds, dig them up in the fall, and keep them in cold storage over the winter. These are the two- to five-eye divisions available in retail nurseries the following spring, packaged in bags with a bit of damp peat and slipped into attractive boxes. Their small size makes it economically feasible for them to be shipped even overseas. If obtained soon after coming out of cold storage, carefully planted, and well cultivated, these divisions eventually grow into acceptable specimens. If shoots have started to emerge before planting, however, the survival rate is severely reduced.

The two- to three-eye division is the typical wholesale size in the United States. These wholesale divisions, usually 50 to 75 percent as large as the standard divisions, generally do well when potted up for the spring trade or lined out in a field to be grown on. The resulting plants take slightly longer to mature than the larger three- to five-eye standard divisions sold by retail peony nurseries.

Other division sizes are sometimes available. Occasionally one-eye liner plants are offered to professional growers. These are very small divisions, simply an eye with a small piece of root. These liners usually take two years longer to mature than the standard three- to five-eye division. Because they have little mass for nutrient storage, liners are especially vulnerable to disease and unfavorable cultural conditions. For the first two years, they should be grown where they can receive extra care; then they can be planted out.

Double- or even triple-sized divisions, the equivalents of two- to three-year-old plants, are often requested by landscapers who are trying to fill out a new installation. Larger divisions are preferred to whole mature plants (four years old or more) because older plants do not transplant well. Some die outright and the survivors take several years to recover.

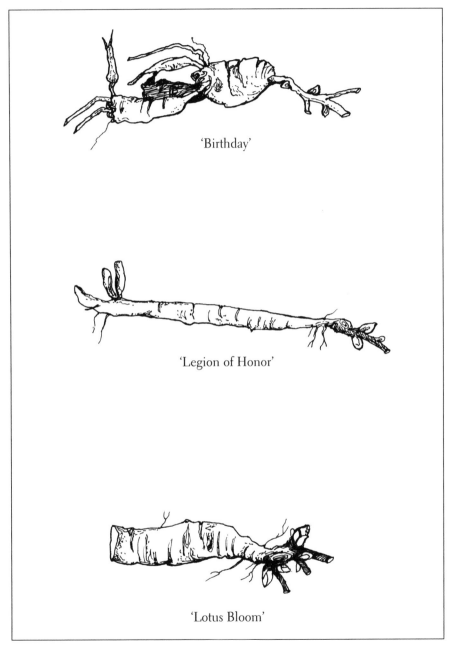

'Birthday'

'Legion of Honor'

'Lotus Bloom'

Shipping roots.

But what of the gardener who has to move an older herbaceous peony or who'd like to share such a plant with a friend? Clearly the plant must be dug up before it is moved or divided, but it must never be moved intact like a woody shrub as, again, it is unlikely to survive. If your aim is to place your peony in another spot, replant only a division of it and give the remaining divisions to gardening friends. Whatever the motivation, propagation or otherwise, dividing peonies is more an art than a science. If you are trying it for the first time, you may want to practice on a few less valuable peonies before disturbing a choice plant.

Begin by thoroughly soaking the surrounding soil if it is dry, several days before lifting the plant. Just before digging, prune off the stems some 2–4 inches above ground level. With a sharp spade, cut straight down through the middle of the crown, splitting the plant into two sections. In addition to easing the plant's removal, this cut will serve for the first division. Next cut the soil all around the plant to the full spade depth and carefully pry out the two underground sections. Take time to do this job, as brute strength and heavy soil often equal a broken shovel and/or shattered roots.

Let the two sections of the lifted plant rest several hours, so that the roots lose some of their brittleness, and then wash them off with a forceful hosing. Remove any soil that the water has not dislodged with a blunt tool, such as a heavy screwdriver. With roots and eyes fully visible, it is easier to further divide the tough crown into the desired number of pieces, each with both eyes and attached roots. For this, you will need a short, stout, stiff-bladed knife for cutting and a heavy screwdriver for prying. Some experienced dividers use a pointed set of pruning shears rather than a knife.

The first step in preparing roots for division is to cut them off about 8 inches from the crown. If the crown has a thin or weak spot, twist, pry, or cut away a division at that point. Try to pry off other divisions with as many eyes as planned, cutting only when absolutely necessary. If only two or three divisions are needed, remove them from the outer edge as this is the most vigorous part of the crown. The older woody center of the clump can be used if it contains any living eyes, but dead tissue is common in older plants and should be cut out and discarded when dividing.

The crowns and roots of herbaceous peony cultivars come in a variety of shapes and sizes and so are often more difficult to divide than the species. Some have huge roots; others, such as 'Cytherea', yield comparatively poor-looking divisions with flimsy roots that yet when planted will grow as well as any others. Some, such as 'Campagna', 'Chalice', and 'Magnolia Flower', have clublike roots with eyes clustered at the top; others, such as 'Lovely Rose' and 'Eliza Lundy', are very easy to divide since their crowns branch. The obliging 'Sea Shell' often has an eye at the top of each root where it comes off the crown.

I have sometimes divided a hybrid peony only to discover that all the eyes have ended up on one piece and all the roots on the other; in the case of a costly cultivar, such a growth pattern could spell disaster. The rare and valuable 'Old Faithful', for instance, is an especially challenging peony to divide. It has a huge main root, and sometimes the only way to get two good divisions on such a plant is to split its single main root lengthwise, using a fine-bladed pruning saw, knife, or shears. But even this surgery does not guarantee success.

As for yield, most of the popular cultivars of *Paeonia lactiflora* presently in commerce provide a reasonable number of divisions. Yields from each plant of the fastest-increasing lactiflora cultivars, such as 'Fire Opal' or 'Louise Marx', average four or five standard retail divisions and the same number of wholesale or planting pieces. Slower-growing cultivars, such as 'Petite Renee', yield only two or three retail divisions and perhaps four smaller pieces. Results further vary with differing soil and climatic conditions, but yield does not seem to correlate with plant growth or vigor. Though 'Walter Marx' and 'Louise Marx' are both strong growers, 'Walter Marx' is slow to increase while its sister seedling 'Louise Marx' is very prolific.

Hybrid peonies exhibit much more variation in yield. Some are very generous. 'Cytherea', despite the often fragile appearance of its roots, yields four or five standard divisions and six to ten smaller pieces after being in the ground three years. Hybrids that are slower to multiply, such as 'Flame', yield a total of three to six divisions of varying size in the same time period. Since the yield of a cultivar is an important component in production cost, the lower-yielding cultivars will likely remain more expensive.

Propagation of tree peonies by division is of limited use. Like a herbaceous division, a tree peony division must also include eyes, crown, and attached root, but with tree peonies, the eyes may occur on both aboveground and underground stems.

Digging tree peonies is easier than digging herbaceous types. Begin by cutting the soil a foot or so away from the stems, spading straight down and encircling the plant to the depth of the spade. When the plant is carefully separated from the soil, pry up. Usually much less matted crown will be found than on the herbaceous types. Tree peony roots are tough, long, narrow, and cylindrical, but not brittle. After the plant is dug out, remove any damaged or broken root ends.

Examine the plant carefully: younger tree peony stems may have developed their own roots. The new stems of Japanese suffruticosa cultivars usually arise near the main stem, making them difficult to divide, while the suffruticosa cultivars of Chinese origin more commonly develop new stems further away from the crown and so are easier to divide. If stems are growing well away from the main stem, cut or saw these divisions off at the first connecting juncture. Cut or pry other divisions off as with herbaceous peonies. Prune each of the divided above-ground stems back to two or three live eyes.

New tree peony divisions seldom bloom the first year after planting but will develop into healthy flowering plants in the second year. If the division consists of several stems, one terminal bud may be saved. This bud should flower the next spring—resulting in one glorious though small flower— which will not seriously affect plant vigor.

With regard to yield, seventy four- to six-year-old unnamed tree peonies of Chinese origin recently divided here at Caprice Farm Nursery resulted in 500 divisions. They are all on their own root and so will mature somewhat faster than newly grafted tree peonies.

The plant parts of the unique Itoh, or intersectional, hybrids reflect characteristics of both parents. Though the plant dies to the ground each fall in herbaceous style, the roots resemble those of tree peonies. The eyes,

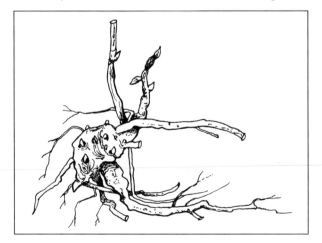

Itoh hybrid root.

often very small, may appear on the crown, as in herbaceous peonies, or on above-ground or underground stems, as in tree peonies. As with tree and herbaceous peonies, a good intersectional division consists of crown, roots, and eyes.

Plant the divisions of Itoh hybrids with the top eye of the crown 1–2 inches deep. The location of the eye does not affect the subsequent growth of the division. For further propagation, plant divisions up to 4 inches deep; on occasion the buried stem eyes may develop their own sets of roots. Roger Anderson, one of the leading hybridizers of intersectional hybrids, divides his plants every two years, believing that rapid growth makes the division of older plants more difficult.

Propagation by root cuttings

A much more recent method of peony propagation is increase by root cuttings. Some other herbaceous perennials, such as *Anemone, Bergenia, Papaver orientale,* and *Phlox,* regenerate readily from pieces of root, but only a limited number of herbaceous peony species possess the genetic ability to successfully regenerate in this fashion. These species are *Paeonia officinalis,* the closely related *P. peregrina,* and *P. tenuifolia,* as well as some selections of these species, such as 'Otto Froebel'.

The first published account of a peony's ability to regenerate from a root piece is found in *Horti Germinal,* published in 1561, in which the author writes, "*Paeonia foemnia* [a name used for *P. officinalis*] grows in many of our gardens where it grows vigorously and if a root is dug up and a small piece left behind it grows again." Surprisingly this phenomenon is not noted again until the 20th century, first in 1907, in *The Peony* by C. S. Harrison, an early peony fancier, and then again in short articles by Reath and Hollingsworth in 1976 and 1977, reprinted in *American Peony Society: Seventy-Five Years* (Kessenich 1979).

The ability of the genus *Paeonia* to regenerate from root parts hangs upon the particular plant's ability to strike adventitious buds, the precursors of eyes and therefore of new shoots. The striking of adventitious buds seems to require the removal of the hormonal influence of the crown, and indeed such buds only develop on roots that have been separated from the old crown. Furthermore, the length of growing season, climatic conditions, and narrowly prescribed soil preferences all seem to be factors in a good outcome as well. For example, consider the conjunction of the heavy clay soils and mild wet winters of Caprice Farm Nursery with *Paeonia tenuifolia.*

This species, which doesn't like to get its feet wet, seldom develops adventitious root buds here, nor is it a strong grower, and yet it produces many adventitious root buds in nurseries in colder climates that have a loamy soil.

Not all hybrids tracing to *Paeonia officinalis*, *P. peregrina*, and *P. tenuifolia* inherit the potential to strike adventitious buds, and not only hybrids from these three species are involved: isolated word-of-mouth reports of adventitious buds found on roots of the species *P. lactiflora* and particularly the lactiflora cultivars 'Westerner' and 'Nippon Gold' have been reported. In fact, the first hybrids displaying this trait in any number were introduced in the 1930s, the result of crosses of *P. lactiflora* and *P. officinalis*. The reason *P. lactiflora* is involved, even if rarely, is most likely attributable to a mutation somewhere along the line, or to the serendipitous bee that first visited another species before alighting upon *P. lactiflora*. In our own extensive lactiflora plantings, we have found large numbers of adventitious buds on 'Imperial Parasol'. Every one of the limited number of lactiflora cultivars possessing this characteristic are of the Japanese form. A complete list of all cultivars known to strike adventitious buds on root pieces concludes this section.

Some cultivar roots make extensive callus formation on root ends the first year and develop adventitious buds the second year, though callus is not necessarily a precursor to new bud formation. Adventitious buds are easily identified on well-washed roots. They first appear as one or more

Callused root.

Adventitious buds.

raised, blisterlike protuberances over the top of the root. These bulging cell masses are white or ivory in color, much lighter than the surface of the root. They may develop on either end of the root, in the middle, or occasionally at two or more locations.

The preparation of root pieces from species and cultivars prone to produce adventitious root buds is relatively simple. Most often, root ends cut off while dividing the plants or root pieces gleaned from the digging area are used. For the best results, use only pieces that are 6–8 inches long and at least half an inch in diameter. Any root pieces recovered in this manner may be stored successfully for several weeks before planting if kept cool and moist.

Plant the root pieces in the fall, laying them crossways in trenches in the peony rows, 4–6 inches apart. Cover them with soil, slightly mounded over the trenches. Leave the root pieces in the ground at least two years; it may take this long for the buds to produce stems. Occasionally one or two root pieces will develop a shoot, evidence that a bit of crown tissue was present, not that the cultivar is adventitious under conditions prevailing at that site.

With favorable environmental conditions, the original cell masses develop into one or more adventitious buds. Some roots will strike adventitious buds by the next fall, others by the second, and the leaf shoots will emerge the following spring. Early growth is supported by the original root piece, but the new plant eventually forms crown tissue from which its own new roots emerge. After the plants have produced above-ground growth for two years, they can be transplanted to the field or placed in their permanent landscape setting. An additional year is required after transplanting for the plant to equal a standard division.

A gardener who owns one of the plants listed below may want to replicate it, or share it with a friend, but may be unwilling to dig and divide it. In such case root propagation can be used and the process couldn't be simpler. In the fall, make one or two cuts with a spade straight down to the depth of the spade, about 12 inches away from the stems. This cut will not injure the plant, but in all likelihood it will sever a root or two. In one or two years—if the plant is adventitious under local conditions—the first shoots of a new plant from one of these severed roots will appear. In another year or two, a satellite plant is ready to dig, fully formed and on its own roots.

The following cultivars will strike adventitious buds on root pieces under optimal environmental conditions:

'Athena'	'Lustrous'
'Birthday'	'Mid May'
'Blaze'	'Nosegay'
'Burning Bright'	'Nova'
'Carina'	'Paladin'
'Chalice'	'Paula Fay'
'Claudia'	'Prairie Moon'
'Constance Spry'	'Red Glory'
'Coral Fay'	'Red Red Rose'
'Cytherea'	'Rose Garland'
'Early Scout'	'Rose Tulip'
'Ellen Cowley'	'Roselette'
'Eventide'	'Rosy Cheek'
'Flame'	'Royal Rose'
'Golden Glow'	'Salmon Glow'
'Laddie'	'Skylark'
'Laura Magnuson'	'Sunlight'
'Legion of Honor'	

Propagation by grafting

In Japan, grafting has been the traditional method of increasing stock of suffruticosa tree peonies for centuries, but only recently has the practice spread beyond that country. In the mid-1900s Brother Charles of Techny Mission Gardens in Techny, Illinois, began grafting in the United States, producing significant numbers of grafted tree peonies. Since then, and following his example, several growers have started grafting programs, but few have proven commercially viable. The Klehm and Reath nurseries share the most notable success stories, and here at Caprice Farm Nursery we have been successful on a more modest scale. We all three have depended primarily on the hybrids of Saunders, Gratwick, and Daphnis, whereas Japanese growers rely almost entirely on suffruticosa cultivars.

As with the grafting of fruit trees and plants in any number of other genera, the obvious way to proceed is to take scions of the desired tree peony cultivar and then to graft them on tree peony roots. This approach has several problems. First, it requires large numbers of seedlings for rootstock;

devoting so much ground and cultural effort to growing rootstock is obviously an expensive undertaking and so leads to costly plants. Another problem is that of matching the scion and stock. The diameter of most scion wood is greater than that of the roots from young tree peonies grown for rootstock, and this makes matching the cambium of the scion to that of the rootstock difficult. Finally, the core of the rootstock is tough, woody, and hard to cut accurately.

A more effective method of tree peony increase—though it also has its frustrations—is to graft scions of the desired cultivar on herbaceous nurse roots, the tissue of which is easily cut. Inevitably, the use of two quite different species causes problems of tissue compatibility, and the success rate is much lower than the one achieved when grafting plants of other genera: a 50-percent graft success is considered satisfactory with tree peonies. Though some tree peony cultivars seem to take more readily than others, plants produced by this method remain scarce and expensive.

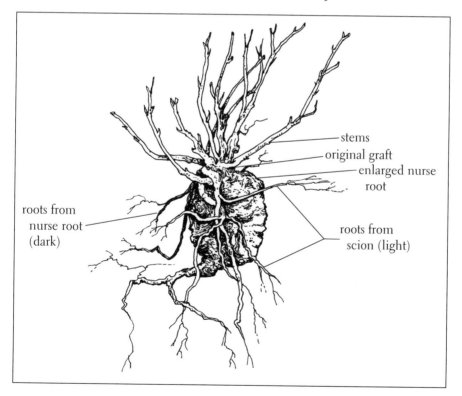

Four-year-old tree peony graft showing enlarged nurse root.

Some grafters use all the roots from four- to five-year-old *Paeonia lacti-flora* seedlings. Such plants often yield forty root pieces 6–8 inches long. Others choose to use roots from specific cultivars. I prefer three-year-old roots from 'Charlie's White', 'Louise Marx', or 'Scarlet O'Hara', one of the most vigorous of peonies, which produces cylindrical roots that can reach 4 feet in length. This allows several pieces to be taken from each root. Cultivars that strike adventitious buds are not possibilities because the growth from the adventitious bud smothers out the scion.

First and above all, grafting requires a very clean work place. I use a kitchen cutting board that has been wiped down with alcohol or a chlorine bleach solution. Necessary supplies include single-edged razor blades, a roll of flexible grafting tape, and tree wound paint. Do not use roofing compound as a substitute for wound paint. Though wound paint is seldom used in the grafting operations of other genera, it seems particularly beneficial with tree peonies. Near aseptic conditions must be maintained while grafting to prevent the spread of disease, so wipe the board and razor blade with disinfectant after every few grafts. Discard each razor blade as necessary; they rapidly become dull, and clean cuts are essential.

To propagate a desirable plant by grafting, take scions of new growth cut after the terminal buds have developed. Terminal buds usually form in August and September. Those of the earliest-flowering species and cultivars, such as the suffruticosa tree peonies, mature first, followed by the later-flowering plants, such as the lutea hybrids, which mature two to three weeks later.

Scions taken from stock plants should be cut just above a node. A scion with a terminal bud and the next lower node work best, though lateral buds can also be used. The scion should be 2–4 inches long. Snip off any leaves and wrap the scions in a damp cloth to prevent their becoming drying before use. If kept cool, shaded, and damp—or in the refrigerator—scions remain viable for several days.

The herbaceous plants from which the rootstocks are taken can be dug any time after mid-August. If the ground is dry, water well before digging so that the plant can be taken out intact. After digging, wash the roots well and set the plant out in a shaded area for a few hours so the roots become less brittle.

If they are of a satisfactory shape and size, roots can be cut right back to the crown, leaving stubs no larger than 2 inches in diameter. The crown can then be divided in the usual manner for increase and the divisions either replanted immediately after the roots are removed or stored in a damp, cool spot for several weeks before replanting.

Cut the roots for grafting into pieces 6–8 inches long, discarding any crooked or diseased sections. Incise a V-shaped wedge into one end of the rootstock, one inch deep. Next, take the scion, and in two strokes, cut its top end so that it forms a matching wedge, one that will fit exactly into the V-shaped opening prepared for it on the rootstock. Make only two clean cuts to both root and scion to minimize tissue damage. If the scion is too large to fit, do not whittle it down; this only increases tissue damage. Rather, make two more clean slices, taking thin slivers with each cut. The two pieces must form a tight joint, and the outer edges of both scion and nurse root should fit smoothly together at their juncture. Finish the graft by wrapping it tightly with overlapping grafting tape. Tuck the end under the last wrap and pull tightly before severing the tape. Cover the exposed cut end of the root with wound paint.

Some grafters plant out immediately after grafting in prepared beds, but my experience is that the knitting process between scion and nurse root is hastened by keeping the grafts in a warm, moist environment for four to six weeks before planting. I place scions from each cultivar in separate, slightly vented plastic bags with damp moss or wood shavings (not cedar) to keep them from drying out. The bags are then kept in a mildly warm location.

At planting, take care that each graft is placed upright and that the graft union is completely covered by 4–6 inches of soil. Heavily mulch the bed for the first winter. I use beds that are 6 feet wide and arrange the grafts 8

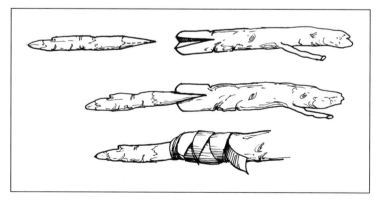

Grafts.

inches apart in 18-inch rows. If only a few grafts are made, tuck them into a corner of a perennial bed for at least three years, where they can easily be kept watered, weeded, and protected against disease.

If the graft is successful, scion growth will be evident the first spring. For at least two or three years, the growth is entirely supported by the enlarging herbaceous nurse root, but the reason the union is planted 4–6 inches deep is to allow for the eventual growth of new roots from the scion itself. After these scion roots have developed, the plant will prove very hardy. Until then, its survival is somewhat precarious. Treat each valuable sapling with the best of care. Regular weeding, watering, fertilizing, and a good disease-control program are absolute requisites to their viability.

The nurse root from the herbaceous plant continues to grow after the graft is planted. When the grafted plant is dug after three years, the herbaceous root should be cut entirely off if the tree peony roots have emerged. If tree peony roots are not in evidence, remove part of the nurse root and replant. If this herbaceous nurse root is not removed, it may grow to one foot in diameter, robbing the tree peony roots—which are, of course, the roots one is after—of growing space and nutrients.

Remember that if a small one-year graft is purchased in the spring, it needs to be dug up in three years and the nurse root removed. Do this in the fall, and seize the opportunity to rework the planting site by adding more organic material. The plant can then be put back in the same spot.

Plants of rare herbaceous cultivars as well as the intersectional hybrids can also be increased by grafting. After dividing the plant, slice off any extra eyes with a piece of crown tissue attached to each. Insert each eye under a flap cut into a root piece from the same cultivar, and handle the root piece as you would a tree peony graft. This method, first described by Reath in 1979, is used by only a few growers; others have had little success with it.

Propagation by layering

A few tree peonies are still propagated by the traditional means of layering. This method of vegetative propagation involves the development of roots while the stem is still attached to the mother plant. Once a common method of commercial production, it is now used almost exclusively by amateur gardeners to propagate a single new tree peony plant.

In the spring, select a young branch growing somewhat horizontally from the mother plant. Carefully bend the stem until part of it touches the ground surface. Remember that tree peony branches and stems are quite brittle and break easily, so bend the stem slowly and in a wide arc. Scrape the bark off the bottom of the stem and dust with rooting hormone where it contacts the soil. Peg the stem down with a stiff wire bent into a U shape, then cover with a shovel or two of soil.

Two years later, after the plant has gone dormant, carefully dig out the soil under the bent stem. If new roots have grown out of the stem, cut the stem off between the new roots and the parent plant. Then transplant the new plant to its permanent location.

Two methods of plant increase widely used in other genera have not yet proven commercially feasible with peonies: tissue culture and vegetative propagation by stem cuttings. With tissue culture, growth is slow and the young plants are susceptible to fungal infection, but a team at the University of London's Wye College has had good results in the micropropagation of certain suffruticosa tree peonies (Harris and Mantell 1991). Their methods may well be adapted to other cultivars. As for vegetative propagation, though limited laboratory success in rooting stem cuttings of *Paeonia lactiflora* has been reported, the achievement has not yet been reproduced in a commercial setting. The Chinese, however, have had some commercial success rooting suffruticosa tree peonies from cuttings. Details of this procedure are not yet available.

Chapter 7

What the Future Holds

Sparked perhaps by the rising interest in all perennials, professional landscape architects and designers—intrigued by the all-season foliage value of peonies and once again entranced by the flowers themselves—are including more and more peonies in their plans. Many new growers of both dried and cut peonies have appeared on the scene in response to this increased demand. While some still rely on the classic, tried-and-true doubles, a significant number are gravitating toward the more unusual colors and lighter forms of hybrid peonies. As well, the keen interest Europeans continue to express for species peonies has stimulated a new respect for species peonies in North America.

I predict that species will increasingly be found in the catalogs of better growers but expect that continued difficulties in propagation will make for only gradual widespread availability of the many fine new cultivars that have been introduced and registered in recent years—the vast number of them the work of such familiar names as Bigger, Daphnis, Klehm, Reath, and Tischler. Who will continue this high level of hybridizing? It remains to be seen, as most of those presently engaged are old-timers and only those few younger hybridizers noted in the pages that follow have appeared on the scene.

For many peony lovers, the fondest hope for the future is that some new recruit will choose to work along the southern edge of what is now thought to be the limits of peony growing. There is tremendous interest in peonies that will flourish under conditions of limited dormancy and whose flowers will open well in heat. At present, few peonies, no matter the degree of humidity, thrive in truly hot conditions. Enough fertile cultivars bearing the genes of the Mediterranean species have been developed in the last few years to form a strong nucleus for any such breeding effort.

HYBRIDIZERS AND GROWERS

In Europe Sir Peter Smithers of Switzerland, along with Michel Rivière in France, is working with tree peonies, and there are a number of active hybridizers in Asia whose work has not been brought to the attention of the West. Of the established North American peony breeders who are still active, Klehm, Reath, and Tischler remain at the fore; members of the new vanguard follow.

Roger Anderson (b. 1938) of Fort Atkinson, Wisconsin, is a latecomer to peonies. Raised on a southern Wisconsin dairy farm, he developed a passion for flowers as a young boy. His grandfather encouraged Anderson's horticultural efforts and taught him how to hybridize gladiolus, but his father—a typical practical farmer—never tired of asking him when his flowers were going to be big enough to eat.

In the early 1980s a local peony enthusiast, Carroll Spangler, interested Anderson in the genus, and most fittingly, a chance Spangler seedling is responsible for Anderson's great successes in developing intersectional hybrids. Spangler found this chance *Paeonia lactiflora* plant growing in an asparagus bed; he moved it and discovered that it bloomed as a pink double at first flowering, but as a pink single the second year. Suspecting that it might have more than the usual amount of genetic diversity, he gave it to Anderson to "fool with."

Anderson divided the plant into three parts. Two divisions reverted back to double flowers. The third, the one he used for his hybridizing, was a single that proved highly fertile as both a pollen parent and a pod parent.

His seedlings, raised under lights in a basement, proved a source for doubleness as seen in the highly praised lemon-yellow Itoh, 'Bartzella'. Others are notable for their striking colors, for example the pure pink 'First Arrival', the very first of his seedlings to bloom; 'Morning Lilac', whose lavender color is enhanced by accents of white and purple; and 'Cora Louise', a white with a striking raspberry center. Intersectional seedlings in other colors are now being propagated for future introduction.

In addition to this exciting work, Anderson has successfully hybridized the rare, shrubby tree peony species, *Paeonia potaninii*. His present pursuits in form and color are a tiny, container-sized plant with teacup size flowers and a true orange.

Ainie and Norm Busse of Busse Gardens, a mail-order perennial nursery in Cokato, Minnesota, have listed a few peonies in their catalogs for a number of years but are now making them one of their major perennial crops. They have diligently collected and propagated a great number of hard-to-find peony cultivars, starting with the purchase of the entire collections of Mervyn Pees of Belle Center, Ohio, and Floyd Miller of Fergus Falls, Minnesota. With these and acquisitions from a number of other growers, they have assembled the largest collection of rare and historic cultivars in North America. Many of these are available nowhere else on the continent.

Don Hollingsworth (b. 1928), who farms the family acreage in Maryville, Missouri, is a leading proponent of hybrid peonies. After receiving his degree in animal science at the University of Missouri he worked with beef cattle breeders for several years before becoming an extension agricultural agent. Now retired, he devotes himself entirely to his advanced-generation peony hybridizing program. His recent introductions of the herbaceous hybrid 'Show Girl' and the Itoh 'Garden Treasure' are welcome harbingers of things to come.

Hollingsworth's interest in plant taxonomy has spurred him to write on various scientific peony subjects. He is a prolific contributor to the American Peony Society Bulletin as well as coauthor of *The American Hybrid Peony*. He has served both as a president and as a longtime director of the American Peony Society.

P. C. (Chris) Laning (b. 1918) of Kalamazoo, Michigan, became interested in peonies in 1969. The following year he purchased a large number of hybrid cultivars from Silvia Saunders, which collection formed the basis for his extensive hybridizing program. His original aim was to develop yellow herbaceous peonies for the garden, a goal he shared with Roy

Pehrson, whose breeding efforts he and William Seidl carry on. The culmination of this effort was the recent introduction of the double yellow hybrids 'Sunny Boy' and 'Sunny Girl'. His present breeding goal is a blue herbaceous peony, based on a color break to purple found in a Krekler seedling.

From 1978 to 1994 he was the editor of *Paeonia*, which under his leadership achieved worldwide distribution and importance. He founded and continues to manage its popular seed exchange program, which works exactly like those of various plant societies: thousands of seeds are contributed by and disseminated among the newsletter's readers. His goal in both undertakings is to develop and encourage interest in peonies and their hybridizing.

William Seidl (b. 1932) of Manitowoc, Wisconsin, has produced peony hybrids that are only now appearing on the market. Long interested in plants, he began by breeding gladioli and daylilies. He started hybridizing peonies in 1968, with *Paeonia lactiflora* crosses. Looking through a Wild catalog, he became intrigued by the pedigrees of some of the hybrid peonies listed and so undertook to assemble a collection of them.

He acquired from Roy Pehrson, a close friend, some of the latter's hybrid seedlings. Of the twenty intersectional seedlings turned over to Seidl, all but one developed only incomplete flowers—a recurring problem with this cross—even though the plants themselves were vigorous and normal.

Seidl soon became involved with the American Peony Society and the newsletter *Paeonia*'s seed exchange program. He has introduced several of Pehrson's hybrid herbaceous seedlings, including the highly sought-after pink double, 'Junior Miss'. His 'Anna Marie', the only true lavender in hybrid tree peonies, is prized for its beautiful color and vigor.

His breeding goals are the development of pure yellow herbaceous doubles and hybrid tree peonies of true pink. The first of his intersectional hybrids to reach the market was 'Rose Fantasy', which achieves the long-elusive fuchsia tone.

The good work of peony hybridizers past and present has produced a number of cultivars that show great promise but are not well known; perhaps they will receive their due sometime in the near future. A few are excellent older forms that for unknown reasons are not widely cultivated. Others are relatively new but in short supply and often expensive. Some have been tested in only a few climatic regions and so need broader trials. Still others offer exciting new color combinations never before available to peony lovers. All are worth a try. Bloom periods and bloom sizes are those described in Chapter 4.

PROMISING HERBACEOUS PEONIES

Unless otherwise noted, all are selections of *Paeonia lactiflora*.

'Bess Bockstoce' (Bockstoce 1955). This medium-sized, fragrant, double hybrid opens a solid dark pink, then changes to a dark pink center surrounded by a wide band of white. A vigorous plant with strong, 24-inch stems. This is the cultivar registered by American Peony Society and offered in the United States; a different plant is sold under the same name in Canada, where this cultivar is known as 'Rose Heart'. Midseason. (Plate 9)

'Bev' (Krekler 1975). A sweetly scented, large double whose petals are deep pink at the base shading to light pink on the edges. Long stems on a narrow plant with warm green foliage. Midseason.

'Blushing Princess' (Saunders–Reath 1991). A pink-blush semi-double hybrid that often displays white petals in the center of its large, intensely fragrant, many-layered bloom. The side buds of its strong, upright stems keep it in bloom for up to six weeks. Early. (Plate 12)

'Bouquet Perfect' (Tischler 1987). A deep but bright pink of anemone form, its rather small flowers are ideal for arrangements. Makes a vigorous, compact bush. Midseason to Late. (Plate 15)

'Camellia' (Saunders 1942). A medium-sized white flower with a peach-pink at the base. Though it is somewhat slow in achieving the state, it becomes a full, but flat, round double once established. This hybrid has an entrancing, heavy fragrance on first opening. Early.

'Fire Opal' (Marx–Rogers 1984). A medium-sized double of fiery red, with each petal set off by a wiry edge of white. One of the fastest-increasing cultivars. Strong stems. Merits trial as a cut flower. Late.

'Heidi' (Tischler 1972). A light and airy flower of Japanese form. The small flowers are pink, and the staminodes are tipped with coral. Usually 26 inches tall. Midseason. (Plate 52)

'Karen Gray' (Krekler 1965). This medium-sized flower of Japanese form is an unusual shade of reddish fuchsia, accented with a creamy yellow center. Dark green foliage. Midseason.

'Little Red Gem' (Reath 1988). A small-flowered, single red hybrid, only 15 inches tall. Ferny foliage forms an attractive low mound, making it an excellent rock garden peony. Very Early.

'Louise Marx' (Marx–Rogers 1981). A very vigorous, large white of Japanese form. Large, dark green leaves. Four side buds per stem keep it in bloom for weeks. Noticeable honey fragrance. Reaches a height of 46–48 inches. Late. (Plate 72)

'Mt. St. Helens' (Marx–Rogers 1981). A medium-sized, dark red double. One of the few really fragrant peonies in its class. Excels in the U.S. Department of Agriculture's hardiness zone 8. Late.

'Myra MacRae' (Tischler 1967). A large, pale pink double with tightly packed petals held on strong stems. The plant reaches a height of 30 inches. A favorite of Myron Bigger. Late.

'Myron D. Bigger' (Bigger 1966). A large, well-formed blush to white double of short stature. Some experienced growers consider it perhaps the best of the double whites. Late.

'Nosegay' (Saunders 1950). A vigorous, medium-sized single hybrid of a pale salmon-pink. The attractive foliage, narrow and deeply divided, shows its *Paeonia tenuifolia* ancestry. Very Early. (Plate 91)

'Pageant' (Saunders 1941). A rich pink single hybrid, 42 inches tall. Very large flowers, each with a great boss of yellow staminodes in the center. Though relatively slow-growing, it matures to one of the largest clumps of any of the herbaceous peonies. Very Early. (Plate 107)

Plate 1. Peony Walk at the Minnesota Arboretum. Photo Michael Heger.

Plate 2. Tree peonies 'Age of Gold' (right) and 'Black Panther' with hostas.
Photo Linda Engstrom.

Plate 3. Herbaceous cultivar 'Alice Harding'. Photo Busse Gardens.

Plate 4. 'America'. Photo Chester Allen.

Plate 5. 'Ann Berry Cousins'. Photo Roy Klehm.

Plate 6. 'Athena'. Photo Linda Engstrom.

Plate 7. 'Banquet'. Photo Michael Dodge, White Flower Farm.

Plate 8. 'Bartzella'. Photo Roger Anderson.

Plate 9. 'Bess Bockstoce'.

Plate 10. 'Big Ben'. Photo Michael Heger.

Plate 11. 'Birthday'.

Plate 12. 'Blushing Princess'. Photo Galen Burrell.

Plate 13. 'Border Charm'. Photo Cliff Weisenhaus.

Plate 14. 'Boreas'. Photo Roy Klehm.

Plate 15. 'Bouquet Perfect'.

Plate 16. 'Bowl of Cream'. Photo Roy Klehm.

Plate 17. 'Bu-Te'. Photo Michael Heger.

Plate 18. 'Burma Ruby'. Photo David Austin Roses.

Plate 19. 'Carina'. Photo Linda Engstrom.

Plate 20. 'Carolina Moon'. Photo Michael Heger.

Plate 21. 'Cincinnati'. Photo Bruce Hamilton.

Plate 22. 'Companion of Serenity'. Photo Roy Klehm.

Plate 23. 'Coral Charm'.

Plate 24. 'Coral Sunset'. Photo B. Hamilton.

Plate 25. 'Coral Supreme'. Photo Roy Klehm.

Plate 26. 'Cream Puff'. Photo Sevald Nursery.

Plate 27. 'Cytherea'.

Plate 28. 'Daystar'. Photo David Austin Roses.

Plate 29. 'Do Tell'. Photo André Viette.

Plate 30. 'Douglas Brand'.
Photo Robert Tischler.

Plate 31. 'Early Scout'.

Plate 32. 'Early Windflower'. Photo Linda Engstrom.

Plate 33. 'Edulis Superba'. Photo Michael Heger.

Plate 34. 'Emma Klehm'. Photo Chester Allen.

Plate 35. 'Etched Salmon'.

Plate 36. 'Eventide'.

Plate 37. 'Fairy's Petticoat'. Photo Michael Heger.

Plate 38. 'Felix Crousse'. Photo Busse Gardens.

Plate 39. 'Feng dan bai'. Photo Zhang Yuexian.

Plate 40. 'First Arrival'. Photo Roger Anderson.

Plate 41. 'Flame'.

Plate 42. 'Frances'. Photo Galen Burrell.

Plate 43. 'Gardenia'. Photo Busse Gardens.

Plate 44. 'Gauguin'. Photo Jack Potter.

Plate 45. 'Gay Paree'.

Plate 46. 'Gene Wild'. Photo Sevald Nursery.

Plate 47. 'Gessekai'. Photo Roy Klehm.

Plate 48. 'Golden Glow'. Photo Linda Engstrom.

Plate 49. 'Great Lady'.

Plate 50. 'Guardian of the Monastery'. Photo A & D Nursery.

Plate 51. 'Hanakisoi'. Photo Roy Klehm.

Plate 52. 'Heidi'. Photo Michael Heger.

Plate 53. 'Helen Matthews'. Photo Michael Heger.

Plate 54. 'Henry St. Clair'. Photo Busse Gardens.

Plate 55. 'High Noon'. Photo Galen Burrell.

Plate 56. 'Honey Gold'. Photo Michael Dodge, White Flower Farm.

Plate 57. 'Horizon'. Photo Peg Goldsmith.

Plate 58. 'Hu Hong'. Photo Zhang Yuexian.

Plate 59. 'Irwin Altman'.

Plate 60. 'Isani-Gidui'. Photo André Viette.

Plate 61. 'Jan van Leeuwen'. Photo André Viette.

Plate 62. 'Kamata-nishiki'. Photo Michael Dodge, White Flower Farm.

Plate 63. 'Kansas'.

Plate 64. 'Kishu Caprice'.
Photo Linda Engstrom.

Plate 65. 'Krinkled White'.
Photo André Viette.

Plate 66. 'L'Etincelante'. Photo A & D Nursery.

Plate 67. 'Lady Alexandra Duff'. Photo André Viette.

Plate 68. 'Laura Magnuson'.

Plate 69. 'Le Jour'. Photo André Viette.

Plate 70. 'Leda'. Photo Roy Klehm.

Plate 71. 'Lillian Wild'. Photo A & D Nursery.

Plate 72. 'Louise Marx'. Photo Lola Branham.

Plate 73. 'Lovely Rose'. Photo Michael Heger.

Plate 74. 'Lowell Thomas'. Photo Michael Dodge, White Flower Farm.

Plate 75. 'Lustrous'.

Plate 76. 'Madame Andre de Villers'. Photo Roy Klehm.

Plate 77. 'Mandarin's Coat'.

Plate 78. 'Marchioness'. Photo Michael Dodge, White Flower Farm.

Plate 79. 'Mary Jo Legere'.

Plate 80. 'Minuet'. Photo Michael Heger.

Plate 81. 'Miss America'. Photo Michael Dodge, White Flower Farm.

Plate 82. 'Mons. Jules Elie'. Photo Michael Heger.

Plate 83. 'Moonstone'. Photo Michael Heger.

Plate 84. 'Mother's Choice'. Photo Roy Klehm.

Plate 85. 'Mrs. Franklin D. Roosevelt'. Photo Sevald Nursery.

Plate 86. 'Mrs. Livingston Farrand'. Photo Busse Gardens.

Plate 87. 'Myrtle Gentry'. Photo André Viette.

Plate 88. 'Nice Gal'. Photo Roy Klehm.

Plate 89. 'Nick Shaylor'. Photo André Viette.

Plate 90. 'Norma Volz'. Photo Roy Klehm.

Plate 91. 'Nosegay'.

Plate 92. 'Old Faithful'.

Plate 93. *Paeonia anomala*. Photo Michael Heger.

Plate 94. *Paeonia brownii*. Photo Galen Burrell.

Plate 98. *Paeonia mascula* subsp. *mascula*. Photo Leo Fernig.

Plate 99. *Paeonia mascula* subsp. *arietina*. Photo Leo Fernig.

Plate 100. *Paeonia mascula* subsp. *triternata*. Photo Leo Fernig.

Plate 101. *Paeonia mlokosewitschii*.

Plate 102. *Paeonia officinalis.*

Plate 103. *Paeonia peregrina*. Photo Leo Fernig.

Plate 104. *Paeonia rockii*. Photo Roy Klehm.

Plate 105. *Paeonia tenuifolia*. Photo Leo Fernig.

Plate 106. *Paeonia veitchii*. Photo Leo Fernig.

Plate 107. 'Pageant'.

Plate 108. 'Paul M. Wild'. Photo A & D Nursery.

Plate 109. 'Paula Fay'. Photo Michael Heger.

Plate 110. 'Pillow Talk'. Photo Sevald Nursery.

Plate 111. 'Pink Hawaiian Coral'. Photo B. Hamilton.

Plate 112. 'Prairie Moon'. Photo Busse Gardens.

Plate 113. 'Princess Margaret'.

Plate 114. 'Raspberry Sundae'. Photo Chester Allen.

Plate 115. 'Red Charm'. Photo Linda Engstrom.

Plate 116. 'Red Glory'.

Plate 117. 'Red Red Rose'. Photo Michael Heger.

Plate 118. 'Renkaku'. Photo Roy Klehm.

Plate 119. 'Requiem'. Photo A & D Nursery.

Plate 120. 'Rose Garland'.

Plate 121. 'Rosedale'. Photo Linda Engstrom.

Plate 122. 'Roselette'. Photo Michael Heger.

Plate 123. 'Rushlight'. Photo A & D Nursery.

Plate 124. 'Sarah Bernhardt'. Photo A & D Nursery.

Plate 125. 'Scarlet O'Hara'. Photo Chester Allen.

Plate 126. 'Sea Shell'.

Plate 127. 'Shawnee Chief'. Photo Busse Gardens.

Plate 128. 'Shintenchi'. Photo Roy Klehm.

Plate 129. 'Shirley Temple'. Photo A & D Nursery.

Plate 130. 'Show Girl'.

Plate 131. 'Snow Mountain'. Photo A & D Nursery.

Plate 132. 'Stardust'. Photo Sevald Nursery.

Plate 133. 'Sword Dance'. Photo Michael Dodge, White Flower Farm.

Plate 134. 'Top Brass'. Photo Michael Dodge, White Flower Farm.

Plate 135. 'Tria'. Photo Michael Dodge, White Flower Farm.

Plate 136. 'Vesuvian'. Photo Michael Dodge, White Flower Farm.

Plate 137. 'Vivid Rose'. Photo Roy Klehm.   Plate 138. 'Walter Faxon'.
Photo Michael Heger.

Plate 139. 'Walter Marx'.

Plate 140. 'White Innocence'. Photo A & D Nursery.

Plate 141. 'Wu long peng-sheng'. Photo Zhang Yuexian.

Plate 142. 'Yae Zakura'. Photo Linda Engstrom.

Plate 143. 'Yellow Crown'.

'Papilio' (Saunders 1950). Another of Saunders' quadruple hybrids, this is an ivory single with pink veins resembling butterfly markings. A specimen plant that well rewards close observation of its medium-sized blooms. Very Early.

'Picotee' (Saunders 1949). A medium-sized white single, each petal of which is edged in lavender-pink. The only known cultivar selected from *Paeonia mascula* subsp. *russii*, this 24-inch plant has mounded foliage to the ground. The large, ruffled, dark green leaves are accented with red stems and veins and stay attractive all season. Strong grower in zone 8, but not fully tested elsewhere. Early.

'Pink Derby' (Bigger 1966). A platform of rose-red guard petals support a high-built center of light pink to white petals. The large blooms are well supported by strong stems. Late.

'Pink Hawaiian Coral' (R. Klehm 1981). A hybrid, the large, fragrant double flowers are coral-pink, changing to soft pink as the flower ages. Compact, mounded foliage, 36 inches in height. Early to Early Midseason. (Plate 111)

'Pink Pearl' (Reath 1991). This large double is a light and luminous shade of pink. At only 24 inches tall, it is worth a trial for both its low growth habit and unusual color. Late.

'Rivida' (Harrell–Varner 1985). Large and unusual fuchsia-rose flowers (nearest to lavender) of single form. Pods are widely used in dried arrangements. Midseason to Late.

'Royal Rose' (Reath 1980). This hybrid is the result of a cross between 'Moonrise' and 'Paula Fay'. The medium-sized, semi-double pink blooms show traces of cream. Fine plant habit similar to its pod parent, 'Paula Fay'. Wonderful in the landscape. Pod and pollen fertile. Early.

'Show Girl' (Hollingsworth 1984). Large hybrid flowers of Japanese form. The petals are of a warm, opaque pink with cream staminodes. Often contains many center petaloids of pink, making it appear nearly double. Midseason. (Plate 130)

'Sparkling Windflower' (Saunders–Reath 1971). A diamond-dusted, single red hybrid. Medium-sized flowers borne on an arching bush with finely divided foliage, much like the other members of the Windflower strain. Early.

'Walter Marx' (Marx–Rogers 1981.) A very large, floriferous white single. It forms a large bush, 44–48 inches high, with up to eight side buds on each stem, making for a long period of bloom. Highly fragrant. Midseason to Very Late. (Plate 139)

'White Frost' (Reath 1991). A beautiful, large, symmetrically shaped white double. Very strong stems. Late.

'Windchimes' (Reath 1984). A *Paeonia tenuifolia* hybrid with signature cut-leaved foliage. The small single flowers, borne on a relatively large bush, are lavender-pink. Early.

PROMISING TREE PEONIES

'Anna Marie' (Seidl 1984). A large single hybrid, the petals are a soft lavender to orchid with dark burgundy flares. Sturdy, vigorous growth, to 30 inches high. Occasionally sets seed and excels in ease of grafting. Early.

'Duchesse de Morny' (ex France pre-1955). A large double suffruticosa, blush to light pink. The large, dense bush holds as many as 280 flowers. Foliage to the ground. Early.

'Golden Era' (Reath 1984). A single yellow hybrid, whose very large flowers are carried on strong stems. Fertile both ways and of great value in breeding. Early Midseason.

'Kishu Caprice' (ex Japan via Rogers 1991). Large double flowers of dusty pink with a silvered effect. A tree peony of round habit, it flowers some two weeks earlier than most other suffruticosa forms. Very Early. (Plate 64)

PROMISING ITOHS (INTERSECTIONALS)

'Bartzella' (Anderson 1986). A very large double, the first intersectional to usually take this form. Each plant carries up to sixty frilly, lemon-yellow blooms and may reach a height of 24–36 inches. Midseason. (Plate 8)

'Garden Treasure' (Hollingsworth 1984). A large semi-double yellow. An improvement on the early Itohs, this hybrid grows to a larger size and produces larger flowers. Its lush foliage maintains a fresh appearance all summer long. Midseason.

'Rose Fantasy' (Seidl 1989). An unusual, medium-sized fuchsia-rose single whose petals are outlined in silver. Arching foliage. Particularly sought-after for unusual arrangements. Midseason.

'Yellow Crown' (Itoh–Smirnow 1974). A dwarf semi-double, its medium-sized blooms are bright yellow with red flares. 'Yellow Dream', 'Yellow Emperor', and 'Yellow Heaven' are all comparable semi-double yellow Itohs. Midseason. (Plate 143)

Chapter 8

Getting Started Commercially

Commercial peony production involves the same basic principles of culture as the ones given for home gardening in Chapter 5, though methods will differ slightly depending upon whether the grower's aim is to produce new plants, cut flowers, or dried flowers. Full sun and proper drainage are musts for optimum performance in all cases. Well-prepared ground is also necessary. If production is to begin on the site of an existing commercial nursery, presumably the soil will have been tested and the standard recommendations for liming and fertilization followed; peony production may, therefore, be started at once. The one crop peonies should never follow is alfalfa, as the levels of nitrogen it leaves behind in the soil are too high. If alfalfa was the most recent crop, grow something else for a year before planting peonies.

Schedule final cultivation or rototilling as soon before planting as possible. If subsequent spraying and cultivating will be done by tractor, make each row as long as possible while still allowing sufficient space at the end of each row for turning. Plant at any time during the fall before the ground freezes.

In commercial fields, where plants are often crowded, fungal infections may be a problem in wet springs, particularly with first-year plants. Bordeaux mixtures may be used but are not always as effective as the newer fungicides. Several new chemicals are under trial, including Fore, which is labeled for use on peonies, but none have yet been proven commercially. Consult an agricultural plant pathologist for up-to-date recommendations.

Rootknot nematode control is essential in commercial production. Set up a separate quarantine area for all new plants, destroying any that are suspected of harboring this pest. The nematodes can also be carried in soil, so all tools and boots used in a contaminated area must be sterilized. Products such as methyl bromide or Vapam can be used to fumigate a suspected area before planting.

At one time nematodes were quite prevalent in commercial plantings, which led to the industrywide practice of trimming off all fibrous roots on each division before sale or replanting. This not only rid roots of most nematodes, but as an unlooked-for bonus made for stronger and more vigorous divisions as well—one of the few cases where good cultural practice led to other horticultural benefits.

Production of new plants

For commercial new-plant production any size of division can be used, even small pieces of root with one eye, but do remember that plants from smaller divisions will take an additional year to mature. To prevent carrying over disease, make certain that no above-ground parts remain attached to the roots. Drop in small planting pieces at intervals of 12–18 inches; larger divisions need more room, 24 inches between them.

New roots grow from the terminal ends of the old ones, so if the planting stock consists of single root divisions with eyes at one end, plant with all eyes oriented in the same direction. This pattern allows adequate space for the plants to develop, while keeping roots of adjacent plants from growing together—which would be a problem if a single plant were to be removed from a row. Tiny planting pieces of valuable cultivars should be grown for two years in a special bed before lining out.

After planting the root pieces, cover the rows with soil and hill up in a ridge 2–3 inches high. The hilled-up soil acts as a mulch the first winter. Spring rain and normal soil compaction will level the planting area by the time the shoots emerge.

In milder areas, where grasses and weeds grow through the winter, herbicides can be applied at any time during the winter that weather allows, but before the peonies emerge from the ground. I use a mixture of Roundup with either Surflan or Dacthal at the rates prescribed on the label. Surflan builds up over time, so it is best to switch to another product two years before removing peonies and putting in a cover crop. These mixtures not only control winter-growing grasses but also prevent weed seeds from germinating the following spring. Neither mixture will totally control clover, however. Weed growth between planting rows is best controlled by mechanical cultivation. Be careful not to damage the plants if a tractor is used; broken tissue promotes the growth of fungi. Weeds can be controlled in smaller plantings by hand hoeing and shallow rototilling.

In commercial new-plant production, a plant propagation cycle of three to four years from planting to salable stock is the rule. In the last year, the oldest plants are dug and divided. After dividing, the grower is left with large numbers of root pieces with eyes that are too small to market. These are replanted as part of the rootstock used in the new cycle. Such an everlasting production regime can become a curse in that the temptation to keep inferior cultivars is strong. Succumbing to this temptation accounts, in part, for the many older, second-rate cultivars that are still found in the market in great numbers and often at low prices. Few such cultivars bloom reliably or yield first-class flowers.

Production of cut flowers

With the renewed demand for peonies as cut flowers, the large, long-stemmed doubles are again starting to sell well, and the fresh colors and lighter forms of modern hybrids are finding their way into commerce. Designers working with table arrangements seek the informal look that single, semi-double, and Japanese forms provide and often make use of the smaller side buds of single cultivars such as 'Sea Shell' and 'Walter Marx'. Semi-doubles of unusual coloring pack a double punch: such cultivars as 'Coral Charm' and 'Cytherea' are eagerly sought and command a premium price. And an entirely new market has opened because many end-users, particularly florists and designers, now use peony flowers on shorter stems. This encourages the production of the lower-growing cultivars, which do not require staking.

Peony cut flower production requires in general the same cultural practices as growing for other uses. Remember though that the market requires a high-quality flower, so proper fertilization and the control of pests and diseases are more important than ever. The subsequent quality and vase life of the peony flower is just as dependent upon the cultural conditions experienced by the plant during growth as it is upon the postharvest handling of the plant material.

If fertilized with excessive nitrogen, the plant will produce fine, dark green foliage but its flowers will have a relatively shorter vase life. If on the other hand the plant is properly fed with a balanced fertilizer, containing adequate amounts of phosphorus and potash (both of which enhance flower development), a flower of higher quality will be produced.

As for pests and diseases, an active control program must be maintained to assure the highest possible quality. Flea beetles (*Epitrix* and *Phyllotreta* spp.) are of particular concern to cut flower growers. These pests chew on unopened buds, disfiguring the flowers. In severe infestations the opened flowers have a ragged appearance. Scout the field on warm sunny afternoons, when the beetles are most active, to determine levels of infestation. Both rotenone and pyrethrum give satisfactory control. Spray in mid-afternoon.

The one departure that some cut flower growers make from root production guidelines is in planting. Roots intended for cut flower production must be placed at least 3.5 feet apart. Annuals for the cut flower market may be grown between the young peony plants for the first two years. If maximum flower production is the goal, plant the top eyes no more than two inches deep.

Some growers plant in double rows, some in triple rows, or beds. When grown in these hedgelike conditions, the plants provide support for each other, and of course, the number of plants grown in a given area is markedly increased. The downside is that plants grown so tightly cannot be machine-cultivated, and better disease control is required.

If commercial cut flower production is your aim, remove all but one bud on each plant the first year after planting. This allows more of the plant's energy to be devoted to growth, but still gives you positive identification of the plant. After that single bud flowers, cut the flower off just above the top leaf. In the course of the first year a network of feeder roots develops, which augments the water and nutrient uptake of the old root; new storage roots take an additional year or two to develop. In the second year these newly developed feeder roots become well established and the original roots begin to wither and then rot.

Conventional wisdom holds that no flowers should be taken the first two years, leaving all the foliage to produce a strong plant. By the end of the third year the old roots will have completely rotted, and the new root system is extensive enough to develop a number of stems, enough to permit a light picking—about 30 percent of the stems. By the fourth year the plant should produce ten or more stems. The plant becomes completely mature when five to seven years old.

The yield from older plants ranges from 50 to 75 percent of the available stems. At least the two lowest leaves must be left on each stem, but if peony flowers with longer stems are required they may be cut at ground level, in which case fewer stems can be removed from the plant. It is possible to hasten the flowering season by covering the plants with cloches (plastic tunnels) before growth starts. Remove the covering before harvesting.

The market for commercial cut flowers typically requires one flower per stem, yet most peony flowers marketed are cultivars of *Paeonia lactiflora*, a species that characteristically produces side buds on short stems below the terminal bud. Significant time must be spent, then, removing these side buds. Nip the side buds off as soon as possible after they have formed. The full strength of the plant can then be devoted to the terminal bud, producing the largest possible flower.

To open properly after cold-storage, buds must be harvested at the proper point of development. The flowers of some cultivars, such as 'Mons. Jules Elie', open quickly and so should be harvested when the buds are still tight. Most, however, can be harvested when the first petal starts to curl. A few, like 'Red Charm' and 'Sarah Bernhardt', need to be more nearly open before cutting.

Cut as early in the morning as possible, using a sharp knife or clippers. Not only is the stem most turgid at this time of day, but metabolic activities are low as well. Carry flowers to the work area, strip their leaves, and place them in a cold room that has been previously chilled. Alternatively, place stems directly in buckets of water in the field and quickly put them under refrigeration.

Growers and arrangers alike must remember that even after cut, the flower and stem remain alive and are actively metabolizing and transpiring water. It is essential therefore to cool the flowers as quickly as possible after cutting to slow down respiration, reduce ethylene production, and minimize the utilization of carbohydrates. The longest possible cut flower storage life can be realized at 32°F; at this temperature, the carbohydrates in the flower cells prevent damage to the flowers. Peonies can be successfully stored for up to four weeks at temperatures up to 45°F, but the lower the temperature, the longer the storage life.

It is also important that the concentration of ethylene in the cooler be kept as low as possible. Peony buds should never be stored with vegetables, fruits, or opened flowers, all of which are heavy producers of ethylene. For more information, see *Postharvest Handling and Storage of Cut Flowers, Florist Greens, and Potted Plants* (Nowak and Rudnicki 1990), a practical rather than scientific book on the postharvest care of cut flowers in general.

The following cultivars are recommended for commercial cut flower production:

> *Double white*
> > 'Charlie's White'
> > 'Duchesse de Nemours'
> > 'Elsa Sass'
> > 'Festiva Maxima'
> > 'Gardenia'
> > 'Mary E. Nicholls'
> > 'Mme. de Verneville'
> > 'Mother's Choice'
> > 'Mrs. Frank Beach'
> > 'Snow Mountain'
>
> *Double red*
> > 'Big Ben'
> > 'Chippewa'
> > 'Felix Crousse'
> > 'Felix Supreme'
> > 'Henry St. Clair'
> > 'Kansas'
> > 'Karl Rosenfield'
> > 'Mt. St. Helens'
> > 'Paul M. Wild'
> > 'Red Charm'
> > 'Red Comet'
> > 'Shawnee Chief'
>
> *Double pink*
> > 'Doris Cooper'
> > 'Duchesse d'Orleans'
> > 'Gene Wild'
> > 'Hansina Brand'

'Minuet'
'Mons. Jules Elie'
'Nick Shaylor'
'Raspberry Sundae'
'Sarah Bernhardt'
Lighter forms
    'Coral Charm' (semi-double pink)
    'Cytherea' (semi-double rose)
    'Gay Paree' (Japanese pink and white)
    'Louise Marx' (Japanese white)
    'Miss America' (semi-double white)
    'Red Goddess' (semi-double red)
    'Rosedale' (semi-double or double rose)
    'Sea Shell' (single pink)

Production of dried flowers

Peonies are grown specifically for dried flowers by growers around the world, and millions of dried peony flowers are sold each year through specialist commercial firms. Most of these commercially produced flowers are dried in special rooms fitted with carefully controlled, forced-warm-air systems. Recently a successful, though very expensive, process of removing water by freeze-drying has been employed. This method produces flowers with color and form identical to fresh-cut flowers.

There is a ready market for fresh-cut peonies for drying. Indeed the demand—particularly for fairly well-opened reds or dark pinks in double or anemone form—exceeds the supply. Though the price paid is low compared to what a grower could command in the fresh flower market, it is the best market for short stems of 4–8 inches. This means that blooms can be taken from some one- and two-year-old plants without reducing the number of leaves, which are so necessary for the plant's continued growth and development.

Biodynamic production

Growers who want to avoid the use of chemical fertilizers and sprays should consider an alternative method of peony production, the biodynamic method. This system is based on the pioneering work of the Austrian

Rudolph Steiner, back in the 1940s. To Steiner, the farm was a living organism; if its soil was brought to an optimum level, the result would be sustained yields over long periods of time.

One grower who uses this system is Paul Sansone of Gales Creek, Oregon. His Here and Now Garden is a certified biodynamic operation that produces many different cut flowers for the wholesale market. He grows four and one half acres of peonies, including such cultivars as 'Charlie's White', 'Felix Crousse', 'Sarah Bernhardt', and various single peonies.

He starts by devoting at least one year to soil preparation before planting. During this time he grows a succession of cover crops, including buckwheat and a combination of annual rye and vetch. These are mowed when in flower, then tilled into the soil.

He also adds large amounts of compost composed of soil, cow manure, plant trimmings, and all the carbonaceous material he can acquire, such as straw and spoiled hay. Green sand, rock phosphate, oyster shell, and kelp are added at the rate of two pounds each per ton of compost. The compost piles are inoculated with biodynamic starter. After ripening a year, the finished product is rich in trace elements, humus, and microflora, which help protect plants against fungus and disease. This compost is the basic ingredient of Sansone's raised beds.

The beds are 3 feet wide and raised 10 inches above ground level. Raised beds improve drainage and provide a much-enlarged upper soil zone for increased root growth. Once formed, the beds are covered with woven black polypropylene cloth, pegged down. Round holes 6 inches in diameter are burned into this covering in a matrix pattern. This spacing gives each plant a deep root space, 16 inches in diameter. In the fall a two-to three-eye peony division is planted in each hole and covered with an inch of soil.

After planting, the beds are covered with 1–2 inches of horse bedding (manure and shavings), which smothers any weeds that may come up in the planting holes. Each succeeding spring and fall, more horse bedding is added as well as a half inch of ripened compost. Specialized tractor-pulled equipment is used to spread these materials. The third spring, before growth starts, the polypropylene is stripped off for reuse (Sansone estimates a ten-year life for the material). By this time the plant foliage is so dense that weeds are all but eliminated.

The paths between beds are 2 feet wide and are completely covered with a black ultraviolet-resistant polypropylene pot cloth. This material prevents weed growth but allows air and water penetration. It can withstand foot and even tractor traffic.

Such a system keeps all but wind-blown weed seeds from germinating. Any weeds present are removed by hand, three or four times a year. One person can weed one acre in a single day.

The peony beds are interspersed with beds devoted to other genera to prevent the spread of disease. At the end of each season, the foliage from all beds is cut and composted. The composting pile is hot enough to destroy any pathogens that may be present.

The large amount of organic material added annually to the soil produces a stable humus that improves aeration, enhancing the availability of nutrients to the plants. It also encourages soil microbial activity, which draws fungal activity away from the foliage. Biodynamic sprays are used to further stimulate root and foliage growth. The healthier and more vigorous the plant, the better able it is to resist pathogens such as *Botrytis*.

Sansone employs a two-way watering system: a computerized drip system is used during the flowering season so the foliage stays dry, and an overhead sprinkling system is used to provide larger amounts of water during dry spells and to distribute soluble fertilizers. During cold, wet weather in the spring, the plants receive foliar feedings every ten days.

A general reference to the biodynamic farming process is *Agriculture* (Steiner 1958); more specific information on biodynamic growing is found in *How to Grow More Vegetables* (Jenvons 1974) and may be had from the following excellent groups:

Association of Specialty Cut Flower Growers
155 Elm Street, Box 268
Oberlin, Ohio 44074 U.S.A.

Bio Dynamic Farming and Gardening Association
Box 550
Kimberton, Pennsylvania 19442 U.S.A.

Appendix I

Peonies in Cultivation Worldwide

Peonies are grown virtually universally in the temperate regions of the world, but the levels of interest and the scope of uses vary widely from country to country, and up-to-date information is not available for some regions, such as the former Soviet Union, Argentina, and Chile. The extent of known national interest in peonies can be summarized as follows.

Australia

Most of Australia is too warm to grow peonies, but they have been found in the southern state of Victoria at higher elevations, within 300 miles of Melbourne (Hutton 1992). They can also be found on the island of Tasmania and scattered locations along the southern coast of the main continent. Several general nurseries offer them in very limited numbers. Tree peonies fare better than do the herbaceous forms.

Canada

The federal government's Northern Research Group in Beaverlodge, Alberta, has grown peonies since 1922, with detailed performance studies dating back to 1947. A new peony bed, the Beaverlodge Bed, was planted at that time and has never been disturbed. Dr. J. G. N. Davidson (1991) reports on the history and management of that bed and recommends cultivars best suited to that region.

Despite climatic difficulties, the Beaverlodge Bed is considered the finest floral display in the Peace River Region. Beaverlodge is located at latitude 55°N, in the U.S. Department of Agriculture's hardiness zone 2b. In addition to severely low temperatures and long winters, it is subject to violent chinook winds, which may quickly—but temporarily—raise temperatures by 40°F in the winter months. The peonies do have the protection of a windbreak, which also helps trap and retain snow cover.

The Beaverlodge Bed has received only minimal care over the years. It is weeded with some regularity, the bushes are tied up in the spring, the flowers are deadheaded after blooming, and the foliage is removed in the fall. Fertilizer is seldom applied, and the bed has never been irrigated.

The cultivars used in the planting were donated by Cyril M. Clarke, a leading Alberta peony enthusiast who reportedly farmed only to support his passion for peonies. They were chosen as the finest of his collection of more than 200 prized cultivars, purchased from leading growers in Canada, France, Great Britain, and the United States.

The Beaverlodge collection now consists of forty select cultivars—select in the sense that all those not thoroughly suited to the climate have long since died and only the hardy remain. All are lactiflora cultivars introduced before World War II. Many are classic peonies that remain available today, such as 'Festiva Maxima' and 'Marietta Sisson'. The single and semi-double forms do exceptionally well and are very consistent from year to year. Many of the cultivars classed as double, however, show great variability in form and change from bush to bush and even from stem to stem on the same plant.

There does not seem to be any active peony hybridizing going on in Canada at this time, but a large number of growers and vendors offer a wide range of peonies, and Canadian gardeners can readily procure plants domestically. Many of these growers can be found in Appendix II.

Germany

The German public is devoted to plants, and perennial plants in particular are considered an essential part of every landscape there. It is not unusual to find drought-resistant perennials, including peonies, in the traffic islands at center-city intersections. Peonies also figure in the traditional farm gardens of the countryside, together with phlox, bleeding heart, larkspur, and pinks. The German common name for peony is *Pfingstrose* as they usually bloom during *Pfingsten* (Whitsuntide). In southern Germany the village fountains are decorated with peonies on Whitsunday, the seventh Sunday after Easter.

Germany is the home of three perennial nurseries noted for their peony offerings. The largest, the renowned Staudengärtnerei Heinz Klose, has been active in hybridizing the modern peony and is discussed in Chapter 2. The oldest is the internationally acclaimed Staudengärtnerei Gräfin von Zeppelin. This mail-order nursery, founded by the Countess Helene von Stein-Zeppelin, was established in 1929. It is located in the southwestern corner of Germany between Freiburg and Basel, Switzerland, amid the vineyards of the rolling hills bordered by the Rhine Plain and the mountains of the Black Forest.

The von Zeppelin nursery offers a selection of more than 4000 species and cultivars of hardy perennial plants of which about 300 are cultivars and species of peonies. Many of the latter appear in their general catalog, but a separate catalog for the peony connoisseur is issued annually.

The newest peony nursery is that of Wolfgang Linnemann, of Bonn-Beuel. This nursery was started as a hobby and has only recently been converted to commercial production. They sell only tree peonies, specializing in Chinese cultivars.

Japan

A measure of the value and symbolic significance of both herbaceous and tree peonies to the Japanese is their longstanding tradition of presenting peonies as a final gift, a living reminder of someone who has recently died. For hundreds of years Japanese gardeners have especially revered the Botan (tree peony). They are the best-known growers of the plant, and naturally enough, Japan is a leading exporter of tree peony grafts.

Before World War II about 200 acres of precious land were devoted to the commercial production of tree peonies. These fields were located in the prefectures of Niigata, Shimane, and Osaka. Production has picked up since about 1970, and presently some 250 acres are under cultivation. The fields are primarily given over to scion stock plants and grafted saplings, some of which are forced for the domestic market. These are dug from the field, potted, pre-cooled, and then brought into heated greenhouses, where they are kept until the buds are ready to open (Aoki and Yoshino 1984). Tree peonies in bloom are a winter feature in Japanese flower shops, as they are in Chinese markets.

From late August through early September, hundreds of farmers graft suffruticosa scions on rootstock from wild herbaceous peony seedlings and grow them on in their small plots. These are sometimes marketed by the farmers themselves, but more frequently they are offered through agricultural cooperatives. The number of saplings produced has increased to one million per year; between 20 and 30 percent of these are exported to the United States.

Cut flower peonies, primarily lactiflora cultivars, are another major crop. They go to market from the end of December through April and are forced in either heated or unheated plastic houses. No specific sales figures are available (Hosaki 1992).

The Japan Botan Society—headed by Ryoji Hashida, Honcho 1-2-11, Tatebayashi City, Gumma Prefecture, Japan—published *A Book of Tree and Herbaceous Peonies in Modern Japan* (1990), an authoritative reference work on identification and nomenclature. Its excellent color illustrations clearly show the distinctive floral and foliar features of more than 400 Chinese and Japanese tree peony species and cultivars, including winter-flowering forms, as well as a number of herbaceous cultivars now being grown in Japan.

Great Britain

England is the home of the world-renowned Hardy Plant Society. Its Paeony Specialty Group is open to all members of the parent society worldwide and publishes a quarterly newsletter. Mrs. Margaret Baber, Green Cottage, Redhill Lane, Lydney, Gloucestershire, GL15 6BS, United Kingdom, is currently the head of this specialty group.

Three official National Reference Collections for peonies have been established. These are gardens governed by the National Council for the Conservation of Plants and Gardens, created to ensure that valuable species and important historic cultivars of most garden forms are not lost in cultivation. In addition, these National Reference Collection gardens serve as reference centers for cultivars in commerce. If the accuracy of a particular cultivar's name is questioned, here it can be compared and validated. The council strongly emphasizes education and conservation as well as identification. Collection holders—private gardens in most cases—must meet rigid council requirements: records must be kept, collections must be continually expanded and open to the public, and plants must be propagated and offered for sale. Private individuals fund these collections.

Mrs. Baber holds the collection devoted to pre- and post-1900 peony cultivars. The Species Paeonia Collection is held by Mr. and Mrs. R. J. Mitchell, Branklyn, Dundee Road, Perth, Perthshire, PH2 7BB, United Kingdom. The Species and Primary Hybrid Collection is held by Paul Nichols, The National Trust, Hidecote Bartrim, Chipping, Camden, Gloucestershire, GL55 6LR, United Kingdom.

Roots are produced commercially by only two nurseries, Kelway's and Austin's. Cut flower production is in the main a cottage industry except for those turned out by one firm, La Hougette. Started by Theodore Person and now run by his son-in-law, La Hougette is located in the town of St. Lawrence on the island of Jersey. Several acres there are devoted to cut flower peony production, two acres alone of 'Sarah Bernhardt'. Other cultivars regularly grown include 'Felix Crousse', 'Festiva Maxima', and 'Paula Fay'.

For about twenty years after World War II, one of the features at the world-famous Chelsea Flower Show was the peony display of Maurice Prichard. He specialized in cultivars of *Paeonia officinalis* and bred several noteworthy single red cultivars including 'Crimson Globe'. The nursery, unfortunately, was dissolved upon his death.

The Netherlands

Although the climate is poorly suited to the growing of tree peonies, some five million herbaceous peony roots are grown for sale each year by Dutch nurseries. Twelve firms dominate this market and three others maintain extensive collections of rare cultivars. Most of the peony roots grown in the Netherlands are exported. It is estimated that 65 percent go to the United States, 25 percent to European destinations, and 10 percent to Japan.

Cut flower peonies are sold through flower auctions, where nearly two million stems are marketed by cultivar name. 'Sarah Bernhardt' sells more than all other cultivars combined; the other most popular forms are 'Dr. Alexander Fleming', 'Karl Rosenfield', and *Paeonia officinalis*.

In addition some 800,000 are sold by color—not name—with white being the most popular color. Another three million stems are sold annually as dried flowers.

New Zealand

Pam Simpson, Box 67, Geraldine, is the secretary of the New Zealand Paeony Growers Group, whose members are commercial growers involved in the production of both roots and cut flowers. The flowering season there peaks in December, giving New Zealand the off-season opportunity to market cut flowers to the Northern Hemisphere. Their principal markets are Japan, Sweden, and the United States.

Most of the commercial root nurseries grow only the more recently introduced cultivars; the Klehm introductions are the most widely available.

People's Republic of China

China is the ancestral home of *Paeonia lactiflora*, the most extensively cultivated peony species in the world. From time immemorial the herbaceous peony—originally called Shoyao, which translates as both "charming and beautiful" and "wealthy and honorable"—has been grown in China, and lactiflora cultivars in particular were well developed as garden flowers there by the 18th century.

The shrubby tree peony was known by several names: Mow Tan ("red blossom"), Hwa Wang ("king of flowers"), and Fu Gui ("wealthy and honorable"). The Chinese presently use the word *Mudan* to identify both herbaceous and tree peonies. In the West the derived term, Moutan, refers only to tree peonies.

China is becoming a major grower and exporter of ornamental tree peonies. The work is centered outside the city of Heze—known as Caozhou in ancient times—in the southwest part of Shandong Province. This fertile area, in what used to be the flood plains of the Huang He (Yellow River), has been home to tree peonies since 1550. Today, peony nurseries are located in most of the provinces and cities of China, but the Huang He valley remains the major production area.

The blooming period of the Caozhou peony is from mid-April to early May. During the period of peak bloom, Heze is ablaze with color. Every year nearly a million people come to visit the fields east of the city, to make literary or artistic presentations, and to exchange scientific information. Professor Hong of the Chinese Academy of Forestry (woody tree peonies are considered forest species in China) describes it as "a magnificent scene, with flowers like the ocean and people like the surf."

The Chinese government has taken a great interest in the Caozhou peony of late and is the official sponsor of the International Peony Flower Fair, held each year from 20–26 April (Zhang 1992). The General Developing Company of Caozhou Peony Flowers and Trees in Shandong was set up to manage the production, scientific research, and marketing of the Caozhou peony. Currently some 1080 acres of peonies are being grown in this area.

Each winter some 200,000 plants are induced to set flower buds early and then sent to the large southern cities where the climate is too hot to grow them. There they are brought into flower and sold. Invariably, the demand exceeds the supply. More than 100,000 plants from Heze are sold to other cities in China as well as exported to Japan, Korea, North America, the former Soviet Union, France, and southeast Asian countries. A trade in cut flowers, of both tree and herbaceous peonies, is also being developed (Chen 1992).

Peonies are cultivated in most of the public gardens of China. The Shanghai Botanical Garden, for example, maintains a separate peony garden, which includes collections of both tree and herbaceous cultivars. There is also a pavilion for the display of unusual peonies, grown in containers and brought into the pavilion only when in full bloom. This garden attracts up to a million visitors annually.

Because of the widespread medicinal use of the genus *Paeonia* in China, botanical gardens generally display their peonies in their herb garden exhibits along with other curatives. Such herb gardens are not infrequently the most extensive specialized areas in Chinese botanical gardens.

Paeonia ostii, the species believed by Hong and his associates to be the wild progenitor of many tree peony cultivars thus far attributed to *P. suffruticosa*, is now endangered due to the excessive digging, over a long period of time, of its roots for use as the medicinal herb, mu-dan-pi. Its distribution has been seriously reduced, and as a result, few examples of this species remain in the wild.

'Phoenix White' is a very precious, beautiful, and fragrant cultivar of what Hong has described as "Osti's peony cultivar group" (see the discussion of his thesis in Chapter 3). Its root bark (dan-pi) is a specialty herbal product of Tongling City in Anhui Province. Ninety acres of this cultivar are in cultivation there for Chinese herbal medicines. The quantity of dan-pi exported each year exceeds 300 tons, and the profit on this export alone is reported to exceed $500,000 per year.

Wanhua Mountain in Yanan City, Shaanxi Province, is the apparent center of both *Paeonia jishanensis* and *P. yananensis*. These two species, distributed over a wide area in ancient times, are seldom found in the wild today, but as with endangered parent *P. ostii*, many unique cultivars have been developed from them. The high-quality cultivars of the Jishan and Yanan peony are quite different from those developed in Heze and Luoyang, the capital of the Sung dynasty and ancient center of tree peony production.

Species Peonies International Network

On the subject of vanishing species, one worldwide network is committed to making a difference and has assumed responsibility for preserving species—in cultivation at least. SPIN (the acronym for Species Peonies International Network) is an informal group of enthusiasts located throughout the temperate world who share a common purpose: to identify and preserve peony species and encourage their cultivation in the landscape. The organization, an informal subset of the American Peony Society, was established in 1976 on the initiative of members living in Australia and France. It is composed of amateur gardeners in the main, but also reaches out to nurserymen, seed growers, and scientists at botanical gardens.

Major individual efforts have been undertaken to collect seed from wild plants, and every member is encouraged to cultivate several species. The resultant plants are used not only to validate the authenticity of plants offered by growers but as breeding material for controlled hybridizing. As a part of its work, the group is endeavoring to positively identify and stabilize the nomenclature of all peony species, based on the exhaustive survey of Ray Cooper of Oldham, England.

The responsibility for issuing the group's newsletter rests with Leo Fernig, La Fougere, Lucinges, 74380 Bonne, France. This useful publication contains news of the activities of the members and frequently updates the activities of Ray Cooper's work. Seed exchange listings are included as well. Contacts for the group are as follows:

Alan Matchett
Dunedin Botanic Gardens
Box 5045
Dunedin, New Zealand

Irmtrud Reick
Friedrichstrasse 8
74906 Bad Rappenau-Babstadt, Germany

Galen Burrell
Box 754
Ridgefield, Washington 98642 U.S.A.

The following lists of cultivated and commercially available peony species and cultivars were derived from the catalogs and price lists of the principal peony nurseries in North America, Europe, New Zealand, Japan, and China. Additional information may be found in updated editions of the Andersen Horticultural Library's *Source List of Plants and Seeds*, Anne and Peter Ashley's *The Canadian Plant Sourcebook*, and the Royal Horticultural Society's *The Plant Finder*, for the British Isles.

The lists are presented in the following sequence: Herbaceous Species, Tree Peony Species, Herbaceous Cultivars, Suffruticosa Tree Peony Cultivars, Hybrid Tree Peony Cultivars, and Itoh Hybrids.

In the case of cultivars listed by one nursery or another under an invalid name ('Mrs. F. D. R.' or 'Mrs. F. D. Roosevelt' rather than 'Mrs. Franklin D. Roosevelt'), I provide a cross-reference to the valid name as published by the American Peony Society. Whatever the name assigned by the nursery, I list all sources under the valid name. If there is a question as to the name intended—especially where species are concerned, and even more especially in light of recent nomenclatural reassignments—I use the nursery's own designation, even to retaining trinomials. It is hard to know exactly what plant is being offered in these cases.

Whenever I knew or could locate the parentage of a cultivar, I include the information. But growers sometimes submit incomplete information for registration; even more painful to report, some cultivars introduced by leading breeders were never registered, and the known parentage of some of those reported was not disclosed. The world of peonies is much poorer for want of this information.

It is worth noting that many cultivar parents are no longer in commerce, and as a consequence, it is unlikely that the same cross could be repeated. The problem of the extinction of breeding lines of hybrid cultivars is, although not as serious, analogous to loss of species in their native habitats. It is imperative that collectors and specialized growers adopt a more responsible and acute sense of the need to preserve breeding lines.

As it was in the case of parentage, likewise spotty information on hybridizer, date, form, or color exists for some of the plants cataloged. In these cases I pass on all the information provided by the original source. Because the information supplied in some catalogs is inadequate, it is possible that some old cultivars may have been given new names or that they may never have been registered. Finally, the catalog description does not always match that of the registered plant. Although I was not able to identify every such instance, I note whenever possible the registered name and description to minimize confusion or disappointment on the buyer's part.

The catalogs utilize a variety of words, often far-fetched, for colors. For the most part, in the interest of consistency, I standardize color descriptions to the nearest commonly employed term—yellow, white, blush, lavender, pink, purple, rose, or red—except in the case of the hybrid and Itoh tree peonies. Their complex colors occasionally demand a more subtle accounting, but despite the expanded descriptive palette, only the principal color for each is listed.

Cultivars that have been awarded the annual Gold Medal by the American Peony Association for all-around excellence are noted. This award requires the unanimous decision of the society's board of directors and so is usually a reliable—but not an unfailing—guide to quality.

The names of the growers who make the plants available and whose catalogs were used to create these lists are given following each flower description. If a nursery is located outside the United States, the country is included in parentheses. If a cultivar is offered by more than seven different sources, I show it as "widely available." The reader should keep in mind, however, that some firms may not offer all the cultivars they grow in any particular year.

The full names and addresses of all growers mentioned as well as many other likely nursery sources are found in Appendix II.

HERBACEOUS SPECIES

Names are presented as they are given in the catalogs; they do not necessarily appear in the taxonomic literature, and some are in all likelihood invalid.

Paeonia anemoniflora. A single pink, available from Pivoinerie (France).

Paeonia anomala. A single red, available from Pivoinerie (France).

Paeonia bakeri. A single pink, available from Austin Roses (U.K.).

Paeonia banatica. A single red, available from Austin Roses (U.K.).

Paeonia coriacea. A single red, available from Gärtnerei und Staudenkulturen (Switzerland).

Paeonia emodi. A single white, available from Pivoinerie (France) and Marsal (New Zealand).

Paeonia humilis. A single red, available from Austin Roses (U.K.) and Caprice Farm.

Paeonia humilis var. *villosa*. A single red, available from Gärtnerei und Staudenkulturen (Switzerland).

Paeonia japonica. A single white, available from Brand Peony Farm.

Paeonia lactiflora. A single white, available from Austin Roses (U.K.).

Paeonia lobata. Possibly *P. peregrina*. A single red, available from Busse Gardens and Viette Farm and Nursery.

Paeonia mlokosewitschii. A single yellow, available from Caprice Farm; Klose (Germany); von Zeppelin (Germany); Gärtnerei und Staudenkulturen (Switzerland); and Marsal (New Zealand).

Paeonia officinalis. A single pink, available from Marsal (New Zealand).

Paeonia officinalis var. *lobata*. Possibly *P. peregrina*. A single red, available from Busse Gardens.

Paeonia officinalis mollis. A single pink, available from Klose (Germany).

Paeonia peregrina. A single red, available from von Zeppelin (Germany) and Austin Roses (U.K.).

Paeonia peregrina lobata. Possibly *P. peregrina*. A single red, available from Pivoinerie (France).

Paeonia russii. A single pink, available from Pivoinerie (France).

Paeonia tenuifolia. A single red, available from Piroche Plants (Canada) and Tischler Peony Garden.

Paeonia veitchii var. *woodwardii*. A single red, available from Caprice Farm; Peony Gardens (New Zealand); and Holden Clough (U.K.).

TREE PEONY SPECIES

With the exception of *Paeonia rockii*, names are presented as they are given in the catalogs; they do not necessarily appear in the taxonomic literature, and some are in all likelihood invalid.

Paeonia delavayi. A single red, available from Hillier (U.K.); Pivoinerie (France); and Marsal (New Zealand).

Paeonia lutea. A single yellow, available from Hillier (U.K.) and Pivoinerie (France).

Paeonia lutea var. *ludlowii*. A single yellow, available from Caprice Farm; Hillier (U.K.); Craigmore (New Zealand); and Marsal (New Zealand).

Paeonia potaninii var. *trollioides*. A single yellow, available from Reath's.

Paeonia rockii (ex China). Offered as 'Joseph Rock'. A single white suffruticosa, available from Craigmore (New Zealand) and Reath's.

Paeonia suffruticosa. A single red-purple, available from Rivière (France).

Paeonia suffruticosa var. *Rocks*. Possibly *Paeonia rockii*. A single white, available from Reath's.

Paeonia suffruticosa var. *Rocks*. Possibly *Paeonia rockii*. A semi-double white, available from Klehm Nursery and Reath's.

HERBACEOUS CULTIVARS

The lactiflora cultivars are selections of *Paeonia lactiflora*, a late-flowering species. Cultivars identified as hybrids are from two or more species (most likely a combination of *P. lactiflora* and *P. officinalis*) and as such flower earlier. When parentage is given as "linebred" it indicates that both parents are descended from the same cultivar; when it is given as "selfed," a parent and the same parent's own pollen was used to produce the new plant. "Origin unknown" includes unregistered plants.

'A. B. C. Nicholls' (Nicholls 1937). A double white lactiflora, available from Busse Gardens.

'A. B. Franklin' (Franklin 1928). Gold Medal. A double white lactiflora, available from New Peony Farm; Brand Peony Farm; and Busse Gardens.

'A. G. Perry' (Brand 1933). A semi-double or double pink lactiflora, available from Hildebrandt's; Adamgrove; Ferncliff Gardens (Canada); and Cruickshank's (Canada).

'A la Mode' (R. Klehm 1981). A single white lactiflora, available from Viette Farm and Nursery; Klehm Nursery; Terrace Peonies (New Zealand); and Craigmore (New Zealand).

'Abalone Pink' (Krekler–R. Klehm 1978). A single pink hybrid, available from Klehm Nursery.

'Accent' (Franklin 1928). A double red lactiflora, available from Bigger Peonies and New Peony Farm.

'Achille' (Calot 1835). A double pink lactiflora, available from von Zeppelin (Germany).

'Ada Priscilla' (Guille 1928). A double white lactiflora, available from Viette Farm and Nursery.

'Adolphe Rousseau' (Dessert–Mechin 1890). A semi-double or double red lactiflora, available from Mount Arbor; Austin Roses (U.K.); Cannon Nurseries (Canada); Country Squires (Canada); Sheridan Nurseries (Canada); Maison des Fleurs (Canada); and Pivoinerie (France).

'Adonis' (Sass 1930). A double pink lactiflora, available from Bigger Peonies.

'Aerie' (Bigger 1949). A semi-double white lactiflora, available from Bigger Peonies; Busse Gardens; and Craigmore (New Zealand).

'Afterglow' (origin unknown). A double rose lactiflora, available from Kelways (U.K.).

'Agida' (origin unknown pre-1930). A double red lactiflora, available from Austin Roses (U.K.) and Pivoinerie (France).

'Aglow' (Nicholls–Wild 1959). A double white lactiflora, available from Wild and Son.

'Airway' (Wild 1967). A Japanese rose lactiflora, available from Wild and Son.

'Akalu' (Dessert). A Japanese rose lactiflora, available from Pivoinerie (France).

'Akasjhigata' (origin unknown). A Japanese pink lactiflora, available from Ferncliff Gardens (Canada) and Brickman's (Canada).

'Alba'. Offered as a cultivar of *Paeonia veitchii*. A single white, available from Austin Roses (U.K.).

'Alba Plena'. Offered as a cultivar of *Paeonia officinalis*. A double white, widely available.

'Albert Crousse' (Crousse 1893). A double white to blush lactiflora, widely available.

'Alberta Kelsey' (Kelsey 1937). A double pink lactiflora, available from Cedar Creek (Canada).

'Alecia Kunkel' (Tischler 1987). A Japanese pink lactiflora, available from Tischler Peony Garden and Caprice Farm.

'Alesia' (Lemoine 1927). A double white lactiflora, available from Anderson Iris; Busse Gardens; and Rivière (France).

'Alexander Fleming'. See 'Dr. Alexander Fleming'

'Alexander Steffen' (Steffen). A single rose hybrid, available from Klose (Germany).

'Alexander Woollcott' (Saunders 1941). A cross between *Paeonia lactiflora* and *P. peregrina*. A semi-double red, available from Caprice Farm; Cedar Creek (Canada); Reath's; and Klehm Nursery.

'Alexandre Dumas' (Guerin 1862). A double pink lactiflora, available from Pivoinerie (France) and Mount Arbor.

'Alice Crousse' (Calot 1893). A double pink lactiflora, available from Rivière (France).

'Alice Harding' (Lemoine 1922). A double blush lactiflora, available from Heschke Gardens; Klose (Germany); Austin Roses (U.K.); Rivière (France); and Pivoinerie (France).

'Alice Reed Bates' (Franklin 1939). A double pink lactiflora, available from Brand Peony Farm.

'Alice Roberts' (Krekler). A Japanese pink lactiflora, available from Klehm Nursery.

'Alix Fleming'. See 'Dr. Alexander Fleming'

'Alma Hansen' (Cooper 1946). A double pink lactiflora, available from Rivière (France).

'Alpine Air' (Minks 1985). A sport of 'Festiva Maxima'. A double white, available from Wild and Son.

'Ama-No-Sode' (ex Japan pre-1928). A Japanese pink lactiflora, available from Weston Nurseries; Ferncliff Gardens (Canada); von Zeppelin (Germany); and Pivoinerie (France).

'Amabilis' (Calot 1856). A double blush lactiflora, available from Pivoinerie (France).

'Amalia Olson' (Olson 1959). A double white lactiflora, available from Hollingsworth Peonies; Busse Gardens; and Reath's.

'America' (Rudolph 1976). A 'Burma Ruby' cross. Gold Medal. A single red, available from Wayside Gardens; Caprice Farm; Hildebrandt's; Peony Gardens (New Zealand); and Klehm Nursery.

'Anemoniflora Rosea'. Offered as a cultivar of *Paeonia officinalis*. A single pink, available from Austin Roses (U.K.).

'Angel Cheeks' (C. G. Klehm). A double pink lactiflora, widely available.

'Angelika Kauffmann' (Goos–Koenemann 1912). A Japanese white lactiflora, available from Klose (Germany).

'Angelo Cobb Freeborn' (Freeborn 1943). A double red hybrid, widely available.

'Angelus' (Auten 1933). A single white lactiflora, available from Viette Farm and Nursery.

'Ann Berry Cousins' (Cousins–R. Klehm 1972). A semi-double pink hybrid, available from Craigmore (New Zealand) and Klehm Nursery.

'Ann Cousins' (Cousins 1946). A double white lactiflora, widely available.

'Ann Pfeiffer' (Pfeiffer 1932). A double white lactiflora, available from Busse Gardens.

'Anne Zaylor' (Mains 1956). A semi-double red lactiflora, available from Busse Gardens.

'Annisquam' (Thurlow–Stranger 1951). A double pink lactiflora, available from Busse Gardens and Klehm Nursery.

'Antwerpen' (origin unknown). A single pink lactiflora, available from Klose (Germany); Gärtnerei und Staudenkulturen (Switzerland); Maison des Fleurs (Canada); and Pivoinerie (France).

'Apache' (Wolfe–Bigger 1966). A single red hybrid, available from Bigger Peonies.

'Arabian Prince' (Kelway). A double rose lactiflora, available from Kelways (U.K.).

'Archangel' (Saunders 1950). A second-generation hybrid resulting from a cross between *Paeonia lactiflora* and *P. macrophylla*. A single white, available from Reath's; A & D Nursery; and Busse Gardens.

'Argentine' (Lemoine). A double white lactiflora, available from Brand Peony Farm and Maison des Fleurs (Canada).

'Armistice' (Kelsey 1938). A double pink lactiflora, available from Weston Nurseries; Wild and Son; Craigmore (New Zealand); Hortico (Canada); and Maison des Fleurs (Canada).

'Arroway' (origin unknown). A Japanese pink lactiflora, available from A & D Nursery.

'Asa Gray' (Crousse 1886). A double pink lactiflora, available from Craigmore (New Zealand); Aimers (Canada); Pepieniere Charlevoix (Canada); Pivoinerie (France); and Marsal (New Zealand).

'Astarte' (Saunders 1951). Descended from *Paeonia lactiflora*, *P. macrophylla*, *P. mlokosewitschii*, and *P. peregrina* crosses. An anemone pink, available from Wild and Son.

'Athelstane' (Brown 1935). A double pink lactiflora, available from Country Squires (Canada).

'Athena' (Saunders 1955). Descended from *Paeonia lactiflora*, *P. macrophylla*, *P. mlokosewitschii*, and *P. peregrina* crosses. A single white and rose, available from Reath's; A & D Nursery; Busse Gardens; Caprice Farm; and Klehm Nursery.

'Atlas' (Gilbertson 1975). A double red lactiflora, available from Brand Peony Farm.

'Attar of Roses' (Murawska 1951). A double pink lactiflora, available from Wild and Son.

'Audrey' (Saunders 1938). A cross between *Paeonia lactiflora* and *P. macrophylla*. A semi-double or double blush, available from Caprice Farm.

'Auguste Dessert' (Dessert 1920). A semi-double pink lactiflora, widely available.

'Augustin d'Hour'. See 'General MacMahon'

'Aureole' (Hollis 1905). A Japanese pink lactiflora, available from Cannon Nurseries (Canada).

'Aureolin' (Shaylor 1917). A Japanese rose lactiflora, available from Brand Peony Farm and Craigmore (New Zealand).

'Auten's 1816' (Auten). A double red hybrid, available from Klehm Nursery and Austin Roses (U.K.).

'Auten's Pride' (Auten 1933). A double pink lactiflora, available from Viette Farm and Nursery; Busse Gardens; and Sherman Nursery.

'Auten's Red Sport' (Auten). A double red lactiflora, available from Klehm Nursery.

'Avalanche' (Crousse 1886). A double white lactiflora, available from Brand Peony Farm; Sherman Nursery; A & D Nursery; Reath's; Craigmore (New Zealand); and Marsal (New Zealand).

'Avant Garde' (Lemoine 1907). A cross between *Paeonia lactiflora* and *P. wittmanniana*. A single pink, available from Ferncliff Gardens (Canada); Brickman's (Canada); and Pivoinerie (France).

'Ave Maria' (Mann–van Steen 1936). A double blush lactiflora, available from Klehm Nursery and Busse Gardens.

'Avis Varner' (Varner 1981). A double red lactiflora, available from Varner and Caprice Farm.

'Ballerina' (Kelway). A double blush lactiflora, available from Kelways (U.K.).

'Balliol' (origin unknown). A single red lactiflora, available from Klose (Germany).

'Banatica'. Offered as a cultivar of *Paeonia officinalis*. A single red, available from Gärtnerei und Staudenkulturen (Switzerland).

'Bandit' (Krekler 1986). A double blush lactiflora, available from Klehm Nursery.

'Banner Bright' (Franklin). Originally called 'Fluffy Ruffles'. A semi-double or double pink lactiflora, available from Brand Peony Farm.

'Barbara's White' (origin unknown). A single white lactiflora, available from Peony Gardens (New Zealand).

'Baron' (Krekler). A single pink hybrid, available from Klehm Nursery.

'Baroness Schroeder' (Kelway 1889). A double blush lactiflora, widely available.

'Baronne de Rothschild' (Kelway 1898). A double pink lactiflora, available from Pivoinerie (France).

'Barrington Belle' (C. G. Klehm 1971). A Japanese or anemone rose lactiflora, available from Peony Gardens (New Zealand); Klehm Nursery; Adamgrove; Hildebrandt's; Gardenimport (Canada); Pivoinerie (France); and Marsal (New Zealand).

'Battle Flag' (Nicholls 1941). A Japanese red lactiflora, available from Brand Peony Farm.

'Beacon Hill' (Auten 1937). A single red hybrid, available from Viette Farm and Nursery.

'Beersheba' (Kelway). A single rose lactiflora, available from Kelways (U.K.).

'Belle' (Glasscock 1931). A double or anemone pink lactiflora, available from Pivoinerie (France).

'Belle Center' (Mains 1956). A semi-double red lactiflora, available from Busse Gardens; Klehm Nursery; Austin Roses (U.K.); and Pivoinerie (France).

'Benjamin Franklin' (Brand 1907). A double red lactiflora, available from Carroll Gardens and Mount Arbor.

'Bess Bockstoce' (Bockstoce 1955). Called 'Rose Heart' in Canada. A double rose hybrid, available from Caprice Farm and Cedar Creek (Canada).

'Bess Bockstoce' (origin unknown). Invalid name. A double pink hybrid, available from Cedar Creek (Canada).

'Bessie' (Krekler 1958). A double pink lactiflora, available from Busse Gardens; Wayside Gardens; and Klehm Nursery.

'Best Man' (C. G. Klehm). A double red lactiflora, available from Klehm Nursery; Hildebrandt's; and Ferncliff Gardens (Canada).

'Better Times' (Franklin 1941). A double rose lactiflora, widely available.

'Betty Warner' (Krekler). A Japanese red lactiflora, available from Klehm Nursery.

'Bev' (Krekler 1975). A double pink lactiflora, available from Reath's; Wayside Gardens; and Klehm Nursery.

'Big Ben' (Auten 1943). A double red lactiflora, widely available.

'Big Red Boomer Sooner' (Wild 1962). A double red lactiflora, available from A & D Nursery.

'Bill Krekler' (Mains–Krekler). A cross between 'Alice Harding' and *Paeonia officinalis*. A double pink, available from Cedar Creek (Canada) and Country Squires (Canada).

'Birthday' (Saunders 1935). A cross between *Paeonia lactiflora* and *P. peregrina* 'Otto Froebel'. A single pink, available from Caprice Farm.

'Black Swan' (Murawska 1968). A 'Chocolate Soldier' cross. A double red, available from Cedar Creek (Canada).

'Blanche King' (Brand 1922). A double pink lactiflora, available from Caprice Farm; Brand Peony Farm; Busse Gardens; and Rivière (France).

'Blaze' (Fay 1973). 'Bravura' selfed. A semi-double red, available from Caprice Farm; Peony Gardens (New Zealand); Busse Gardens; Klehm Nursery; von Zeppelin (Germany); and Pivoinerie (France).

'Blush Queen' (Hoogendoorn 1949). A double white lactiflora, available from Viette Farm and Nursery; Austin Roses (U.K.); Cheyenne Tree Farms (Canada); and Pivoinerie (France).

'Blushing Princess' (Saunders–Reath 1991). A third-generation, semi-double blush hybrid, available from Caprice Farm.

'Bo-Peep' (Auten 1944). A Japanese or anemone red lactiflora, available from Wild and Son.

'Bob Krekler' (Krekler 1965). A Japanese pink lactiflora, available from Klehm Nursery.

'Bobby Ann Miller' (Home Garden Co. 1937). A Japanese pink lactiflora, available from Viette Farm and Nursery.

'Bonanza' (Franklin 1947). A double red lactiflora, available from Brand Peony Farm; Reath's; Tischler Peony Garden; Busse Gardens; Klehm Nursery; and Ferncliff Gardens (Canada).

'Border Gem' (Hoogendoorn 1949). A Japanese pink lactiflora, available from Viette Farm and Nursery.

'Bouquet Perfect' (Tischler 1987). An anemone pink lactiflora, available from Tischler Peony Garden and Caprice Farm.

'Bowl of Beauty' (Hoogendoorn 1949). A Japanese pink lactiflora, widely available.

'Bowl of Cream' (C. G. Klehm 1963). Gold Medal. A double white lactiflora, widely available.

'Bravura' (Saunders 1943). A cross between *Paeonia lactiflora* and *P. peregrina*. A single red, available from Viette Farm and Nursery and Klehm Nursery.

'Bravura Supreme' (Krekler). A single red lactiflora, available from Reath's.

'Break o' Day' (Murawska 1947). A Japanese pink lactiflora, available from Busse Gardens; Klehm Nursery; Ferncliff Gardens (Canada); and Brickman's (Canada).

'Bridal Gown' (C. G. Klehm 1981). Linebred 'Charlie's White'. A double white, available from Klehm Nursery; Wayside Gardens; Hildebrandt's; and Austin Roses (U.K.).

'Bridal Icing' (R. Klehm 1981). A cross between 'Alice Harding' and 'Charlie's White'. A double white, available from Viette Farm and Nursery; Hildebrandt's; and Klehm Nursery.

'Bridal Shower' (R. Klehm 1981). Linebred 'Charlie's White'. A double white, available from Klehm Nursery; Wayside Gardens; and Craigmore (New Zealand).

'Bridal Veil' (Kelway). A double pink lactiflora, available from Kelways (U.K.).

'Bride's Dream' (Krekler 1965). A Japanese white lactiflora, available from Busse Gardens; Hildebrandt's; and Klehm Nursery.

'Bridesmaid'. See 'Marie Jacquin'

'Bright Knight' (Glasscock 1939). A semi-double red hybrid, available from Cedar Creek (Canada); Busse Gardens; Brand Peony Farm; Austin Roses (U.K.); and Pivoinerie (France).

'Brightness' (Glasscock 1947). A single red hybrid, available from Reath's; Busse Gardens; and Brand Peony Farm.

'British Beauty' (Kelway 1926). A double rose lactiflora, available from Kelways (U.K.).

'Bu-Te' (Wassenberg 1954). A cross between 'Isani-Gidui' and 'Tamate-Boku'. Gold Medal. A Japanese white, available from Anderson Iris and Craigmore (New Zealand).

'Buccaneer' (Saunders 1929). A single red hybrid, available from Busse Gardens.

'Buckeye Belle' (Mains 1956). A semi-double red hybrid, widely available.

'Bunker Hill' (Hollis 1906). A double red lactiflora, widely available in Europe.

'Burma Midnight' (R. Klehm). A 'Burma Ruby' cross. A semi-double red, available from Klehm Nursery.

'Burma Ruby' (Glasscock 1951). Gold Medal. A cross between *Paeonia lactiflora* and *P. peregrina*. A single red, available from Adamgrove; Viette Farm and Nursery; Hollingsworth Peonies; Cedar Creek (Canada); Klehm Nursery; and Marsal (New Zealand).

'Burning Bright' (Saunders–Rogers 1986). A single pink hybrid, available from Caprice Farm.

'Burst of Joy' (Auten 1968). A single red hybrid, available from Busse Gardens and Pivoinerie (France).

'Butch' (Krekler 1959). A semi-double or double pink lactiflora, available from Austin Roses (U.K.) and Klehm Nursery.

'Butter Bowl' (Rosenfield 1955). A Japanese pink lactiflora, available from Terrace Peonies (New Zealand) and Klehm Nursery.

'Butterball' (origin unknown). A Japanese pink lactiflora, available from Bluebird Nursery and Austin Roses (U.K.).

'Camden' (Krekler 1965). A single red lactiflora, available from Klehm Nursery.

'Camellia' (Saunders 1942). A double white hybrid, available from Caprice Farm.

'Campagna' (Saunders 1941). Descended from *Paeonia lactiflora, P. macrophylla,* and *P. officinalis* crosses. A single white, available from Reath's; Caprice Farm; A & D Nursery; and Busse Gardens.

'Canari' (Guerin 1861). A double white lactiflora, available from Pivoinerie (France).

'Candidissima' (Calot 1856). A double white lactiflora, available from Pivoinerie (France).

'Candy Heart' (Bigger 1961). A 'Mons. Jules Elie' cross. A double white, available from New Peony Farm; Wild and Son; Bigger Peonies; and Klehm Nursery.

'Candy Stripe' (Anderson 1992). A double red and white lactiflora, available from Beaux Jardins.

'Captivation' (Kelway). A single rose lactiflora, available from Kelways (U.K.).

'Cardinal's Robe' (Saunders 1940). A cross between *Paeonia lactiflora* and

P. peregrina. A semi-double red, available from Tischler Peony Garden; Peony Gardens (New Zealand); Busse Gardens; and Klehm Nursery.

'Carina' (Saunders 1944). A cross between *Paeonia lactiflora* and *P. peregrina*. A semi-double red, widely available.

'Carmen' (Lemoine 1898). A double rose lactiflora, available from Kelways (U.K.).

'Carmin'. Offered as a cultivar of *Paeonia officinalis*. A semi-double pink, available from Pivoinerie (France).

'Carol' (Bockstoce 1955). An advanced-generation, double red hybrid, available from Reath's; Viette Farm and Nursery; A & D Nursery; Busse Gardens; Klehm Nursery; von Zeppelin (Germany); and Austin Roses (U.K.).

'Carolina' (Saunders 1950). A single white hybrid, available from Reath's.

'Carolina Moon' (Auten 1940). A double white lactiflora, available from Busse Gardens; Viette Farm and Nursery; and Hildebrandt's.

'Caroline Mather' (Pfeiffer). A double red lactiflora, available from Sherman Nursery.

'Carrara' (Bigger 1952). A Japanese white lactiflora, widely available.

'Casablanca' (Lins 1942). A double white lactiflora, available from Tischler Peony Garden; Wild and Son; Brand Peony Farm; and Rivière (France).

'Cascade Gem' (Marx–Rogers 1987). A Japanese white, available from Caprice Farm.

'Cathedral Supreme' (origin unknown). A Japanese pink, available from Klehm Nursery.

'Cavatina' (Saunders 1935). A single rose hybrid, available from A & D Nursery; Busse Gardens; Ferncliff Gardens (Canada); and Brickman's (Canada).

'Celebration' (Nicholls–Wild 1964). A double rose lactiflora, available from Wild and Son.

'Centennial' (Bigger 1961). A double pink lactiflora, available from Wild and Son.

'Centerpoint' (Saunders). A double white hybrid, available from Caprice Farm.

'Chalice' (Saunders 1929). A cross between *Paeonia lactiflora* and *P. macrophylla*. A single white, available from Klose (Germany).

'Chalice' (Blacklock). Invalid name. A single rose hybrid, available from A & D Nursery.

'Chaminade' (Auten 1933). A Japanese pink lactiflora, available from Wild and Son.

'Charles Burgess' (Krekler 1963). A Japanese red lactiflora, available from Hildebrandt's; Klehm Nursery; Ferncliff Gardens (Canada); and Pivoinerie (France).

'Charles McKellup' (Brand 1907). A double red lactiflora, available from Heschke Gardens and Busse Gardens.

'Charlie's White' (C. G. Klehm 1951). A double white lactiflora, widely available.

'Charm' (Franklin 1931). A Japanese red lactiflora, available from New Peony Farm; Park Seed; Anderson Iris; Klehm Nursery; and Austin Roses (U.K.).

'Cheddar Charm' (R. Klehm 1992). A Japanese white lactiflora, available from Klehm Nursery.

'Cheddar Cheese' (C. G. Klehm 1973). A double white lactiflora, available from Klehm Nursery; Peony Gardens (New Zealand); Anderson Iris; Hildebrandt's; and Pivoinerie (France).

'Cheddar Gold' (R. Klehm 1971). A 'Charlie's White' cross. A double white, available from Anderson Iris; Klehm Nursery; Terrace Peonies (New Zealand); and Gardenimport (Canada).

'Cheddar Regal' (R. Klehm). A 'Mons. Jules Elie' cross. A Japanese white, available from Klehm Nursery.

'Cheddar Supreme' (R. Klehm). A Japanese white lactiflora, available from Klehm Nursery and Terrace Peonies (New Zealand).

'Cheddar Surprise' (R. Klehm 1980). A 'Bowl of Cream' cross. A semidouble or double white, available from Peony Gardens (New Zealand); Klehm Nursery; and Craigmore (New Zealand).

'Cherry Bomb' (origin unknown). A double red lactiflora, available from Sherman Nursery.

'Cherry Hill' (Thurlow 1915). A double red lactiflora, available from Bluebird Nursery; Busse Gardens; Wild and Son; Brand Peony Farm; Austin Roses (U.K.); Craigmore (New Zealand); and Pivoinerie (France).

'Cherry Red' (Glasscock 1939). A double red hybrid, available from Cedar Creek (Canada); Reath's; Klehm Nursery; and Pivoinerie (France).

'Cherry Royal' (Wild 1967). A double pink lactiflora, available from Ferncliff Gardens (Canada) and Wild and Son.

'Chestine Gowdy' (Brand 1913). A double pink lactiflora, available from New Peony Farm; Brand Peony Farm; and Kelways (U.K.).

'Chief Justice' (Auten 1941). A semi-double red hybrid, available from Busse Gardens; Ferncliff Gardens (Canada); and Rivière (France).

'Chief Logan' (Mains 1961). A semi-double red hybrid, available from Busse Gardens.

'Chiffon Parfait' (C. G. Klehm 1981). A double pink lactiflora, available from Klehm Nursery; Park Seed; Viette Farm and Nursery; Terrace Peonies (New Zealand); Craigmore (New Zealand); and Marsal (New Zealand).

'China Rose' (ex England). A double pink lactiflora, available from Swedberg Nurseries and Austin Roses (U.K.).

'China Rose'. Offered as a cultivar of *Paeonia officinalis*. A single red, available from Klose (Germany) and Pivoinerie (France).

'Chinook' (Marx–Rogers 1981). A double blush lactiflora, available from Caprice Farm.

'Chippewa' (Murawska 1943). A double red lactiflora, available from Busse Gardens; Craigmore (New Zealand); Country Squires (Canada); and Marsal (New Zealand).

'Chocolate Soldier' (Auten 1939). A single red hybrid, widely available.

'Christmas Holiday' (Wild 1983). A single red lactiflora, available from Wild and Son.

'Christmas Holiday' (origin unknown). Invalid name. A single pink lactiflora, available from Ferncliff Gardens (Canada).

'Christopher's Coral' (Hall 1991). A single pink lactiflora, available from Granville Hall.

'Cincinnati' (Krekler 1962). A double pink lactiflora, available from Park Seed; Peony Gardens (New Zealand); Klehm Nursery; and Cedar Creek (Canada).

'Cinderella' (Jones 1938). A single pink lactiflora, available from Busse Gardens.

'Circus Clown' (Wild 1970). A Japanese rose lactiflora, available from Wild and Son.

'Claire de Lune' (White–Wild 1954). A cross between 'Mons. Jules Elie' and *Paeonia mlokosewitschii*. A single yellow, available from Caprice Farm; Cedar Creek (Canada); Reath's; Klose (Germany); Wild and Son; Klehm Nursery; and Pivoinerie (France).

'Claire Dubois' (Crousse 1886). A double pink, available from Pivoinerie (France).

'Claudia' (Saunders 1944). A cross between *Paeonia lactiflora* and *P. pere-*

grina. A semi-double pink, available from Cedar Creek (Canada); Reath's; and Caprice Farm.

'Clemenceau' (Dessert 1920). A double pink lactiflora, available from Pivoinerie (France).

'Cloud Cap' (Bigger 1974). A double blush lactiflora, available from Bigger Peonies.

'Colleen Marie' (Gilbertson 1981). A double red lactiflora, available from Bluemount Nurseries.

'Colonel Owen Cousins' (Cousins 1972). A double blush hybrid, available from Klehm Nursery.

'Comanche' (Bigger 1957). A Japanese red lactiflora, available from Wild and Son; New Peony Farm; Bigger Peonies; and Reath's.

'Commando' (Glasscock 1944). A double red hybrid, available from Klehm Nursery.

'Constance Spry' (Saunders 1941). A cross between *Paeonia lactiflora* and *P. peregrina*. A semi-double red, available from Cedar Creek (Canada); Wild and Son; Caprice Farm; Ferncliff Gardens (Canada); and Klehm Nursery.

'Convoy' (Glasscock 1944). A double red hybrid, available from Sherman Nursery and Klehm Nursery.

'Cora Stubbs' (Krekler). A Japanese pink lactiflora, available from Klehm Nursery; Hildebrandt's; and Ferncliff Gardens (Canada).

'Coral Charm' (Wissing 1964). Linebred 'Minnie Shaylor' crossed with hybrid lines. Gold Medal. A semi-double pink, widely available.

'Coral Fay' (Fay 1973). 'Laddie' selfed. A semi-double pink, available from Reath's; Peony Gardens (New Zealand); Klehm Nursery; von Zeppelin (Germany); Austin Roses (U.K.); Pivoinerie (France); and Marsal (New Zealand).

'Coral Isle' (Kelsey 1939). A semi-double pink lactiflora, available from Busse Gardens.

'Coral 'n Gold' (Cousins–R. Klehm 1981). A single or semi-double pink hybrid, widely available.

'Coral Queen' (Sass 1937). A double blush lactiflora, available from New Peony Farm.

'Coral Sunset' (Wissing–C. G. Klehm 1981). A cross between *Paeonia lactiflora* and *P. peregrina* 'Otto Froebel'. A semi-double pink, available from Caprice Farm; Viette Farm and Nursery; Peony Gardens (New Zealand); Klehm Nursery; and Craigmore (New Zealand).

'Coral Supreme' (Wissing 1964). Linebred 'Minnie Shaylor'. A single or double pink, available from Klehm Nursery; Terrace Peonies (New Zealand); Peony Gardens (New Zealand); Craigmore (New Zealand); and Marsal (New Zealand).

'Coral Tide' (R. Klehm). A single pink hybrid, available from Klehm Nursery.

'Cornelia Shaylor' (Shaylor 1919). A double pink lactiflora, available from Kelways (U.K.); Busse Gardens; Harrison's (Canada); Cedar Creek (Canada); and Pivoinerie (France).

'Countess of Altamont' (Kelway). A single blush lactiflora, available from Kelways (U.K.).

'Country Girl' (Kelway). A single pink lactiflora, available from Kelways (U.K.).

'Courage' (Bigger 1968). A double blush lactiflora, available from Bigger Peonies.

'Couronne d'Or' (Calot 1873). A double white lactiflora, available from Country Squires (Canada); Pepieniere Charlevoix (Canada); Busse Gardens; Mount Arbor; Klose (Germany); Rivière (France); and Pivoinerie (France).

'Cream Delight' (Reath 1971). A single white hybrid, available from Reath's.

'Cream Puff' (Marx–Rogers 1981). A Japanese blush lactiflora, available from Sevald Nursery and Caprice Farm.

'Crimson Globe' (Prichard). A selection from *Paeonia officinalis*. A single red, available from Klose (Germany).

'Crimson Globe'. Offered as a cultivar of *Paeonia peregrina*. A single red, available from Pivoinerie (France).

'Crusader' (Glasscock 1940). A semi-double red hybrid, available from Hildebrandt's; Sherman Nursery; Busse Gardens; Wild and Son; Reath's; and Klehm Nursery.

'Cuckoo's Nest' (Krekler 1992). A Japanese red lactiflora, available from Klehm Nursery.

'Cytherea' (Saunders 1953). A cross between *Paeonia lactiflora* and *P. peregrina*. Gold Medal. A semi-double rose, widely available.

'Dad' (Glasscock–Krekler). A semi-double red hybrid, available from Wild and Son; Hildebrandt's; A & D Nursery; Bigger Peonies; Peony Gardens (New Zealand); Busse Gardens; and Klehm Nursery.

'Dai-Jo-Kuhan' (Millet). A Japanese pink lactiflora, available from Cramer Nursery (Canada) and Mount Arbor.

'Dainty Lass' (Glasscock 1935). A Japanese pink hybrid, available from Klehm Nursery.

'Daisy B' (Nicholls–Wild 1957). A double white lactiflora, available from Wild and Son.

'Dakota' (Auten 1941). A single red hybrid, widely available.

'Dakota Princess' (Gilbertson 1977). A 'Laura Dessert' cross. A double pink, available from Brand Peony Farm.

'Dandy Dan' (Auten 1946). A semi-double red hybrid, available from Cedar Creek (Canada); Viette Farm and Nursery; Tischler Peony Garden; Hildebrandt's; Busse Gardens; Austin Roses (U.K.); and Ferncliff Gardens (Canada).

'Darling o' Mine' (Good–Reese 1930). A double pink lactiflora, available from Caprice Farm.

'Dauntless' (Glasscock 1944). A single red hybrid, available from Sherman Nursery and Klehm Nursery.

'David Harum' (Brand 1907). A double red lactiflora, available from Tischler Peony Garden; Busse Gardens; Heschke Gardens; Brand Peony Farm; Terrace Peonies (New Zealand); Craigmore (New Zealand); and Marsal (New Zealand).

'Dawn Glow' (Saunders–Hollingsworth 1986). A third-generation, semi-double white to lavender hybrid, available from Caprice Farm.

'Dawn Pink' (Sass 1946). A single pink lactiflora, available from Hollingsworth Peonies.

'Dayspring' (Kelway). A single pink lactiflora, available from Kelways (U.K.).

'Daystar' (Saunders 1949). A third-generation hybrid resulting from a cross between *Paeonia mlokosewitschii* and *P. tenuifolia*. A single yellow, available from Caprice Farm.

'Daystar' (origin unknown). Invalid name. A double rose lactiflora, available from Kelways (U.K.).

'Dayton' (Krekler 1962). A double pink lactiflora, available from Brickman's (Canada) and Reath's.

'Dazzler' (Auten 1956). A single red hybrid, available from Busse Gardens.

'Dearest' (origin unknown). A single white hybrid, available from Hollingsworth Peonies.

'Deer Creek' (Bigger 1952). A double pink lactiflora, available from Bigger Peonies and Wild and Son.

'Defender' (Saunders 1929). A cross between *Paeonia officinalis* and 'Primevere'. A single red, available from Klehm Nursery and Austin Roses (U.K.).

'Delachei' (Delache 1856). Also sold as 'Emperor of Russia'. A double red lactiflora, available from Pivoinerie (France).

'Detroit' (Auten 1948). A double red lactiflora, available from Wild and Son; Anderson Iris; Heschke Gardens; and Harrison's (Canada).

'Dia-Jo-Kuhan'. See 'Dai-Jo-Kuhan'

'Diana Parks' (Bockstoce 1942). A double red hybrid, widely available.

'Dignity' (Murawska 1943). A Japanese red lactiflora, available from Anderson Iris.

'Dinner Plate' (C. G. Klehm 1968). A double pink lactiflora, widely available.

'Divine Gift' (Krekler 1978). A double pink lactiflora, available from Klehm Nursery.

'Dixie' (Franklin 1931). A double red lactiflora, available from Hildebrandt's; Busse Gardens; Heschke Gardens; Reath's; and Ferncliff Gardens (Canada).

'Do Tell' (Auten 1946). A Japanese pink lactiflora, widely available.

'Dolorodell' (Lins 1942). Gold Medal. A double pink lactiflora, available from Klehm Nursery; Reath's; Anderson Iris; and Hildebrandt's.

'Don Richardson' (Krekler 1975). A Japanese red lactiflora, available from Klehm Nursery.

'Doreen' (Sass 1949). A Japanese rose lactiflora, widely available.

'Doris Cooper' (Cooper 1946). Gold Medal. A double pink lactiflora, widely available.

'Dorothy J.' (Jones 1938). A double blush lactiflora, available from Brand Peony Farm; Reath's; Anderson Iris; Viette Farm and Nursery; and Wild and Son.

'Douglas Brand' (Tischler 1972). Gold Medal. A double red lactiflora, available from New Peony Farm; Brand Peony Farm; Reath's; Tischler Peony Garden; Bigger Peonies; and Busse Gardens.

'Dr. Alex Fleming'. See 'Dr. Alexander Fleming'

'Dr. Alexander Fleming' (ex England). A double pink lactiflora, widely available.

'Dr. F. G. Brethour' (Sass 1938). A double white lactiflora, available from Sherman Nursery and Mount Arbor.

'Dr. F. R. Huxley' (Brand 1936). A double white lactiflora, available from Reath's.

'Dr. H. Barnsby' (Dessert 1913). A double red lactiflora, available from Kelways (U.K.).

'Dr. J. Crenshaw'. See 'Dr. John L. Crenshaw'

'Dr. J. H. Neeley' (Neeley 1930). A double white lactiflora, available from Anderson Iris and Busse Gardens.

'Dr. John L. Crenshaw' (Brand 1936). A double red lactiflora, available from Ferncliff Gardens (Canada) and Brand Peony Farm.

'Dr. Lee W. Pollock'. See 'Lee W. Pollock'

'Dr. Walter Rumph' (Brand 1967). A double pink lactiflora, available from Brand Peony Farm.

'Dragon's Nest' (Auten 1933). A Japanese or double red lactiflora, available from Klose (Germany); Ferncliff Gardens (Canada); and Brickman's (Canada).

'Dream Mist' (Wild 1970). A Japanese pink lactiflora, available from Wild and Son.

'Dresden' (Kelway). A single pink lactiflora, available from Kelways (U.K.).

'Dresden Pink' (Wild 1957). A double pink lactiflora, available from Reath's and Wild and Son.

'Duchesse de Nemours' (Calot 1856). A double white lactiflora, widely available.

'Duchesse d'Orleans' (Guerin 1846). A double pink lactiflora, available from A & D Nursery and Sherman Nursery.

'Duke of Devonshire' (Kelway 1895). A double white lactiflora, available from Kelways (U.K.).

'Duluth' (Franklin 1931). A double white lactiflora, available from Busse Gardens; Brand Peony Farm; and Reath's.

'Dunlora' (Peyton 1943). A single white lactiflora, available from Tischler Peony Garden.

'Dürer' (Goos–Koenemann 1910). A Japanese white lactiflora, available from Klose (Germany).

'Early Bird'. See 'Earlybird'

'Early Daybreak' (Saunders 1949). Descended from *Paeonia lactiflora*, *P. macrophylla*, *P. mlokosewitschii*, and *P. peregrina* crosses. A single white, available from Reath's.

'Early Glow' (Hollingsworth 1992). A single white hybrid, available from Hollingsworth Peonies.

'Early Scout' (Auten 1952). A cross between *Paeonia tenuifolia* and 'Richard Carvel'. A single red, widely available.

'Early White' (origin unknown). A single white lactiflora, available from A & D Nursery.

'Early Windflower' (Saunders 1939). A cross between *Paeonia emodi* and *P. veitchii*. A single white, available from Reath's; Caprice Farm; Pivoinerie (France); and Marsal (New Zealand).

'Earlybird' (Saunders 1939). A cross between *Paeonia tenuifolia* and *P. veitchii* var. *woodwardii*. A single red, available from Peony Gardens (New Zealand); Klehm Nursery; and Marsal (New Zealand).

'Eastern Star' (Bigger 1975). A double white lactiflora, available from Reath's and Bigger Peonies.

'Easy Lavender' (Tischler–Rogers 1994). A Japanese or anemone lavender lactiflora, available from Caprice Farm and Tischler Peony Garden.

'Echo' (Saunders 1951). A second-generation hybrid resulting from a cross between *Paeonia anomala* and *P. lactiflora*. A single pink, available from Busse Gardens.

'Edgar Jessup' (Bockstoce 1958). A double red hybrid, available from Bigger Peonies; Cedar Creek (Canada); and Pivoinerie (France).

'Edith Cavell' (Kelway 1916). A double white lactiflora, available from Kelways (U.K.); Austin Roses (U.K.); and Pivoinerie (France).

'Edouard Andre' (Mechin 1874). A double red lactiflora, available from Pivoinerie (France).

'Edulis Superba' (Lemon 1824). A double pink lactiflora, widely available.

'Edulis Supreme' (Kriek). A double pink lactiflora, available from Busse Gardens; Bigger Peonies; and Klehm Nursery.

'Edward F. Flynn' (Brand 1942). A double red lactiflora, available from Brand Peony Farm; Busse Gardens; and Harrison's (Canada).

'Edward Steichen' (Saunders 1941). A cross between *Paeonia lactiflora* and *P. peregrina*. A semi-double red, available from Klehm Nursery.

'Edwin C. Bills' (Murawska 1959). A cross between 'Beth Ann' and 'Rosalie'. A double red, available from Klehm Nursery.

'Edwin C. Shaw' (Thurlow 1919). A double pink lactiflora, available from Busse Gardens.

'El Dorado' (Auten 1956). A semi-double or double red hybrid, available from Cedar Creek (Canada) and Busse Gardens.

'Elgin' (Brown 1952). A double pink lactiflora, available from Cedar Creek (Canada).

'Elise Renault' (Doriat 1927). A double purple lactiflora, available from Rivière (France).

'Eliza Lundy' (Krekler 1975). Either a hybrid of or a selection from *Paeo-*

nia officinalis. A double red, available from Busse Gardens; Klehm Nursery; and Caprice Farm.

'Elizabeth Cahn' (Saunders 1942). A cross between *Paeonia lactiflora* and *P. macrophylla*. A single white, available from Caprice Farm; A & D Nursery; and Busse Gardens.

'Elizabeth Foster' (Saunders 1941). A cross between *Paeonia lactiflora* and *P. peregrina*. A single pink, available from A & D Nursery and Hollingsworth Peonies.

'Elizabeth Huntington' (Sass 1925). A double pink lactiflora, available from Busse Gardens.

'Elizabeth Nourrisson' (Doriat 1931). A single pink lactiflora, available from Pivoinerie (France).

'Elizabeth Peninger' (Nicholls 1958). A double pink lactiflora, available from Wild and Son.

'Elizabeth Price' (Nicholls–Wild 1958). A double pink lactiflora, available from Ferncliff Gardens (Canada); Wild and Son; and Country Squires (Canada).

'Ella Christiansen' (Brand 1925). A double pink lactiflora, available from Busse Gardens; New Peony Farm; Brand Peony Farm; Reath's; Viette Farm and Nursery; and Bigger Peonies.

'Ellen Cowley' (Saunders 1940). A cross between *Paeonia lactiflora* and *P. peregrina*. A semi-double red, available from Anderson Iris; Hollingsworth Peonies; A & D Nursery; Peony Gardens (New Zealand); Klehm Nursery; Caprice Farm; and Craigmore (New Zealand).

'Ellen Foster' (Brand 1937). A double pink lactiflora, available from Busse Gardens.

'Elsa Sass' (Sass 1930). Gold Medal. A double white lactiflora, widely available.

'Elsie Pickett' (Tischler 1967). A double pink lactiflora, available from New Peony Farm; Brand Peony Farm; and Tischler Peony Garden.

'Emblem' (Saunders 1941). A single red hybrid, available from A & D Nursery and Busse Gardens.

'Emma Klehm' (C. G. Klehm 1951). A double pink lactiflora, available from Klehm Nursery; Wild and Son; Busse Gardens; Hildebrandt's; and Peony Gardens (New Zealand).

'Emmeline Sellers' (Bockstoce 1962). A double or semi-double red hybrid, available from Bigger Peonies.

'Emperor of Russia'. See 'Delachei'

'Enchantress' (Lemoine 1903). A double white lactiflora, available from Pivoinerie (France).

'Ensign Moriarty' (Lins). A double pink lactiflora, available from Rivière (France) and Hildebrandt's.

'Ermenegilda Mantagna' (origin unknown). A single blush lactiflora, available from A & D Nursery.

'Etched Salmon' (Cousins–R. Klehm 1981). A double pink hybrid, available from Caprice Farm; Klehm Nursery; Hildebrandt's; and Beaux Jardins.

'Ethel Mars' (Murawska 1943). A semi-double white lactiflora, available from Busse Gardens; Klehm Nursery; and Cedar Creek (Canada).

'Etienne Mechin' (Mechin 1880). A double red lactiflora, available from Klose (Germany).

'Eugenie Verdier' (Calot 1864). A double pink lactiflora, available from Klose (Germany).

'Evelyn Tibbits' (Krekler 1965). A Japanese white lactiflora, available from Klehm Nursery; Tischler Peony Garden; and Peony Gardens (New Zealand).

'Evening Star' (Sass 1937). A double white lactiflora, available from Busse Gardens; New Peony Farm; and Sherman Nursery.

'Eventide' (Glasscock 1945). A cross between *Paeonia lactiflora* and *P. peregrina*. A single pink, available from Busse Gardens and Caprice Farm.

'Exotic' (Kelsey 1936). A semi-double pink lactiflora, available from New Peony Farm.

'Exquisite' (Kelway 1902). A double pink lactiflora, available from Heschke Gardens.

'F. Koppius' (Rijnstroom 1931). A double red lactiflora, available from Klose (Germany).

'Fairbanks' (Auten 1945). A Japanese blush lactiflora, available from Wild and Son; White Flower Farm; Sunny Border Nursery; Heschke Gardens; and von Zeppelin (Germany).

'Fairy Princess' (Glasscock–Falk 1945). A single red hybrid, available from Busse Gardens; Klehm Nursery; and Marsal (New Zealand).

'Fairy Tale' (Auten). A double red lactiflora, available from Reath's.

'Fairy's Petticoat' (C. G. Klehm). A double pink lactiflora, widely available.

'Fancy Nancy' (Auten 1944). A Japanese pink lactiflora, available from Viette Farm and Nursery; Klehm Nursery; Ferncliff Gardens (Canada); Klose (Germany); Wild and Son; and Brickman's (Canada).

'Fanny Crosby' (Brand 1907). A double pink lactiflora, available from Rivière (France).

'Fantasia' (Saunders 1931). A second-generation hybrid resulting from a cross between *Paeonia lactiflora* and *P. macrophylla*. A single pink, available from Busse Gardens.

'Fantastic' (Tischler 1972). A Japanese or single pink lactiflora, available from New Peony Farm; Brand Peony Farm; and Tischler Peony Garden.

'Faribo Gold' (Gilbertson). A Japanese white lactiflora, available from Tischler Peony Garden.

'Fause' (Miellez 1855). A double rose lactiflora, available from Pivoinerie (France).

'Favorita' (Auten 1956). A single red hybrid, available from Busse Gardens.

'Fayette' (Fay 1970). 'Laddie' selfed. A semi-double red, available from Reath's.

'Feather Top' (Wild 1967). A Japanese rose lactiflora, available from Wild and Son; Ferncliff Gardens (Canada); and Brickman's (Canada).

'Felix Crousse' (Crousse 1881). A double red lactiflora, widely available.

'Felix Supreme' (Kriek 1955). A double red lactiflora, widely available.

'Festiva Maxima' (Miellez 1851). A double white lactiflora, widely available.

'Festiva Pixie' (R. Klehm). A double pink lactiflora, available from Klehm Nursery.

'Festiva Powder Puff' (R. Klehm). A double white lactiflora, available from Klehm Nursery.

'Festiva Supreme' (R. Klehm 1981). An 'Alice Harding' cross. A double white, available from Hildebrandt's and Klehm Nursery.

'Fibrio Gold' (Gilbertson). A Japanese white lactiflora, available from Klehm Nursery.

'Fiery Crater' (Marx–Rogers 1981). A single red lactiflora, available from Caprice Farm.

'Fine Lady' (Kelway 1909). A single white lactiflora, available from Busse Gardens.

'Fire Bird' (Auten 1956). A double red hybrid, available from Wild and Son; Ferncliff Gardens (Canada); Brickman's (Canada); Klehm Nursery; and Pivoinerie (France).

'Fire King'. Offered as a cultivar of *Paeonia peregrina*. A single orange-red, available from Klose (Germany) and Pivoinerie (France).

'Fire Opal' (Marx–Rogers 1984). A double red lactiflora, available from American Daylily and Caprice Farm.

'Fireball' (Brand 1938). A semi-double red lactiflora, available from Wild and Son.

'Firebell' (Mains 1959). A double red hybrid, available from Cedar Creek (Canada); Tischler Peony Garden; and Klehm Nursery.

'Firelight' (Saunders 1950). Descended from *Paeonia lactiflora, P. macrophylla, P. mlokosewitschii,* and *P. peregrina* crosses. A single rose, widely available.

'First Lady' (C. G. Klehm). A double pink lactiflora, available from Klehm Nursery; White Flower Farm; Hildebrandt's; Terrace Peonies (New Zealand); Craigmore (New Zealand); and Ferncliff Gardens (Canada).

'Flame' (Glasscock 1939). A cross between *Paeonia lactiflora* and *P. peregrina.* A single pink, widely available.

'Flamingo' (Andrews 1925). A double pink lactiflora, available from Kelways (U.K.).

'Flanders Fields' (Brand 1928). A single red lactiflora, available from Busse Gardens and Brand Peony Farm.

'Flora Plena'. Offered as a cultivar of *Paeonia tenuifolia.* A single red, available from Brand Peony Farm; Sherman Nursery; and Tischler Peony Garden.

'Florence Bond' (Gumm 1936). A double white lactiflora, available from Wild and Son.

'Florence Ellis' (Nicholls 1948). A double pink lactiflora, available from Busse Gardens; Wild and Son; and Craigmore (New Zealand).

'Florence MacBeth' (Sass 1924). A double blush lactiflora, available from Heschke Gardens.

'Florence Nicholls' (Nicholls 1938). A double white lactiflora, available from Klehm Nursery; Carroll Gardens; Reath's; Wild and Son; Anderson Iris; A & D Nursery; and Hollingsworth Peonies.

'Floro Plena'. Offered as a cultivar of *Paeonia tenuifolia.* A double red, available from Pivoinerie (France).

'Flower Girl' (Auten 1935). A double white lactiflora, available from Busse Gardens.

'Fluffy' (R. Klehm 1992). Linebred 'Bowl of Cream'. A single white, available from Klehm Nursery.

'Fluffy Ruffles'. See 'Banner Bright'

'Fokker' (Ruys 1928). A double red lactiflora, available from von Zeppelin

(Germany); Gärtnerei und Staudenkulturen (Switzerland); and Maison des Fleurs (Canada).

'Fortune Teller' (Auten 1936). A single red lactiflora, available from Busse Gardens and Heschke Gardens.

'France' (Kelway 1917). A double pink lactiflora, available from Kelways (U.K.).

'Frances' (Saunders). A cross between *Paeonia lactiflora* and *P. macrophylla*. A single pink, available from Caprice Farm.

'Frances Mains' (Mains 1955). A cross between 'Alice Harding' and 'General Gorgas'. A double pink, available from Busse Gardens and Klehm Nursery.

'Frances Willard' (Brand 1907). A double blush lactiflora, available from Busse Gardens; New Peony Farm; Brand Peony Farm; Sherman Nursery; and Pivoinerie (France).

'Francois Ortegat' (Parmentier 1850). A double red lactiflora, widely available.

'Frank Keith' (Moots 1962). A cross between 'Matilda Lewis' and *Paeonia peregrina*. A semi-double red, available from Rivière (France).

'Friendship' (Glasscock–Falk 1955). A single or semi-double pink hybrid, available from Brand Peony Farm; Caprice Farm; Reath's; Busse Gardens; and Klehm Nursery.

'Fringed Ivory' (R. Klehm). Linebred 'Bowl of Cream'. A double white, available from Klehm Nursery.

'Fruit Bowl' (Bigger 1979). A Japanese pink lactiflora, available from Bigger Peonies.

'Fuyajo' (origin unknown). A Japanese red lactiflora, available from Pivoinerie (France) and Bluebird Nursery.

'Gail Tischler' (Brand 1964). A Japanese pink lactiflora, available from Tischler Peony Garden.

'Garden Glory' (Auten 1956). A double red lactiflora, available from Busse Gardens.

'Garden Lace' (Hollingsworth 1992). A Japanese pink hybrid, available from Hollingsworth Peonies.

'Garden Peace' (Saunders 1941). A second-generation hybrid resulting from a cross between *Paeonia lactiflora* and *P. macrophylla*. A single white, available from Busse Gardens; A & D Nursery; Reath's; Viette Farm and Nursery; and Klehm Nursery.

'Gardener's Joy' (Neeley 1936). A semi-double pink lactiflora, available from Viette Farm and Nursery.

'Gardenia' (Lins 1955). A double white lactiflora, widely available.

'Gay Cavalier' (Glasscock 1944). A single red hybrid, available from Busse Gardens.

'Gay Ladye' (Kelway). A single rose lactiflora, available from Kelways (U.K.).

'Gay Paree' (Auten 1933). A Japanese pink and white lactiflora, widely available.

'Gayborder June' (Hoogendoorn 1949). A double or semi-double pink lactiflora, available from Viette Farm and Nursery; Austin Roses (U.K.); and Pivoinerie (France).

'Gene Wild' (Cooper 1956). A double pink lactiflora, widely available.

'General MacMahon' (Calot 1867). Originally called 'Augustin d'Hour'; also sold as 'Marechal MacMahon'. A double red lactiflora, widely available.

'George W. Peyton' (Nicholls 1938). A 'Lady Alexandra Duff' cross. A double blush, available from Brand Peony Farm; Craigmore (New Zealand); and Marsal (New Zealand).

'Georgiana Shaylor' (Shaylor 1908). A double pink lactiflora, available from Reath's.

'Germaine Bigot' (Dessert 1902). A semi-double pink lactiflora, available from Austin Roses (U.K.).

'Gerry' (Glasscock–R. Klehm 1988). A double red hybrid, available from Klehm Nursery.

'Gibraltar' (Bigger 1958). A double red lactiflora, available from Bigger Peonies.

'Gigantea'. See 'Lamartine'

'Gilbert Barthelot' (Doriat 1931). A double pink lactiflora, available from Austin Roses (U.K.) and Pivoinerie (France).

'Gilbert H. Wild' (Nicholls–Wild). A double rose lactiflora, available from Wild and Son; Ferncliff Gardens (Canada); Brickman's (Canada); and Harrison's (Canada).

'Gladys Hodson' (Krekler 1961). A double white lactiflora, available from Klehm Nursery.

'Globe of Light' (Kelway 1928). A Japanese pink lactiflora, available from Marsal (New Zealand).

'Glory Hallelujah' (C. G. Klehm). A double red lactiflora, available from

A & D Nursery; Hildebrandt's; Klehm Nursery; and Craigmore (New Zealand).

'Glory of Somerset' (Kelway 1887). A double pink lactiflora, available from Kelways (U.K.).

'Glowing Candles' (Wild 1966). A Japanese pink lactiflora, available from Caprice Farm; Cannon Nurseries (Canada); A & D Nursery; Wild and Son; and Ferncliff Gardens (Canada).

'Glowing Embers' (Kelsey 1936). A Japanese rose lactiflora, available from Wild and Son.

'Glowing Raspberry Rose' (Cousins–R. Klehm). A double red hybrid, available from Klehm Nursery.

'Go-Daigo' (Millet 1926). A Japanese rose lactiflora, available from Pivoinerie (France).

'Gold Rush' (R. Klehm 1992). A Japanese white lactiflora, available from Klehm Nursery.

'Gold Standard' (Rosenfield 1934). A Japanese white lactiflora, available from Adamgrove; White Flower Farm; Terrace Peonies (New Zealand); Klehm Nursery; and Pivoinerie (France).

'Gold Star' (Kelsey 1938). A Japanese pink lactiflora, available from Pivoinerie (France).

'Golden Bracelet' (Brand 1939). A double white lactiflora, available from Busse Gardens; Ferncliff Gardens (Canada); Brickman's (Canada); and Harrison's (Canada).

'Golden Dawn' (Gumm 1923). An anemone white lactiflora, available from Busse Gardens; Brand Peony Farm; and Tischler Peony Garden.

'Golden Glow' (Glasscock 1935). Gold Medal. A cross between *Paeonia lactiflora* and *P. peregrina* 'Otto Froebel'. A single pink, available from Busse Gardens; Hildebrandt's; and Caprice Farm.

'Goldilocks' (Gilbertson 1975). A cross between 'Claire de Lune' and 'Oriental Gold'. A double yellow, available from A & D Nursery; Klehm Nursery; Caprice Farm; and Beaux Jardins.

'Golly' (Krekler 1966). A Japanese white lactiflora, available from Hildebrandt's; Klehm Nursery; and Marsal (New Zealand).

'Good Cheer' (Saunders 1942). A cross between *Paeonia officinalis* and *P. peregrina*. A single red, available from Cedar Creek (Canada) and Country Squires (Canada).

'Good Double Deep Red' (origin unknown). A double red lactiflora, available from Viette Farm and Nursery.

'Good News' (Auten 1946). A single red hybrid, available from Busse Gardens and A & D Nursery.

'Grace Batson' (Sass 1927). A double pink lactiflora, available from Busse Gardens and Viette Farm and Nursery.

'Grace Gedge' (Kelsey 1934). A double white lactiflora, available from Busse Gardens.

'Grace Kelsey' (Kelsey 1940). A **double pink** lactiflora, available from Cedar Creek (Canada).

'Grace Lewis' (Lewis 1922). A double blush lactiflora, available from Country Squires (Canada) and Maison des Fleurs (Canada).

'Grace Loomis' (Saunders 1920). A double white lactiflora, available from Pivoinerie (France).

'Grace Root' (Saunders 1940). A cross between *Paeonia lactiflora* and *P. peregrina*. A single pink, available from Caprice Farm.

'Granat' (Goos–Koenemann 1951). A single red lactiflora, available from Klose (Germany).

'Grandiflora'. See 'Henry Woodward'

'Great Lady' (Saunders 1943). A cross between *Paeonia lactiflora* and *P. peregrina*. A single or semi-double pink, available from Busse Gardens.

'Grover Cleveland' (Terry 1904). A double red lactiflora, available from Sherman Nursery; Busse Gardens; and Pivoinerie (France).

'Guidon' (Nicholls 1941). A double pink lactiflora, available from Carroll Gardens; Wild and Son; von Zeppelin (Germany); and Country Squires (Canada).

'Gypsy Rose' (Franklin 1939). A Japanese pink lactiflora, available from Brand Peony Farm and Tischler Peony Garden.

'Hakodate' (Millet). A Japanese white lactiflora, available from Pivoinerie (France).

'Hans P. Sass' (Sass 1937). A double blush lactiflora, available from Heschke Gardens and Viette Farm and Nursery.

'Hansina Brand' (Brand 1925). Gold Medal. A double pink lactiflora, available from Wild and Son; Viette Farm and Nursery; Sherman Nursery; Busse Gardens; and Caprice Farm.

'Hardy Giant' (Freeborn 1943). A double pink hybrid, available from Cedar Creek (Canada).

'Hargrove Hudson' (Wild 1949). A double pink lactiflora, available from

Busse Gardens; Wild and Son; Ferncliff Gardens (Canada); Country Squires (Canada); and Brickman's (Canada).

'Hari-Ai-Nin' (Babcock 1929). A Japanese red lactiflora, available from Bigger Peonies; Klose (Germany); and Wild and Son.

'Harriet Olney' (Brand 1920). A single pink lactiflora, available from Ferncliff Gardens (Canada) and Brickman's (Canada).

'Harry F. Little' (Nicholls 1933). Gold Medal. A double white lactiflora, available from Busse Gardens.

'Harry L. Smith' (Smith–Krekler 1953). A double red lactiflora, available from Klehm Nursery.

'Hawaii' (Murawska 1960). A Japanese or double pink lactiflora, available from Peony Gardens (New Zealand).

'Hazel Brand' (Brand). A Japanese pink lactiflora, available from New Peony Farm and Tischler Peony Garden.

'Hazel Kinny' (Brand 1925). A double pink lactiflora, available from Busse Gardens.

'Heavenly Pink' (origin unknown). A double pink hybrid, available from Cedar Creek (Canada).

'Heidi' (Tischler 1972). A Japanese pink lactiflora, available from Tischler Peony Garden and Caprice Farm.

'Heimburg' (Goos–Koenemann 1926). A double red lactiflora, available from Klose (Germany).

'Heirloom' (Kelway). A double pink lactiflora, available from Kelways (U.K.).

'Helen' (Thurlow 1922). A single pink lactiflora, available from Busse Gardens and Heschke Gardens.

'Helen Hayes' (Murawska 1943). A double pink lactiflora, available from Reath's; Austin Roses (U.K.); and Klehm Nursery.

'Helen Matthews' (Saunders–Krekler 1953). A semi-double or double red hybrid, available from Caprice Farm; Cedar Creek (Canada); Tischler Peony Garden; and Marsal (New Zealand).

'Helen Sears' (Smith–Krekler 1928). A Japanese pink lactiflora, available from Marsal (New Zealand).

'Henri Potin' (Doriat 1924). A Japanese pink lactiflora, available from Pivoinerie (France); Brand Peony Farm; and Maison des Fleurs (Canada).

'Henry Bockstoce' (Bockstoce 1955). An advanced-generation, double red hybrid, widely available.

'Henry Poitin'. See 'Henri Potin'

'Henry Sass' (Sass–Interstate 1948). A double white lactiflora, available from New Peony Farm; Mount Arbor; and Bigger Peonies.
'Henry St. Clair' (Brand 1941). A double red lactiflora, available from New Peony Farm; Brand Peony Farm; and Busse Gardens.
'Henry Woodward' (Richardson–Jackson). Also sold as 'Grandiflora'. A double pink lactiflora, available from Sheridan Nurseries (Canada).
'Heritage' (Saunders 1950). A cross between *Paeonia lactiflora* and *P. peregrina*. A double red, widely available.
'Hermione' (Sass 1932). A double pink lactiflora, widely available.
'Hi-Mabel' (Bockstoce 1961). A semi-double pink hybrid, available from Bigger Peonies and Rivière (France).
'Hiawatha' (Franklin 1931). A double red lactiflora, available from Busse Gardens.
'Hifalutin' (Bigger 1960). A double red lactiflora, available from Bigger Peonies.
'High Fashion' (origin unknown). A double pink lactiflora, available from Ferncliff Gardens (Canada) and Brickman's (Canada).
'Highlight' (Auten–Wild 1952). A double red lactiflora, widely available.
'Hit Parade' (Nicholls 1965). A Japanese pink lactiflora, available from Carroll Gardens; Klose (Germany); and Wild and Son.
'Hogarth' (Goos–Koenemann 1912). A single pink lactiflora, available from Klose (Germany).
'Holbein' (Goos–Koenemann 1910). A single pink lactiflora, available from Klose (Germany).
'Hollywood' (Auten 1937). A Japanese pink lactiflora, available from Wild and Son.
'Honey Gold' (C. G. Klehm). A double white lactiflora, available from Klehm Nursery; Wayside Gardens; Anderson Iris; Hildebrandt's; Caprice Farm; Adamgrove; and Craigmore (New Zealand).
'Honor' (Saunders 1941). A cross between *Paeonia lactiflora* and *P. peregrina* 'Otto Froebel'. A single or semi-double pink, available from Caprice Farm.
'Hoosierland' (C. G. Klehm 1968). A semi-double red lactiflora, available from Klehm Nursery; Peony Gardens (New Zealand); and Marsal (New Zealand).
'Hope' (Saunders 1929). A cross between *Paeonia lactiflora* and *P. peregrina* 'Otto Froebel'. A semi-double pink, available from Caprice Farm.
'Horizon' (Saunders 1943). A single white hybrid, available from Caprice

Farm; Busse Gardens; A & D Nursery; Klehm Nursery; Terrace Peonies (New Zealand); and Austin Roses (U.K.).

'Hot Chocolate' (Sass 1971). A Japanese red lactiflora, available from Klehm Nursery.

'Howdy' (Auten). A double red lactiflora, available from Klehm Nursery.

'Humilis'. Offered as a cultivar of *Paeonia officinalis*. A single rose, available from Austin Roses (U.K.).

'Hyperion' (origin unknown). A single red lactiflora, available from Kelways (U.K.).

'Illini Belle' (Glasscock 1941). A semi-double or double red hybrid, available from Cedar Creek (Canada); Klehm Nursery; Busse Gardens; and Austin Roses (U.K.).

'Illini Warrior' (Glasscock–Falk 1955). An advanced-generation, single or semi-double red hybrid, available from Busse Gardens; Cedar Creek (Canada); Wild and Son; Klehm Nursery; Country Squires (Canada); Austin Roses (U.K.); and Pivoinerie (France).

'Illustrous' (Brown 1952). A double pink lactiflora, available from Country Squires (Canada).

'Immaculee' (origin unknown). A double white lactiflora, available from Pivoinerie (France).

'Imperial Divinity' (Marx–Rogers 1978). A Japanese rose lactiflora, available from Caprice Farm.

'Imperial Parasol' (Marx–Rogers 1979). A Japanese pink lactiflora, available from Carroll Gardens; Caprice Farm; and Pivoinerie (France).

'Imperial Princess' (Marx–Rogers 1978). A double pink lactiflora, available from Caprice Farm.

'Imperial Red' (Sass 1932). A single red lactiflora, available from Busse Gardens; Anderson Iris; New Peony Farm; and Heschke Gardens.

'Indian Hill' (Glasscock 1950). A cross between *Paeonia lactiflora* and *P. peregrina* 'Otto Froebel'. A double red, available from Cedar Creek (Canada); Ferncliff Gardens (Canada); Country Squires (Canada); and Brickman's (Canada).

'Insigny' (origin unknown). A double pink lactiflora, available from Pivoinerie (France).

'Inspecteur Lavergne' (Doriat 1924). A double red lactiflora, widely available.

'Instituteur Doriat' (Doriat 1925). A Japanese red lactiflora, available from

Country Squires (Canada); Pepieniere Charlevoix (Canada); Maison des Fleurs (Canada); and Pivoinerie (France).

'Irving Flint' (Kelsey 1935). A double pink lactiflora, available from Busse Gardens.

'Irwin Altman' (Kelsey 1940). A double red lactiflora, available from Reath's; Busse Gardens; Caprice Farm; and Rivière (France).

'Isani-Gidui' (ex Japan pre-1928). A Japanese white lactiflora, widely available.

'Israel' (Krekler 1975). A single red hybrid, available from Klehm Nursery.

'Iwo' (Nicholls 1946). A Japanese red lactiflora, available from Craigmore (New Zealand).

'J. C. Legg' (Wild 1950). A double white lactiflora, available from Busse Gardens.

'J. C. Weguelin'. Offered as a cultivar of *Paeonia officinalis*. A single red, available from Klose (Germany).

'J. H. Wigell'. See 'John Howard Wigell'

'Jack Frost' (Krekler 1978). A double white lactiflora, available from Klehm Nursery.

'Jacob Styer' (Styer 1948). A double white lactiflora, available from Busse Gardens and Wild and Son.

'Jake's Tall Red' (origin unknown). A double red lactiflora, available from Sherman Nursery.

'James Kelway' (Kelway 1900). A double blush lactiflora, available from Pivoinerie (France).

'James Pillow' (Pillow 1936). A double pink lactiflora, available from Klehm Nursery; Sunny Border Nursery; Busse Gardens; and Wild and Son.

'James R. Mann' (Thurlow 1920). A double pink lactiflora, available from Mount Arbor.

'Jan van Leeuwen' (van Leeuwen 1928). A Japanese white lactiflora, widely available.

'Janice' (Saunders 1939). A cross between *Paeonia lactiflora* and *P. peregrina*. A semi-double pink, available from Cedar Creek (Canada).

'Japanese Beauty' (Sass 1937). A Japanese red lactiflora, available from Sherman Nursery.

'Jappensha-Ikhu' (ex Japan). A Japanese pink lactiflora, available from Ferncliff Gardens (Canada); Hillier (U.K.); and Brickman's (Canada).

'Jay Cee' (C. G. Klehm 1959). A cross between 'Mons. Jules Elie' and 'Mr. L. van Leeuwen'. A double red, available from Klehm Nursery; Wild and Son; Reath's; and Brickman's (Canada).

'Jayhawker' (Bigger 1949). A double pink lactiflora, available from New Peony Farm; Bigger Peonies; Busse Gardens; and Heschke Gardens.

'Jean E. Bockstoce' (Bockstoce 1933). A double red hybrid, available from Viette Farm and Nursery; Hildebrandt's; and Klehm Nursery.

'Jean Lapandry' (origin unknown). A double rose lactiflora, available from Terrace Peonies (New Zealand).

'Jeanne d'Arc' (Calot 1858). A double pink lactiflora, available from Kelways (U.K.) and Pivoinerie (France).

'Jeannot' (Dessert 1918). A double pink lactiflora, available from Adamgrove; Ferncliff Gardens (Canada); and Brickman's (Canada).

'Jessie' (Krekler 1965). A Japanese red lactiflora, available from Klehm Nursery.

'Jessie Gist' (Nicholls–Wild 1953). A double pink lactiflora, available from Wild and Son.

'Jewel' (Glasscock 1931). A single or Japanese red hybrid, available from Cedar Creek (Canada).

'Jo Hanratty' (Gardiner pre-1951). A double pink lactiflora, available from Busse Gardens.

'John H. Wigell'. See 'John Howard Wigell'

'John Harvard' (Auten 1939). A semi-double red hybrid, available from A & D Nursery; Brand Peony Farm; and Cedar Creek (Canada).

'John Harward' (origin unknown). A Japanese red lactiflora, available from New Peony Farm and Viette Farm and Nursery.

'John Howard Wigell' (Wigell 1942). A double pink lactiflora, widely available.

'John Whitis' (Krekler 1965). A double pink lactiflora, available from Klehm Nursery.

'Joseph Christie' (Rosenfield 1939). A double white lactiflora, available from Peony Gardens (New Zealand) and Klehm Nursery.

'Joseph Plagne' (Doriat 1928). A Japanese red lactiflora, available from Pivoinerie (France).

'Josette' (Brethour 1937). A single blush lactiflora, available from Country Squires (Canada).

'Joyce Ellen' (Moots 1960). A cross between *Paeonia peregrina* and 'Rose Shaylor'. A single or semi-double pink, available from Cedar Creek (Canada).

'Judy Ann' (Wild 1964). A double rose lactiflora, available from Wild and Son; Ferncliff Gardens (Canada); and Brickman's (Canada).

'Judy Becker' (Sass 1941). A double red lactiflora, available from New Peony Farm and Sherman Nursery.

'Julia Grant' (Saunders 1939). A semi-double pink hybrid, available from Cedar Creek (Canada).

'June Brilliant' (Auten 1938). A double red lactiflora, available from Wild and Son and Viette Farm and Nursery.

'June Rose' (Jones 1938). A double pink lactiflora, available from Bigger Peonies; Hildebrandt's; Busse Gardens; Klehm Nursery; and Austin Roses (U.K.).

'Junior Miss' (Pehrson–Seidl 1989). A 'Laura Dessert' cross. A double pink, available from Caprice Farm.

'Kakoden' (ex Japan). A double white lactiflora, available from Caprice Farm.

'Kansas' (Bigger 1940). Gold Medal. A double red lactiflora, widely available.

'Karen Gray' (Krekler 1965). A Japanese red lactiflora, available from Klehm Nursery; Hildebrandt's; and Pivoinerie (France).

'Karl Rosenfield' (Rosenfield 1908). A double red lactiflora, widely available.

'Kaskaskia' (Auten 1931). A single red lactiflora, available from Wild and Son.

'Kate Berry' (Nicholls 1938). A Japanese pink lactiflora, available from Busse Gardens and Wild and Son.

'Kate Smith' (Murawska 1950). A double pink lactiflora, available from Wild and Son.

'Kathalo' (Kelsey 1934). A Japanese pink lactiflora, available from Craigmore (New Zealand) and Busse Gardens.

'Katherine Fonteyn' (origin unknown). A double blush lactiflora, available from Rivière (France); Terrace Peonies (New Zealand); Breifne Flowers (New Zealand); and Marsal (New Zealand).

'Katherine Havemeyer' (Thurlow 1921). A double pink lactiflora, available from Rivière (France).

'Kaw Valley' (Bigger 1944). A double red lactiflora, available from Cedar Creek (Canada).

'Kaye Tischler' (Brand–Tischler 1964). A Japanese pink lactiflora, available from Tischler Peony Garden.

'Kelway's Glorious' (Kelway 1909). A double white lactiflora, available from Caprice Farm; A & D Nursery; Ferncliff Gardens (Canada); and Pivoinerie (France).

'Kelway's Gorgeous' (Kelway). A single rose lactiflora, available from Kelways (U.K.).

'Kelway's Lovely' (Kelway). A double pink lactiflora, available from Pivoinerie (France).

'Kelway's Supreme' (Kelway). A double or semi-double blush lactiflora, available from Kelways (U.K.).

'Kevin' (Krekler 1975). A double pink lactiflora, available from Klehm Nursery.

'Kickapoo' (Auten 1931). A single red lactiflora, available from Cedar Creek (Canada) and Rivière (France).

'Kimo Kimo' (origin unknown). A Japanese pink lactiflora, available from Pivoinerie (France).

'King Midas' (Lins 1942). A double red lactiflora, available from Busse Gardens.

'King of England' (Kelway 1902). A Japanese red lactiflora, available from Craigmore (New Zealand).

'Knighthood' (origin unknown). A double red lactiflora, available from Kelways (U.K.).

'Kojiki' (Millet 1926). A Japanese pink lactiflora, available from Pivoinerie (France).

'Krinkled White' (Brand 1928). A single white lactiflora, widely available.

'Kukenu-Jishia' (ex Japan). A Japanese pink lactiflora, available from Ferncliff Gardens (Canada) and Brickman's (Canada).

'Kukini Jishi' (ex Japan). A single pink lactiflora, available from Klehm Nursery.

'L. W. Pollock'. See 'Lee W. Pollock'

'L'Eclatante' (Calot 1860). A double red lactiflora, available from Aimers (Canada) and Pivoinerie (France).

'L'Etincelante' (Dessert 1905). A single pink lactiflora, available from Busse Gardens; A & D Nursery; Kelways (U.K.); and Pivoinerie (France).

'L'Etincelante' (Calot 1860). Invalid name. A double red lactiflora, available from Klose (Germany).

'La Fiancee' (Dessert 1902). A single white lactiflora, available from Pivoinerie (France).

'La France' (Lemoine 1901). A double pink lactiflora, available from Klose (Germany); Country Squires (Canada); and Pivoinerie (France).

'La Lorraine' (Lemoine 1901). A double white lactiflora, available from Reath's; Tischler Peony Garden; Busse Gardens; Kelways (U.K.); Craigmore (New Zealand); and Klehm Nursery.

'La Perle' (Crousse 1886). A double rose lactiflora, available from Busse Gardens and Craigmore (New Zealand).

'Laddie' (Glasscock 1941). A cross between *Paeonia peregrina* 'Otto Froebel' and *P. tenuifolia*. A single red, available from Caprice Farm; Sherman Nursery; Cedar Creek (Canada); Austin Roses (U.K.); and Country Squires (Canada).

'Lady Alexandra Duff' (Kelway 1902). A double blush lactiflora, widely available.

'Lady Gay' (Saunders 1950). Descended from *Paeonia lactiflora, P. macrophylla, P. mlokosewitschii*, and *P. peregrina* crosses. A single white, available from Cedar Creek (Canada).

'Lady Kate' (Vories 1924). A double pink lactiflora, available from Wild and Son and Craigmore (New Zealand).

'Lady Orchid' (Bigger 1942). A double pink lactiflora, available from Hildebrandt's; Cedar Creek (Canada); Rivière (France); and Pivoinerie (France).

'Lake o' Silver' (Franklin 1920). A double pink lactiflora, available from White Flower Farm and Klehm Nursery.

'Lamartine' (Calot 1860). Also sold as 'Gigantea'. A double pink lactiflora, available from Aimers (Canada).

'Lancaster Imp' (R. Klehm). A double white lactiflora, available from Klehm Nursery and Marsal (New Zealand).

'Langley' (Bockstoce 1955). A semi-double pink hybrid, available from Klehm Nursery.

'Lapinja' (Kelsey 1937). A Japanese pink lactiflora, available from Busse Gardens.

'Largo' (Vories 1929). A Japanese pink lactiflora, available from Busse Gardens; Klehm Nursery; Wild and Son; and Terrace Peonies (New Zealand).

'Late Japanese Red' (origin unknown). A Japanese red lactiflora, available from Viette Farm and Nursery.

'Late Windflower' (Saunders 1939). A cross between *Paeonia beresowskii* and *P. emodi*. A single white, available from Reath's and Caprice Farm.

'Laura Dessert' (Dessert 1913). An anemone or double white lactiflora, widely available in Europe and Canada.

'Laura Dexheimer'. See 'Lora Dexheimer'

'Laura Magnuson' (Saunders 1941). A cross between *Paeonia lactiflora* and *P. peregrina*. A semi-double rose, available from Cedar Creek (Canada) and Caprice Farm.

'Laura Treman' (Nicholls 1943). A double blush lactiflora, available from Busse Gardens.

'Lavender Lace' (Bigger 1979). A Japanese pink lactiflora, available from Bigger Peonies.

'Le Charme' (Eliason 1964). A Japanese pink lactiflora, available from Hollingsworth Peonies.

'Le Cygne' (Lemoine 1907). A double white lactiflora, widely available.

'Le Jour' (Shaylor 1915). A single white lactiflora, available from Klehm Nursery; Busse Gardens; Viette Farm and Nursery; A & D Nursery; and Country Squires (Canada).

'Le Printemps' (Lemoine 1905). A cross between *Paeonia lactiflora* and *P. wittmanniana*. A single yellow, available from Cedar Creek (Canada); Ferncliff Gardens (Canada); Brickman's (Canada); and Pivoinerie (France).

'Leading Lady' (Bigger 1955). A double white lactiflora, available from Bigger Peonies.

'Lee' (Krekler 1965). A double red lactiflora, available from Klehm Nursery.

'Lee W. Pollock' (Brand 1936). A double pink lactiflora, available from Brand Peony Farm; Busse Gardens; and Reath's.

'Legion of Honor' (Saunders 1941). A cross between *Paeonia lactiflora* and *P. peregrina* 'Otto Froebel'. A single or semi-double red, available from A & D Nursery; Wild and Son; McConnell Nurseries (Canada); and Klehm Nursery.

'Leonie'. See 'Mme. Calot'

'Leto' (Neeley 1930). A Japanese white lactiflora, available from Brand Peony Farm; Homestead Nurseries (Canada); Ferncliff Gardens (Canada); and Brickman's (Canada).

'Lettie' (Nicholls–Wild 1956). A double pink lactiflora, available from Busse Gardens and Craigmore (New Zealand).

'Liberty Belle' (Neeley 1926). A double pink lactiflora, available from Busse Gardens.

'Liebchen' (Murawska 1959). A single pink lactiflora, widely available in New Zealand.

'Liebchen' (origin unknown). Invalid name. A double white lactiflora, available from Peony Gardens (New Zealand).

'Lilac Time' (Lins 1958). A Japanese pink lactiflora, available from Rivière (France).

'Lilacina Superba' (Buyck). A double pink lactiflora, available from Maison des Fleurs (Canada) and Pivoinerie (France).

'Lillian Wild' (Wild 1930). A double white lactiflora, available from Ferncliff Gardens (Canada); Carroll Gardens; Wild and Son; and A & D Nursery.

'Linda K. Jack' (Jack). A double red lactiflora, available from Ferncliff Gardens (Canada).

'Little Red Gem' (Reath 1988). A second-generation 'Gwenda' selfed. A single red, available from Reath's.

'Lois Kelsey' (Kelsey 1934). A double white lactiflora, available from A & D Nursery; Peony Gardens (New Zealand); Klehm Nursery; Adamgrove; and Austin Roses (U.K.).

'Longfellow' (Brand 1907). A double red lactiflora, widely available.

'Lora Dex Heimer'. See 'Lora Dexheimer'

'Lora Dexheimer' (Brand 1913). A double red lactiflora, available from Busse Gardens; Klehm Nursery; Sherman Nursery; and Austin Roses (U.K.).

'Lord Avebury' (Kelway 1929). A double red lactiflora, available from von Zeppelin (Germany).

'Lord Calvin' (R. Klehm). A double white lactiflora, available from Gardenimport (Canada); Klehm Nursery; Anderson Iris; Adamgrove; and Pivoinerie (France).

'Lord Kitchener' (Kelway). A single or double red lactiflora, available from Kelways (U.K.); von Zeppelin (Germany); Pivoinerie (France); and Marsal (New Zealand).

'Lottie Dawson Rea' (Rea 1939). A double white lactiflora, available from Brand Peony Farm; Busse Gardens; Heschke Gardens; Caprice Farm; Craigmore (New Zealand); and Marsal (New Zealand).

'Lotus Bloom' (Saunders 1943). A cross between *Paeonia lactiflora* and *P. peregrina* 'Otto Froebel'. A semi-double pink, available from Cedar Creek (Canada); Busse Gardens; and Caprice Farm.

'Lotus Queen' (Murawska 1947). A Japanese white lactiflora, widely available.

'Lou Shenk' (Rosenfield 1927). A Japanese rose lactiflora, available from Sherman Nursery.

'Louis Barthelot' (Doriat 1927). A double white lactiflora, available from Brand Peony Farm; Klose (Germany); and Austin Roses (U.K.).

'Louis van Houtte' (Calot 1867). A double red lactiflora, widely available.

'Louise B. Watts'. See 'Mrs. Lois B. Watts'

'Louise Lossing' (Lossing 1943). A double white lactiflora, available from Country Squires (Canada).

'Louise Marx' (Marx–Rogers 1981). A Japanese white lactiflora, available from Caprice Farm.

'Lovebirds' (origin unknown). A single white hybrid, available from A & D Nursery.

'Lovely Louise' (Murawska 1962). A cross between 'Marie Crousse' and 'Mrs. Livingston Farrand'. A double pink, available from Cedar Creek (Canada).

'Lovely Rose' (Saunders 1942). A cross between *Paeonia lactiflora* and *P. peregrina*. A semi-double rose, available from Caprice Farm; Klose (Germany); and Beaux Jardins.

'Lowell Thomas' (Rosenfield 1934). A semi-double or double red lactiflora, available from New Peony Farm; Bigger Peonies; Klehm Nursery; and Austin Roses (U.K.).

'Lucienne Contassot' (Doriat 1932). A single pink lactiflora, available from Pivoinerie (France).

'Ludovica' (Saunders 1941). A cross between *Paeonia lactiflora* and *P. peregrina*. A semi-double rose, available from Klose (Germany); Cedar Creek (Canada); Wild and Son; Peony Gardens (New Zealand); and Kiwi Gardens (Canada).

'Luella Shaylor' (Shaylor 1917). A double white lactiflora, available from Reath's.

'Lullaby' (Pehrson 1974). A cross between 'Laura Magnuson' and 'Moon of Nippon'. A double blush, available from Peony Gardens (New Zealand) and Klehm Nursery.

'Lustrous' (Saunders 1942). A cross between *Paeonia lactiflora* and *P. peregrina*. A semi-double red, available from Caprice Farm; Cedar Creek (Canada); Wild and Son; Ferncliff Gardens (Canada); Brickman's (Canada); and Country Squires (Canada).

'Luxor' (Sass 1933). A double white lactiflora, available from Klehm Nursery.

'Macrophylla'. Offered as a cultivar of *Paeonia wittmanniana*. A single yellow, available from Pivoinerie (France).

'Madame Antoine Rivière' (A. Rivière 1935). A single red lactiflora, available from Pivoinerie (France).

'Madame Bucquet' (Dessert 1888). A double pink lactiflora, available from Pivoinerie (France).

'Madame Calot'. See 'Mme. Calot'

'Madame Claude Allard' (origin unknown). A double pink lactiflora, available from Pivoinerie (France).

'Madame Claude Tain'. See 'Mme. Claude Tain'

'Madame de Vatry' (Guerin 1863). A double blush lactiflora, available from Pivoinerie (France).

'Madame de Verneville'. See 'Mme. de Verneville'

'Madame Ducel'. See 'Mme. Ducel'

'Madame Emile Debatene'. See 'Mme. Emile Debatene'

'Madame Emile Galle'. See 'Mme. Emile Galle'

'Madame Emile Lemoine'. See 'Mme. Emile Lemoine'

'Madame Gaudichau' (Millet 1902). A double red lactiflora, available from Pivoinerie (France).

'Madame Henri Fuchs' (A. Rivière 1955). A Japanese red lactiflora, available from Pivoinerie (France).

'Madame Jean Bohn' (Doriat 1931). A single red lactiflora, available from Pivoinerie (France).

'Madame Jules Dessert'. See 'Mme. Jules Dessert'

'Madame Lemoine'. See 'Mme. Emile Lemoine'

'Madelon' (Dessert 1922). A double pink lactiflora, available from Ferncliff Gardens (Canada) and Brickman's (Canada).

'Madylone' (van Loon 1966). A cross between 'Mme. Jules Dessert' and 'White Perfection'. A double pink, available from Klehm Nursery.

'Maestro' (Auten). A double red lactiflora, available from Klehm Nursery; Viette Farm and Nursery; Ferncliff Gardens (Canada); Cedar Creek (Canada); and Marsal (New Zealand).

'Magnifica' (Miellez 1953). A double white lactiflora, available from Pivoinerie (France).

'Magnolia Flower' (Saunders 1949). A cross between *Paeonia lactiflora* and *P. macrophylla*. A semi-double pink, available from Caprice Farm.

'Mahogany' (Glasscock 1937). A cross between *Paeonia lactiflora* and *P. peregrina* 'Otto Froebel'. A single red, available from Busse Gardens; Sherman Nursery; Hollingsworth Peonies; Caprice Farm; and Klehm Nursery.

'Mai Fleuri' (Lemoine 1905). A cross between *Paeonia lactiflora* and

P. wittmanniana. A single blush, available from Cedar Creek (Canada); Klose (Germany); Hortico (Canada); and Maison des Fleurs (Canada).

'Maid Marian' (Pees–Busse 1984). A Japanese pink lactiflora, available from Busse Gardens.

'Maison Crousse' (Crousse 1892). A double red lactiflora, available from Pivoinerie (France).

'Majestic Rose' (Franklin 1853). A double rose lactiflora, available from Brand Peony Farm.

'Mandaleen' (Lins 1942). A double pink lactiflora, available from Busse Gardens; Wild and Son; and Cedar Creek (Canada).

'Mandarin's Coat' (Marx–Rogers 1978). A Japanese rose lactiflora, available from Caprice Farm; Carroll Gardens; Klose (Germany); and Country Squires (Canada).

'Many Happy Returns' (Hollingsworth 1990). A cross between 'Little Dorrit' and 'Nippon Splendour'. A double red, available from Hollingsworth Peonies.

'Marcella' (Lins 1952). A double white lactiflora, available from Brand Peony Farm; Reath's; and Sherman Nursery.

'Marechal MacMahon'. See 'General MacMahon'

'Marechal Vallant' (Calot 1867). A double red lactiflora, available from Pivoinerie (France).

'Margaret Lough' (Gumm 1929). A double blush lactiflora, available from Busse Gardens.

'Margaret Trueman' (ex Germany). A single red lactiflora, available from Busse Gardens and Milaeger's.

'Margaret Trueman' (origin unknown). A Japanese red lactiflora, available from Milaeger's.

'Margaret Trueman' (origin unknown). A double pink lactiflora, available from van Hoorn.

'Margarete Klose' (Klose 1972). A double pink lactiflora, available from Klose (Germany).

'Marguerite Gerard' (Crousse). A double pink lactiflora, available from Pivoinerie (France).

'Marie Crousse' (Crousse 1892). A double pink lactiflora, available from Maison des Fleurs (Canada) and Pivoinerie (France).

'Marie Elizabeth' (Guille 1950). A double red lactiflora, available from Busse Gardens and Viette Farm and Nursery.

'Marie Fischer' (origin unknown). A single pink lactiflora, available from Peony Gardens (New Zealand).

'Marie Jacquin' (Verdier). Also sold as 'Bridesmaid' and 'Waterlily'. Registered as pink. A semi-double white lactiflora, available from New Peony Farm.

'Marie Lemoine' (Calot 1869). A double red lactiflora, widely available.

'Marie Lemoine' (Lemoine 1869). A double white lactiflora, available from Austin Roses (U.K.).

'Marie Lemond' (origin unknown). A double white lactiflora, available from van Hoorn.

'Marietta Sisson' (Sass 1933). A double pink lactiflora, available from Klehm Nursery and Wild and Son.

'Mariette Vallee' (origin unknown). A double rose lactiflora, available from Pivoinerie (France).

'Marilla Beauty' (Kelsey 1940). A double blush lactiflora, available from New Peony Farm.

'Marquis C. Lagergren' (Dessert 1911). A double red lactiflora, available from von Zeppelin (Germany).

'Marshmallow Button' (R. Klehm). A double white lactiflora, available from Klehm Nursery.

'Marshmallow Puff' (R. Klehm). A double white lactiflora, available from Klehm Nursery.

'Marshmallow Tart' (R. Klehm 1985). Linebred 'Bowl of Cream'. A double white, available from Klehm Nursery.

'Martha Bulloch' (Brand 1907). A double pink lactiflora, widely available.

'Martha Pollock' (Brand 1907). A double rose lactiflora, available from Brand Peony Farm.

'Martha Reed' (Krekler 1965). A double white lactiflora, available from Klehm Nursery.

'Mary Brand' (Brand 1907). A double red lactiflora, available from Brand Peony Farm; Sherman Nursery; and New Peony Farm.

'Mary E. Nicholls' (Nicholls 1941). A double white lactiflora, available from Caprice Farm; Wild and Son; and Carroll Gardens.

'Mary Eddy Jones' (Nicholls 1961). A double pink lactiflora, available from Ferncliff Gardens (Canada); Homestead Nurseries (Canada); and Brickman's (Canada).

'Mary Jo Legere' (Pehrson 1978). A cross between 'Little Dorrit' and 'Mikado'. A double rose, available from Caprice Farm.

'Mary Nicholls'. See 'Mary E. Nicholls'

'Matilda Lewis' (Saunders 1921). A double red lactiflora, available from Busse Gardens; Ferncliff Gardens (Canada); and Austin Roses (U.K.).

'Mattie Lafuze' (Johnson 1942). A double white lactiflora, available from Wild and Son; Cedar Creek (Canada); and Rivière (France).

'Maxine Wolf' (origin unknown). A Japanese pink lactiflora, available from Brand Peony Farm.

'May Apple' (Wolf–Bigger 1977). A single or Japanese blush lactiflora, available from Bigger Peonies and Klehm Nursery.

'May Morn' (Nicholls 1952). A 'Mme. Calot' cross. A double blush, available from Wild and Son.

'May Music' (Saunders–Reath 1973). Descended from *Paeonia lactiflora*, *P. macrophylla*, *P. mlokosewitschii*, and *P. peregrina* crosses. A single pink, available from Reath's.

'May Treat' (Krekler). A single pink lactiflora, available from Klehm Nursery.

'Meadow Lark' (Bigger 1977). A Japanese pink lactiflora, available from Bigger Peonies.

'Mervyn Pees' (Pees–Busse 1979). A Japanese red lactiflora, available from Anderson Iris and Busse Gardens.

'Messagere' (Lemoine 1909). A cross between *Paeonia lactiflora* and *P. wittmanniana*. A single white, available from Cedar Creek (Canada).

'Mid May' (Saunders 1950). A single pink hybrid, available from Cedar Creek (Canada).

'Midnight Sun' (Murawska 1954). A Japanese red lactiflora, available from A & D Nursery; Busse Gardens; and Klehm Nursery.

'Mikado' (ex Japan 1893). A Japanese red lactiflora, widely available.

'Mildred May' (Murawska). A semi-double white lactiflora, available from Busse Gardens.

'Milton Jack' (Jack). A double rose lactiflora, available from Ferncliff Gardens (Canada).

'Minnie Shaylor' (Shaylor 1919). A semi-double white lactiflora, available from A & D Nursery; Busse Gardens; Klehm Nursery; Wild and Son; Craigmore (New Zealand); and Marsal (New Zealand).

'Minuet' (Franklin 1931). A double pink lactiflora, available from Heschke Gardens; Brand Peony Farm; Sherman Nursery; A & D Nursery; Busse Gardens; and Marsal (New Zealand).

'Mischief' (Auten 1925). A single pink lactiflora, available from Busse Gardens; Brand Peony Farm; Klehm Nursery; A & D Nursery; Garden-import (Canada); and Austin Roses (U.K.).

'Miss America' (Mann–van Steen 1936). Gold Medal. A semi-double white lactiflora, widely available.

'Miss Dainty' (Bigger 1949). A double pink lactiflora, available from Bigger Peonies.

'Miss Eckhart' (Roelof–van der Meer 1928). A double pink lactiflora, available from Rambo Wholesale; von Zeppelin (Germany); Austin Roses (U.K.); Maison des Fleurs (Canada); and Pivoinerie (France).

'Miss Mary' (Krekler 1967). A single red lactiflora, available from Klehm Nursery.

'Mister Ed'. See 'Mr. Ed'

'Mistral' (Dessert 1905). A single red lactiflora, available from Kelways (U.K.).

'Mlle. Leonie Calot'. See 'Mons. Charles Leveque'

'Mme. Butterfly' (Franklin 1933). A Japanese pink lactiflora, available from Busse Gardens; Adamgrove; Wild and Son; New Peony Farm; Klose (Germany); Brand Peony Farm; and Craigmore (New Zealand).

'Mme. Calot' (Miellez 1856). Also sold as 'Leonie'. A double pink lactiflora, available from Rambo Wholesale; Kelways (U.K.); Austin Roses (U.K.); and Pivoinerie (France).

'Mme. Claude Tain' (Doriat 1927). A double white lactiflora, available from Viette Farm and Nursery; Klose (Germany); Country Squires (Canada); Hortico (Canada); Cannon Nurseries (Canada); Maison des Fleurs (Canada); and Pivoinerie (France).

'Mme. de Verneville' (Crousse 1885). A double white lactiflora, widely available.

'Mme. Ducel' (Mechin 1880). A double pink lactiflora, available from Carroll Gardens; Kelways (U.K.); and Klose (Germany).

'Mme. E. Debatene'. See 'Mme. Emile Debatene'

'Mme. Edouard Doriat' (Dessert–Doriat 1924). A double white lactiflora, available from Kelways (U.K.); Maison des Fleurs (Canada); and Pivoinerie (France).

'Mme. Emile Debatene' (Dessert–Doriat 1927). A double pink lactiflora, available from Busse Gardens; von Zeppelin (Germany); Austin Roses (U.K.); Ferncliff Gardens (Canada); and Pivoinerie (France).

'Mme. Emile Galle' (Crousse 1881). A double pink lactiflora, available from von Zeppelin (Germany) and Craigmore (New Zealand).

'Mme. Emile Lemoine' (Lemoine 1899). A double white lactiflora, available from Homestead Nurseries (Canada) and Country Squires (Canada).

'Mme. Jules Dessert' (Dessert 1909). A double blush lactiflora, available from Busse Gardens; Austin Roses (U.K.); and Pivoinerie (France).

'Mme. Julie Berthier' (origin unknown). A double red lactiflora, available from Klose (Germany).

'Mobuchi' (Millet). A single red lactiflora, available from Klose (Germany).

'Modeste Guerin' (Guerin 1845). A double pink lactiflora, available from von Zeppelin (Germany).

'Mons. B. Weum' (origin unknown). A double white lactiflora, available from Brand Peony Farm.

'Mons. Charles Leveque' (Calot 1861). Also sold as 'Mlle. Leonie Calot'. A double pink lactiflora, available from Pivoinerie (France).

'Mons. Jules Elie' (Crousse 1888). A double pink lactiflora, widely available.

'Mons. Krelage' (Crousse 1883). A double red lactiflora, available from Pivoinerie (France).

'Mons. Martin Cahuzac' (Dessert 1899). A double red lactiflora, widely available.

'Monsieur Adam Modzelewski' (Doriat 1935). A double red lactiflora, available from Pivoinerie (France).

'Monsieur Charles Leveque'. See 'Mons. Charles Leveque'

'Monsieur Jules Elie'. See 'Mons. Jules Elie'

'Monsieur Krelage'. See 'Mons. Krelage'

'Monsieur Martin Cahuzac'. See 'Mons. Martin Cahuzac'

'Montezuma' (Saunders 1943). A cross between *Paeonia lactiflora* and *P. peregrina*. A single red, available from Busse Gardens; Cedar Creek (Canada); Reath's; Viette Farm and Nursery; Hildebrandt's; Klehm Nursery; and Pivoinerie (France).

'Moon of Nippon' (Auten 1936). A Japanese white lactiflora, available from Brand Peony Farm; Wild and Son; Viette Farm and Nursery; A & D Nursery; and Adamgrove.

'Moon Over Barrington' (R. Klehm). A double white lactiflora, available from Klehm Nursery.

'Moon River' (C. G. Klehm). A double pink lactiflora, available from Busse

Gardens; Hildebrandt's; Klehm Nursery; Peony Gardens (New Zealand); Craigmore (New Zealand); Pivoinerie (France); and Marsal (New Zealand).

'Moonglow' (Rosenfield 1939). A double white lactiflora, available from Klehm Nursery.

'Moonrise' (Saunders 1949). A second-generation hybrid resulting from a cross between *Paeonia lactiflora* and *P. peregrina*. A semi-double white, available from Cedar Creek (Canada) and Klehm Nursery.

'Moonstone' (Murawska 1943). Gold Medal. A double blush lactiflora, widely available.

'Mother's Choice' (Glasscock 1950). A double white lactiflora, widely available.

'Mount Palomar' (Auten 1939). A Japanese red lactiflora, available from Country Squires (Canada).

'Mr. Ed' (C. G. Klehm 1980). A mutation of 'Mons. Jules Elie'. A double blush, widely available.

'Mr. G. F. Hemerick' (van Leeuwen 1930). A Japanese pink lactiflora, widely available.

'Mr. Thim' (van Leeuwen 1926). A single red lactiflora, available from Klehm Nursery and Busse Gardens.

'Mrs. A. M. Brand' (Brand 1925). Gold Medal. A double white lactiflora, available from Tischler Peony Garden and New Peony Farm.

'Mrs. Bryce Fontaine' (Brand 1916). A double red lactiflora, available from Viette Farm and Nursery.

'Mrs. Edouard Harding'. See 'Mrs. Edward Harding'

'Mrs. Edward Harding' (Shaylor 1918). A double white lactiflora, available from Homestead Nurseries (Canada); Hortico (Canada); Cedar Creek (Canada); and Pivoinerie (France).

'Mrs. Euclid Snow' (Brand). A double blush lactiflora, available from A & D Nursery; Klehm Nursery; and Craigmore (New Zealand).

'Mrs. F. D. R.'. See 'Mrs. Franklin D. Roosevelt'

'Mrs. F. D. Roosevelt'. See 'Mrs. Franklin D. Roosevelt'

'Mrs. Frank Beach' (Brand 1925). A double white lactiflora, available from New Peony Farm; Viette Farm and Nursery; and Mount Arbor.

'Mrs. Franklin D. Roosevelt' (Franklin 1932). Gold Medal. A double pink lactiflora, widely available.

'Mrs. Franklin Roosevelt'. See 'Mrs. Franklin D. Roosevelt'

'Mrs. G. F. Hemerick'. See 'Mr. G. F. Hemerick'

'Mrs. J. H. Neeley' (Neeley 1931). A double white lactiflora, available from Brand Peony Farm.

'Mrs. J. V. Edlund' (Edlund 1929). Gold Medal. A double white lactiflora, available from Pivoinerie (France) and Brand Peony Farm.

'Mrs. James Kelway' (Kelway 1936). A double blush lactiflora, available from New Peony Farm; Sherman Nursery; and Bigger Peonies.

'Mrs. Livingston Farrand' (Nicholls 1935). A double pink lactiflora, widely available.

'Mrs. Lois B. Watts' (Murawska 1965). A double pink lactiflora, available from A & D Nursery and Wild and Son.

'Mrs. Rowland' (Brand 1942). A double red lactiflora, available from Brand Peony Farm.

'Mrs. W. L. Gumm' (Gumm 1929). A double pink lactiflora, available from Wild and Son.

'Mrs. Wilder Bancroft' (Nicholls 1935). A Japanese red lactiflora, available from Viette Farm and Nursery; Heschke Gardens; Country Squires (Canada); Sheridan Nurseries (Canada); and Cedar Creek (Canada).

'Mt. St. Helens' (Marx–Rogers 1981). A double red lactiflora, available from Caprice Farm.

'Multiflora' (Gilbertson 1974). A cross between 'Hedgemaster' and 'Pink n' Yellow'. A double pink, available from Brand Peony Farm and Beaux Jardins.

'Murillio' (Goos–Koenemann 1910). A single pink lactiflora, available from Klose (Germany).

'Music Man' (Wild 1967). A double red lactiflora, available from Wild and Son; Ferncliff Gardens (Canada); and Brickman's (Canada).

'Mutabilis Plena'. Offered as a cultivar of *Paeonia officinalis*. A double pink, available from Klose (Germany); Busse Gardens; and Pivoinerie (France).

'My Love' (Hollingsworth 1992). A double white hybrid, available from Hollingsworth Peonies.

'My Pal Rudy' (C. G. Klehm 1952). Linebred 'Mons. Jules Elie'. A double pink, available from Klehm Nursery; Hildebrandt's; Terrace Peonies (New Zealand); Craigmore (New Zealand); Ferncliff Gardens (Canada); and Brickman's (Canada).

'Myra MacRae' (Tischler 1967). A double pink lactiflora, available from New Peony Farm; Caprice Farm; Brand Peony Farm; Tischler Peony Garden; Bigger Peonies; and Reath's.

'Myron Branson' (Krekler). A Japanese red lactiflora, available from Klehm Nursery.

'Myron D. Bigger' (Bigger 1966). A double white lactiflora, available from Bigger Peonies.

'Myrtle Gentry' (Brand 1925). A double blush lactiflora, widely available.

'Myrtle K. Walgren' (origin unknown). A double rose lactiflora, available from A & D Nursery.

'Myrtle Tischler' (Brand–Franklin 1963). A double rose lactiflora, available from Brand Peony Farm; Tischler Peony Garden; New Peony Farm; and Reath's.

'Nancy Dolman' (Vories 1924). A double rose lactiflora, available from Brand Peony Farm; Ferncliff Gardens (Canada); and Brickman's (Canada).

'Nancy Gedge' (origin unknown). A double pink lactiflora, available from Heschke Gardens.

'Nancy Nicholls' (Nicholls 1941). A double blush lactiflora, available from Klehm Nursery and Hildebrandt's.

'Nancy Nora' (Berstein 1942). A double pink lactiflora, available from Country Squires (Canada).

'Nathalie' (Saunders 1939). A cross between *Paeonia lactiflora* and *P. peregrina*. A semi-double pink, available from Ferncliff Gardens (Canada).

'Nebraska' (Sass 1939). A double white lactiflora, available from Sherman Nursery.

'Nellie Shaylor' (Shaylor 1919). A Japanese red lactiflora, available from Klehm Nursery.

'Neome Demay' (Calot 1867). A double pink lactiflora, available from von Zeppelin (Germany).

'Neon' (Nicholls 1941). A Japanese pink lactiflora, available from Anderson Iris; A & D Nursery; Wild and Son; von Zeppelin (Germany); and Pivoinerie (France).

'Nice Gal' (Krekler 1965). A semi-double pink lactiflora, available from Peony Gardens (New Zealand); Busse Gardens; Klehm Nursery; Brickman's (Canada); and Marsal (New Zealand).

'Nick Shaylor' (Allison 1931). Gold Medal. A double pink lactiflora, widely available.

'Nightwatch' (Saunders 1950). A *Paeonia anomala* cross. A semi-double red, available from Reath's.

'Ninon' (Doriat 1925). A double or anemone pink lactiflora, available from Pivoinerie (France).

'Nippon Beauty' (Auten 1927). A Japanese red lactiflora, available from Brand Peony Farm; Busse Gardens; Viette Farm and Nursery; Homestead Nurseries (Canada); New Peony Farm; Sheridan Nurseries (Canada); and Cedar Creek (Canada).

'Nippon Brilliant' (Auten 1933). A Japanese red lactiflora, available from Rivière (France).

'Nippon Gold' (Auten 1929). A Japanese pink lactiflora, available from Busse Gardens; Hollingsworth Peonies; A & D Nursery; and Heschke Gardens.

'Nippon on Parade'. See 'Nippon Parade'

'Nippon Parade' (Auten 1935). A Japanese red lactiflora, available from Klose (Germany) and Bluebird Nursery.

'Nippon Splendour' (Auten 1931). A Japanese red lactiflora, available from Country Squires (Canada) and Busse Gardens.

'Norma Volz' (Volz 1962). A 'Miss America' cross. Gold Medal. A double blush, available from Klehm Nursery; New Peony Farm; Hollingsworth Peonies; Peony Gardens (New Zealand); Terrace Peonies (New Zealand); and Marsal (New Zealand).

'Northern Glory' (Krekler 1955). A single pink lactiflora, available from Pivoinerie (France).

'Nosegay' (Saunders 1950). A second-generation hybrid resulting from a cross between *Paeonia mlokosewitschii* and *P. tenuifolia*. A single pink, available from Caprice Farm; Country Squires (Canada); and Klehm Nursery.

'Nova' (Saunders 1950). A cross between *Paeonia macrophylla* and *P. mlokosewitschii*. A single yellow, available from Caprice Farm; Busse Gardens; and A & D Nursery.

'Nudicarpa'. Offered as a cultivar of *Paeonia wittmanniana*. A single yellow, available from Pivoinerie (France).

'Nymph'. See 'Nymphe'

'Nymphe' (Dessert 1913). A Japanese pink lactiflora, available from Milaeger's; Bluemount Nurseries; Pivoinerie (France); Aimers (Canada); Pepiniere Charlevoix (Canada); and Kiwi Gardens (Canada).

'Odile' (Doriat 1928). A double blush lactiflora, available from Ferncliff Gardens (Canada) and Brickman's (Canada).

'Okinawa' (origin unknown). A Japanese red lactiflora, available from Sherman Nursery.

'Old Faithful' (Glasscock–Falk 1964). An advanced-generation, double red hybrid, available from Caprice Farm; Reath's; and Klehm Nursery.

'Old Lace' (Lins 1945). A double white lactiflora, available from Busse Gardens.

'Old Siwash' (Auten 1939). A Japanese red lactiflora, available from Viette Farm and Nursery.

'Onahama' (Gumm 1926). A Japanese red lactiflora, available from Country Squires (Canada) and Cedar Creek (Canada).

'Onondaga' (Little 1935). A double red lactiflora, available from Country Squires (Canada).

'Opal Hamilton' (Nicholls–Wild 1957). A Japanese pink lactiflora, available from Wild and Son; Ferncliff Gardens (Canada); and Brickman's (Canada).

'Orange Glory' (Auten 1956). A single red hybrid, available from Brand Peony Farm; Rivière (France); and Klehm Nursery.

'Orange Gold' (Auten). A single or semi-double red lactiflora, available from Busse Gardens.

'Orange Lace' (Bigger 1966). A Japanese pink lactiflora, available from New Peony Farm and Bigger Peonies.

'Oriental Gold' (ex Japan via Smirnow). A double yellow hybrid, available from Country Squires (Canada).

'Orlando Roberts' (Krekler 1962). A double red lactiflora, available from Klehm Nursery.

'Osage' (Bigger 1977). A double red lactiflora, available from Bigger Peonies.

'Otto Froebel'. Offered as a cultivar of *Paeonia officinalis* var. *lobata*. A single red, available from Busse Gardens.

'Ozark Beauty' (Wild 1950). A double pink lactiflora, available from Sarcoxie Nurseries.

'Paddy's Red' (origin unknown). A single red lactiflora, available from Peony Gardens (New Zealand) and Marsal (New Zealand).

'Pageant' (Saunders 1941). Descended from *Paeonia lactiflora, P. macrophylla*, and *P. officinalis* crosses. A single pink, available from A & D Nursery; Busse Gardens; and Caprice Farm.

'Painted Desert' (Nicholls 1965). A double pink lactiflora, available from Wild and Son.

'Paladin' (Saunders 1950). A cross between *Paeonia lactiflora* and *P. peregrina*. A semi-double red, available from Viette Farm and Nursery; Hortico (Canada); and Pivoinerie (France).

'Papilio' (Saunders 1950). Descended from *Paeonia lactiflora*, *P. macrophylla*, *P. mlokosewitschii*, and *P. peregrina* crosses. A single white, available from Caprice Farm.

'Paree Frou Frou' (R. Klehm). A Japanese pink lactiflora, available from Klehm Nursery.

'Party Dress' (Krekler). A single red lactiflora, available from Peony Gardens (New Zealand).

'Pastel Gem' (Bigger 1979). A double pink lactiflora, available from New Peony Farm.

'Pat Victor' (Krekler). A Japanese white lactiflora, available from Anderson Iris and Klehm Nursery.

'Patriot' (Saunders 1943). A single red hybrid, available from Klehm Nursery; Brand Peony Farm; Viette Farm and Nursery; Busse Gardens; and Cedar Creek (Canada).

'Paul Bunyon' (Lins 1955). A double pink lactiflora, available from Brand Peony Farm; Busse Gardens; Hildebrandt's; Klehm Nursery; Reath's; and Rivière (France).

'Paul M. Wild' (Wild 1964). A double red lactiflora, widely available.

'Paula Fay' (Fay 1968). Gold Medal. A semi-double pink hybrid, widely available.

'Payoff' (Krekler–R. Klehm). A Japanese red lactiflora, available from Klehm Nursery.

'Peach Delight' (Smirnow 1978). A semi-double pink lactiflora, available from Peony Gardens (New Zealand).

'Peach Fluff' (Wild 1964). A double pink lactiflora, available from Wild and Son.

'Peachy Rose' (Smirnow). A double rose hybrid, available from Cedar Creek (Canada).

'Pecher Rose' (Calot 1867). A double blush lactiflora, available from Pivoinerie (France).

'Peggy' (Auten 1931). A double rose lactiflora, available from Hildebrandt's and Klehm Nursery.

'Peppermint' (Nicholls–Wild 1958). A double pink lactiflora, available from Wild and Son; Ferncliff Gardens (Canada); and Brickman's (Canada).

'Persephone' (origin unknown). A single pink hybrid, available from A & D Nursery.

'Peter Barr' (origin unknown). A single red hybrid, available from Cedar Creek (Canada).

'Peter Brand' (Seit 1937). A double red lactiflora, available from von Zeppelin (Germany) and Pivoinerie (France).

'Petite Renee' (Dessert 1899). A Japanese pink lactiflora, available from Caprice Farm.

'Petticoat Flounce' (R. Klehm 1985). A double pink lactiflora, available from White Flower Farm and Klehm Nursery.

'Petticoat Parade' (R. Klehm 1989). A double pink, available from Klehm Nursery.

'Pfeiffer's Red Triumph' (Pfeiffer 1937). A double red lactiflora, available from Heschke Gardens; New Peony Farm; Busse Gardens; and Wild and Son.

'Philippe Rivoire' (B. Rivière 1911). A double red lactiflora, available from Heschke Gardens; Anderson Iris; Bigger Peonies; Busse Gardens; and Klehm Nursery.

'Philomele' (Calot 1861). A Japanese or double pink lactiflora, available from Austin Roses (U.K.).

'Phipp's White' (origin unknown). A double white lactiflora, available from Viette Farm and Nursery.

'Phoebe Cary' (Brand 1907). A double pink lactiflora, available from Brand Peony Farm and Cedar Creek (Canada).

'Phyllis Kelway' (Kelway 1908). A semi-double rose lactiflora, available from Busse Gardens.

'Pico' (Freeborn 1934). A single white lactiflora, available from Country Squires (Canada) and Wild and Son.

'Picotee' (Saunders 1949). A selection from *Paeonia mascula* subsp. *russii*. A single white and pink, available from Caprice Farm.

'Pierre Debatene' (Doriat 1935). A single pink lactiflora, available from Pivoinerie (France).

'Pierre Dessert' (Dessert–Mechin 1890). A semi-double or double red lactiflora, available from von Zeppelin (Germany).

'Pillow Talk' (C. G. Klehm 1973). A double pink lactiflora, available from Klehm Nursery; Reath's; Anderson Iris; Hildebrandt's; Terrace Peonies (New Zealand); Craigmore (New Zealand); and Marsal (New Zealand).

'Pink Cameo' (Bigger 1954). A double pink lactiflora, available from Bigger Peonies and Busse Gardens.

'Pink Chiffon' (Glasscock–Falk 1964). A fourth-generation, anemone or Japanese pink hybrid, available from Sherman Nursery.

'Pink Crescendo' (Hollingsworth 1984). A double pink hybrid, available from Hollingsworth Peonies.

'Pink Dawn' (R. Klehm 1990). A single pink lactiflora, available from Austin Roses (U.K.) and Klehm Nursery.

'Pink Derby' (Bigger 1966). A double pink lactiflora, available from Bigger Peonies; Wild and Son; Tischler Peony Garden; and New Peony Farm.

'Pink Formal' (Nicholls 1953). A double pink lactiflora, available from Brand Peony Farm; Wild and Son; Sunny Border Nursery; Reath's; Ferncliff Gardens (Canada); and Terrace Peonies (New Zealand).

'Pink Giant' (origin unknown). A double rose lactiflora, available from Austin Roses (U.K.) and Pivoinerie (France).

'Pink Hawaiian Coral' (R. Klehm 1981). A cross between 'Charlie's White' and *Paeonia peregrina* 'Otto Froebel'. A double pink, available from Klehm Nursery; Craigmore (New Zealand); Gardenimport (Canada); and Marsal (New Zealand).

'Pink Jazz' (C. G. Klehm). A double pink lactiflora, available from Hildebrandt's and Klehm Nursery.

'Pink Lemonade' (C. G. Klehm 1951). An anemone or double pink and yellow, available from Anderson Iris; Viette Farm and Nursery; Hildebrandt's; Klehm Nursery; Terrace Peonies (New Zealand); and Craigmore (New Zealand).

'Pink Monarch' (Auten 1931). A double pink lactiflora, available from Viette Farm and Nursery.

'Pink Parasol Surprise' (R. Klehm 1992). An anemone pink lactiflora, available from Klehm Nursery.

'Pink Parfait' (C. G. Klehm 1975). Linebred 'Mons. Jules Elie'. A double pink, available from Peony Gardens (New Zealand); Klehm Nursery; and Hildebrandt's.

'Pink Patterns' (origin unknown). A single pink hybrid, available from Cedar Creek (Canada).

'Pink Pearl' (Reath 1991). A double pink lactiflora, available from Reath's.

'Pink Pom Pom' (Reath 1992). A double pink lactiflora, available from Reath's.

'Pink Princess' (origin unknown). A single pink lactiflora, available from

Carroll Gardens; White Flower Farm; Wild and Son; New Peony Farm; Hollingsworth Peonies; and Klehm Nursery.

'Pink Radiance' (Wild 1959). A double pink lactiflora, available from Wild and Son; A & D Nursery; and Carroll Gardens.

'Pink Wonder' (Bigger 1950). A double pink lactiflora, available from Bigger Peonies and Cedar Creek (Canada).

'Pinnacle' (Bigger 1970). A double pink lactiflora, available from Bigger Peonies.

'Plainsman' (Bigger 1949). A Japanese blush lactiflora, available from Tischler Peony Garden; New Peony Farm; Bigger Peonies; and Klehm Nursery.

'Playmate' (Saunders 1950). A second-generation hybrid resulting from a cross between *Paeonia mlokosewitschii* and *P. tenuifolia*. A single rose, available from Reath's.

'Plena'. Offered as a cultivar of *Paeonia tenuifolia*. A double red, available from Klose (Germany).

'Plymouth' (Auten 1931). A double white lactiflora, available from Busse Gardens.

'Polar King' (origin unknown). A Japanese white lactiflora, available from Wild and Son.

'Polar Star' (Sass 1932). A Japanese white lactiflora, available from Sherman Nursery.

'Pom Pom' (origin unknown). A Japanese red lactiflora, available from Brand Peony Farm.

'Port Royale' (Krekler–R. Klehm). A Japanese red lactiflora, available from Klehm Nursery.

'Postilion' (Saunders 1941). A semi-double red hybrid, widely available.

'Pottsi Plena' (Calot 1857). A double red lactiflora, available from Klose (Germany).

'Prairie A Fire'. See 'Prairie Afire'

'Prairie Afire' (Brand 1932). A Japanese pink lactiflora, available from Pivoinerie (France); Busse Gardens; Viette Farm and Nursery; New Peony Farm; and Bigger Peonies.

'Prairie Belle' (Bigger 1945). A semi-double pink lactiflora, available from Bigger Peonies.

'Prairie Moon' (Fay 1959). A cross between 'Archangel' and 'Laura Magnuson'. A semi-double or single yellow, widely available.

'Prairie Princess' (Hollingsworth 1984). A double pink hybrid, available from Hollingsworth Peonies.

'President Feuillet' (Doriat 1932). A single blush lactiflora, available from Pivoinerie (France).

'President Lincoln' (Brand 1928). A single red lactiflora, available from Klehm Nursery; Brand Peony Farm; Viette Farm and Nursery; New Peony Farm; A & D Nursery; and Busse Gardens.

'President Poincare' (Kelway). A double red lactiflora, available from Homestead Nurseries (Canada).

'President Roosevelt' (Warnaar–Wild 1905). A double red lactiflora, available from Homestead Nurseries (Canada) and Sheridan Nurseries (Canada).

'President Taft' (Blaauw 1909). A double pink lactiflora, available from Klehm Nursery; Heschke Gardens; and White Flower Farm.

'President Wilson' (Thurlow 1918). A double pink lactiflora, available from Pivoinerie (France).

'Pride of Blasdell' (Kelsey 1934). A Japanese pink lactiflora, available from Cedar Creek (Canada) and Country Squires (Canada).

'Pride of Langport' (Kelway 1909). A Japanese pink lactiflora, available from Ferncliff Gardens (Canada) and Brickman's (Canada).

'Pride of Shenandoah' (origin unknown). A Japanese red lactiflora, available from Viette Farm and Nursery.

'Primevere' (Lemoine 1907). An anemone white lactiflora, widely available.

'Prince of Darkness' (Brand 1907). A double red lactiflora, available from Carroll Gardens and Sunny Border Nursery.

'Princess Margaret' (Murawska 1960). A double rose lactiflora, available from Caprice Farm; Busse Gardens; and Klehm Nursery.

'Princess Margaret Rose' (Brethour 1938). A Japanese pink lactiflora, available from Country Squires (Canada) and Craigmore (New Zealand).

'Princess of Darkness'. See 'Prince of Darkness'

'Professeur Jean-Marie Duvernay' (Doriat 1929). A single red lactiflora, available from Pivoinerie (France).

'Promenade' (Laning–Rogers 1991). A third-generation hybrid resulting from a cross between *Paeonia lactiflora* and *P. wittmanniana*. A semi-double blush, available from Caprice Farm.

'Pure Joy' (origin unknown). A double pink lactiflora, available from Bigger Peonies.

'Quality Folk' (Krekler 1973). A single pink hybrid, available from Marsal (New Zealand).

'Queen of Hamburg' (Sass 1937). A double pink lactiflora, available from Sherman Nursery.

'Queen of Sheba' (Sass 1937). A double pink lactiflora, available from Sherman Nursery; Hildebrandt's; and Klehm Nursery.

'Queen Rose' (Saunders 1949). A cross between *Paeonia lactiflora* and *P. peregrina*. A semi-double pink, available from Klehm Nursery.

'R. A. Napier' (Brand 1939). A double white and rose lactiflora, available from New Peony Farm and Busse Gardens.

'R. W. Auten'. See 'Robert W. Auten'

'Rachel' (Lemoine 1904). A double red lactiflora, available from Carroll Gardens; Bluebird Nursery; and Sherman Nursery.

'Ramona Lins' (Lins 1942). A double blush lactiflora, available from Tischler Peony Garden; Sherman Nursery; Cedar Creek (Canada); Rivière (France); and Reath's.

'Raoul Dessert' (Dessert 1919). A double pink lactiflora, available from Pivoinerie (France).

'Rapture' (Thurlow–Stranger 1937). A double white lactiflora, available from Busse Gardens.

'Rare China' (Kelsey 1935). A semi-double blush lactiflora, available from Country Squires (Canada) and Cedar Creek (Canada).

'Rashoomon' (ex Japan). A Japanese red lactiflora, available from Country Squires (Canada).

'Raspberry Charm' (Wissing–R. Klehm). A semi-double red hybrid, available from Klehm Nursery.

'Raspberry Ice' (C. G. Klehm 1980). A double rose lactiflora, available from Klehm Nursery; Wayside Gardens; and Anderson Iris.

'Raspberry Rose' (Auten 1956). A Japanese rose hybrid, available from Wild and Son.

'Raspberry Sundae' (C. G. Klehm 1968). A double white and red lactiflora, widely available.

'Ray Payton' (Krekler). A Japanese red lactiflora, available from Klehm Nursery; Hildebrandt's; and Marsal (New Zealand).

'Red Beauty' (Auten 1956). A semi-double red hybrid, available from Peony Gardens (New Zealand).

'Red Bird' (Franklin 1921). A semi-double red lactiflora, available from Busse Gardens.

'Red Carpet' (Wild 1965). A double red lactiflora, available from Wild and Son; Ferncliff Gardens (Canada); and Brickman's (Canada).

'Red Charm' (Glasscock 1944). Gold Medal. A double red hybrid, widely available.

'Red Comet' (Auten 1956). A 'Radiant Red' cross. A double red, available from Caprice Farm; Wild and Son; and Reath's.

'Red Dandy' (Auten 1951). A double red hybrid, available from Hildebrandt's.

'Red Dragon in Red Pool' (ex China via Smirnow). A double red lactiflora, available from von Zeppelin (Germany).

'Red Ensign' (Auten 1940). A semi-double red hybrid, available from Klehm Nursery.

'Red Flag' (origin unknown). A single red lactiflora, available from Kelways (U.K.).

'Red Giant' (Glasscock 1939). A double red lactiflora, available from von Zeppelin (Germany).

'Red Glory' (Auten 1937). A semi-double red hybrid, available from Busse Gardens; A & D Nursery; Wild and Son; and Pivoinerie (France).

'Red Goddess' (Brand 1940). A semi-double red lactiflora, available from Busse Gardens and Brand Peony Farm.

'Red Grace' (Glasscock–R. Klehm 1980). A semi-double red hybrid, available from Klehm Nursery; Cedar Creek (Canada); White Flower Farm; and Hildebrandt's.

'Red Imp' (Krekler). A semi-double red hybrid, available from Klehm Nursery.

'Red Japanese' (origin unknown). A Japanese red lactiflora, available from Viette Farm and Nursery.

'Red Red Rose' (Saunders 1942). A cross between *Paeonia lactiflora* and *P. peregrina*. A semi-double red, available from Caprice Farm; Cedar Creek (Canada); Klehm Nursery; Hollingsworth Peonies; A & D Nursery; and Pivoinerie (France).

'Red Romance' (Auten 1968). A single red hybrid, available from Klose (Germany) and Wild and Son.

'Red Triumph'. See 'Pfeiffer's Red Triumph'

'Reine Deluxe' (R. Klehm). A cross between 'Hoosierland' and 'Mr. Ed'. A double pink, available from Klehm Nursery.

'Reine Hortense' (Calot 1857). A double pink lactiflora, available from Heschke Gardens; Brand Peony Farm; Busse Gardens; Boughen Nurseries (Canada); Maison des Fleurs (Canada); Austin Roses (U.K.); and Pivoinerie (France).

'Reliance' (Glasscock 1950). A double pink lactiflora, available from Reath's.

'Renato' (Murawska 1949). A double red lactiflora, available from Klehm Nursery.

'Requiem' (Saunders 1941). A second-generation hybrid resulting from a cross between *Paeonia lactiflora* and *P. macrophylla*. A single white, widely available.

'Reverend H. N. Traggitt' (Brand 1928). A double white lactiflora, available from Sherman Nursery; Bigger Peonies; Ferncliff Gardens (Canada); and Brickman's (Canada).

'Reward' (Saunders 1941). A cross between *Paeonia lactiflora* and *P. peregrina*. A single red, available from Country Squires (Canada) and Klehm Nursery.

'Richard Carvel' (Brand 1913). A double red lactiflora, widely available.

'Rigolette'. See 'Rigoloto'

'Rigolote'. See 'Rigoloto'

'Rigoloto' (Doriat 1931). A Japanese red lactiflora, available from Pivoinerie (France).

'Rita' (Dessert 1922). A double rose lactiflora, available from Ferncliff Gardens (Canada) and Brickman's (Canada).

'Rivida' (Harrell–Varner 1985). A single lavender lactiflora, available from Caprice Farm; Varner; and Pivoinerie (France).

'Robert W. Auten' (Auten 1948). A semi-double red hybrid, available from Wild and Son; Ferncliff Gardens (Canada); Klehm Nursery; and Brickman's (Canada).

'Roberta' (Auten 1936). A Japanese white lactiflora, available from Wild and Son.

'Romona'. See 'Ramona Lins'

'Rosabel' (Sass 1937). A double red lactiflora, available from Busse Gardens and Sherman Nursery.

'Rose Beauty' (Richmond 1949). A double rose lactiflora, available from Viette Farm and Nursery.

'Rose City' (Marx–Rogers 1981). A Japanese rose lactiflora, available from Caprice Farm.

'Rose Crystal' (Saunders 1955). A second-generation hybrid resulting from a cross between *Paeonia lactiflora* and *P. macrophylla*. A single rose, available from Caprice Farm and Country Squires (Canada).

'Rose Diamond' (Saunders 1943). A cross between *Paeonia lactiflora* and

P. peregrina. A single pink, available from Country Squires (Canada); Ferncliff Gardens (Canada); and Austin Roses (U.K.).

'Rose Garland' (Saunders 1943). A cross between *Paeonia lactiflora* and *P. peregrina*. A single rose, available from Caprice Farm.

'Rose Heart'. See 'Bess Bockstoce'

'Rose Marie' (Auten–Glasscock 1936). A double red hybrid, available from Cedar Creek (Canada) and Marsal (New Zealand).

'Rose of Delight' (origin unknown). A single pink and white lactiflora, available from Kelways (U.K.).

'Rose Pearl' (Bigger). A double pink lactiflora, available from Bigger Peonies and Busse Gardens.

'Rose Queen' (Franklin). A double pink lactiflora, available from Busse Gardens.

'Rose Red' (Franklin). A double red lactiflora, available from Busse Gardens.

'Rose Shaylor' (Shaylor 1920). A double pink lactiflora, available from Reath's.

'Rose Tulip' (Saunders 1947). A cross between *Paeonia lactiflora* and *P. peregrina*. A single pink, available from Viette Farm and Nursery.

'Rose Valley' (Scott 1925). A Japanese pink lactiflora, available from Busse Gardens.

'Rosea'. Offered as a cultivar of *Paeonia officinalis*. A double pink, available from Peony Gardens (New Zealand).

'Rosea'. Offered as a cultivar of *Paeonia tenuifolia*. A single pink, available from Klose (Germany) and Pivoinerie (France).

'Rosea Plena'. Offered as a cultivar of *Paeonia officinalis*. A double pink, widely available.

'Rosea Superba' (origin unknown). A double pink lactiflora, available from Ferncliff Gardens (Canada).

'Rosea Superba'. Offered as a cultivar of *Paeonia officinalis*. A double pink, available from Viette Farm and Nursery.

'Rosedale' (Auten 1936). A double or semi-double rose hybrid, widely available.

'Roselette' (Saunders 1950). Descended from *Paeonia lactiflora*, *P. mlokosewitschii*, and *P. tenuifolia* crosses. A single pink, available from Busse Gardens; Hollingsworth Peonies; Caprice Farm; Austin Roses (U.K.); Klehm Nursery; and Pivoinerie (France).

'Roselette's Child' (Saunders 1967). A single pink hybrid, available from Marsal (New Zealand).

'Rosy Cheek' (Saunders 1943). A cross between *Paeonia lactiflora* and *P. peregrina*. A semi-double rose, available from Cedar Creek (Canada); Caprice Farm; and Busse Gardens.

'Rosy Dawn' (Barr). A single white lactiflora, available from New Peony Farm and Bluebird Nursery.

'Rosy Wreath' (Saunders 1941). A cross between *Paeonia lactiflora* and *P. peregrina*. A single rose, available from Busse Gardens.

'Royal Charter' (Wild 1966). A double red lactiflora, available from Wild and Son; Ferncliff Gardens (Canada); and Brickman's (Canada).

'Royal Rose' (Reath 1980). A cross between 'Moonrise' and 'Paula Fay'. A semi-double pink, available from Caprice Farm and Reath's.

'Rozella' (Reath 1991). A double rose lactiflora, available from Reath's.

'Rubens' (Delache 1854). A double red lactiflora, available form Pivoinerie (France).

'Rubio' (Nicholls 1941). A double red lactiflora, available from Busse Gardens.

'Rubra'. Offered as a cultivar of *Paeonia officinalis*. A double red, available from Brand Peony Farm.

'Rubra Flora Plena'. Offered as a cultivar of *Paeonia tenuifolia*. A double red, available from Busse Gardens; Wayside Gardens; and Heschke Gardens.

'Rubra Plena'. Offered as a cultivar of *Paeonia officinalis*. A double red, widely available.

'Rubra Plena'. Offered as a cultivar of *Paeonia tenuifolia*. A double red, available from Busse Gardens; Wayside Gardens; and Heschke Gardens.

'Rubyette' (Wissing–R. Klehm 1992). A single red hybrid, available from Klehm Nursery.

'Rushlight' (Saunders 1950). Descended from *Paeonia lactiflora*, *P. mlokosewitschii*, and *P. tenuifolia* crosses. A single white, available from Cedar Creek (Canada) and Viette Farm and Nursery.

'Ruth Clay' (Kelsey 1935). A double red lactiflora, available from Bluebird Nursery; Country Squires (Canada); and Sheridan Nurseries (Canada).

'Ruth Cobb' (Wild 1963). A double pink lactiflora, available from Wild and Son.

'Ruth Elizabeth' (Brand 1936). A double red lactiflora, available from New Peony Farm; Busse Gardens; and Brand Peony Farm.

'Sagamore' (Jones 1943). A Japanese blush lactiflora, available from Busse Gardens.

'Salmon Chiffon' (Rudolph–R. Klehm 1981). A single pink hybrid, available from Klehm Nursery and Viette Farm and Nursery.

'Salmon Glory' (Glasscock 1947). A double pink hybrid, available from Klehm Nursery.

'Salmon Glow' (Glasscock 1947). A cross between *Paeonia lactiflora* and *P. peregrina*. A single pink, available from Caprice Farm; Sherman Nursery; Cedar Creek (Canada); and Pivoinerie (France).

'Salmon Surprise' (Cousins–R. Klehm 1986). A single pink hybrid, available from Klehm Nursery.

'Sam Donaldson' (Brand 1943). A double red lactiflora, available from Brand Peony Farm; Ferncliff Gardens (Canada); and Harrison's (Canada).

'Sambo' (Auten 1950). A double red hybrid, available from Hildebrandt's and Klehm Nursery.

'Sanctus' (Saunders 1952–1955). An advanced-generation, single white hybrid, available from A & D Nursery; Caprice Farm; and Rivière (France).

'Sang Gaulois' (A. Rivière 1958). A double red lactiflora, available from Pivoinerie (France).

'Santa Fe' (Auten 1937). A double red lactiflora, available from Hildebrandt's and Austin Roses (U.K.).

'Sarah Bernhardt' (Lemoine 1906). A double pink lactiflora, widely available.

'Sarah M. Napier' (Vories 1930). A double red lactiflora, available from Bigger Peonies.

'Sarah Napier'. See 'Sarah M. Napier'

'Saunders 4992' (Saunders). A single red hybrid, available from Klehm Nursery.

'Scarlet O'Hara' (Glasscock–Falk 1956). A single red hybrid, widely available.

'Scarlet Tanager' (Saunders 1942). A cross between *Paeonia officinalis* and *P. peregrina*. A single red, available from Cedar Creek (Canada).

'Schaffe' (Krekler 1965). A double pink lactiflora, available from Klehm Nursery.

'Schwindt' (Goos–Koenemann 1910). A single pink lactiflora, available from Klose (Germany).

'Sea Shell' (Sass 1937). Gold Medal. A single pink lactiflora, widely available.

'Seraphim' (Saunders 1929). A cross between *Paeonia lactiflora* and *P. macrophylla*. A single white, available from Caprice Farm and A & D Nursery.

'Shannon' (Brown 1952). A double pink lactiflora, available from Country Squires (Canada).

'Shawnee Chief' (Bigger 1940). A double red, widely available.

'Shawnee Rose' (Bigger 1979). A double pink lactiflora, available from New Peony Farm and Bigger Peonies.

'Shaylor's Sunburst' (Allison 1931). A Japanese white lactiflora, available from Ferncliff Gardens (Canada); Brickman's (Canada); Country Squires (Canada); and Klehm Nursery.

'Shell Pink' (Saunders 1939). A single pink hybrid, available from Country Squires (Canada).

'Sheyenne Chief' (Gilbertson 1981). A double red lactiflora, available from Brand Peony Farm.

'Shirley Temple' (origin unknown). A double blush lactiflora, widely available.

'Show Girl' (Hollingsworth 1984). A cross between 'Dawn Pink' and 'Echo'. A Japanese pink, available from Hollingsworth Peonies and Caprice Farm.

'Siam' (origin unknown). A double pink lactiflora, available from Marsal (New Zealand).

'Siloam' (Auten 1933). A single white lactiflora, available from Busse Gardens.

'Silver Daubed' (Krekler 1977). A double pink lactiflora, available from Klehm Nursery.

'Silver Shell' (Wild 1962). A double white lactiflora, available from Wild and Son.

'Silvia Saunders' (Saunders 1921). Not registered. A semi-double white lactiflora, available from Viette Farm and Nursery.

'Simplex'. Offered as a cultivar of *Paeonia tenuifolia*. A single red, available from New Peony Farm and Pivoinerie (France).

'Sioux Chief' (Gilbertson 1984). A single red lactiflora, available from Brand Peony Farm.

'Sir Edward Elgar' (Kelway). A single red lactiflora, available from Kelways (U.K.).

'Sir John Franklin' (Franklin 1939). A double red lactiflora, available from Anderson Iris and Busse Gardens.

'Sister Margaret' (Cooper–Wild 1953). A double white lactiflora, available from Wild and Son.

'Sitka' (Auten 1945). A Japanese white lactiflora, available from White Flower Farm; Sunny Border Nursery; Wild and Son; Ferncliff Gardens (Canada); von Zeppelin (Germany); and Brickman's (Canada).

'Sky Pilot' (Auten 1939). A Japanese pink lactiflora, available from Viette Farm and Nursery; A & D Nursery; and Klose (Germany).

'Skylark' (Saunders 1942). A cross between *Paeonia lactiflora* and *P. peregrina*. A single pink, available from Caprice Farm.

'Smouthi' (Smout–Malines 1843). A cross between *Paeonia lactiflora* and *P. tenuifolia*. A double red, available from Brand Peony Farm.

'Snow Mountain' (Bigger 1946). A double white lactiflora, available from Busse Gardens; Carroll Gardens; Wild and Son; Anderson Iris; A & D Nursery; Bigger Peonies; and Heschke Gardens.

'Snow Princess' (R. Klehm). A 'Bowl of Cream' cross. A semi-double white, available from Klehm Nursery.

'Snow Swan' (R. Klehm 1987). A single white lactiflora, available from Klehm Nursery.

'Solange' (Lemoine 1907). A double blush lactiflora, available from Homestead Nurseries (Canada); Klose (Germany); Ferncliff Gardens (Canada); Cruickshank's (Canada); Rivière (France); and Pivoinerie (France).

'Solfatare' (Calot 1861). A double white lactiflora, available from Pivoinerie (France).

'Solo Flight' (Saunders 1935). A Japanese blush lactiflora, available from Tischler Peony Garden.

'Sophie' (Saunders 1940). A cross between *Paeonia lactiflora* and *P. peregrina*. A semi-double pink, available from Peony Gardens (New Zealand).

'Souvenir d'A. Millet' (Millet 1924). A double red lactiflora, available from Pivoinerie (France).

'Souvenir de Louis Bigot' (Dessert 1913). A double rose lactiflora, available from A & D Nursery; Maison des Fleurs (Canada); Cedar Creek (Canada); and Pivoinerie (France).

'Sparkling Star' (Bigger 1953). An anemone or Japanese pink lactiflora, available from Bigger Peonies and Busse Gardens.

'Sparkling Windflower' (Saunders–Reath 1971). A single red hybrid, available from Caprice Farm.

'Spell Binder'. See 'Spellbinder'

'Spellbinder' (Bigger 1960). A single white lactiflora, available from Bigger Peonies; Craigmore (New Zealand); and Klehm Nursery.

'Splendida' (Guerin 1850). A double pink lactiflora, available from Brand Peony Farm and New Peony Farm.

'Spring Beauty' (Nicholls 1933). A semi-double or double pink lactiflora, available from Craigmore (New Zealand) and Marsal (New Zealand).

'Springfield' (Krekler 1962). A double pink lactiflora, available from Klehm Nursery and White Flower Farm.

'Sprite' (Saunders 1950). An advanced-generation hybrid descended from *Paeonia lactiflora*, *P. mlokosewitschii*, and *P. tenuifolia* crosses. A single white and rose, available from Cedar Creek (Canada).

'Stardust' (Glasscock–Falk 1964). Descended from 'Le Cygne'. A single white, available from Reath's; Sherman Nursery; Caprice Farm; and Klehm Nursery.

'Starlight' (Saunders 1949). Descended from *Paeonia lactiflora*, *P. macrophylla*, *P. mlokosewitschii*, and *P. peregrina* crosses. A single yellow, widely available.

'Strawberry Ripple' (Bigger 1979). A double white and red lactiflora, available from New Peony Farm.

'Strephon' (Kelway). A single rose lactiflora, available from Kelways (U.K.).

'Sugar n' Spice' (Rogers 1988). An advanced-generation, single or semi-double pink hybrid, available from Caprice Farm.

'Summer Snow' (origin unknown). A single white hybrid, available from Sherman Nursery.

'Sunbright' (Glasscock). A cross between *Paeonia lactiflora* and *P. peregrina*. A single red, available from Klehm Nursery and Reath's.

'Sunburst'. See 'Shaylor's Sunburst'

'Sunlight' (Saunders 1950). Descended from *Paeonia lactiflora*, *P. macrophylla*, *P. mlokosewitschii*, and *P. peregrina* crosses. A single yellow, available from American Daylily; Caprice Farm; and Pivoinerie (France).

'Sunny Side Up' (Bigger 1979). A Japanese white lactiflora, available from Bigger Peonies.

'Super Glow' (Hollingsworth 1992). A double yellow hybrid, available from Hollingsworth Peonies.

'Superior' (Reath 1984). A *Paeonia lactiflora* cross. A single pink available from A & D Nursery and Reath's.

'Suruga' (origin unknown). A single red lactiflora, available from Klose (Germany); Country Squires (Canada); and Maison des Fleurs (Canada).

'Susan B. White' (Brand 1933). A double white lactiflora, available from Brand Peony Farm.

'Susie Q' (C. G. Klehm). A double pink lactiflora, available from Klehm Nursery; Adamgrove; Busse Gardens; Wayside Gardens; White Flower Farm; Hildebrandt's; and Peony Gardens (New Zealand).

'Susie Smith' (Brown 1950). A Japanese pink lactiflora, available from Country Squires (Canada).

'Sweet 16' (C. G. Klehm). A double pink lactiflora, available from White Flower Farm; Hildebrandt's; A & D Nursery; Peony Gardens (New Zealand); Terrace Peonies (New Zealand); Austin Roses (U.K.); and Klehm Nursery.

'Sweet May' (Saunders 1955). Descended from *Paeonia lactiflora*, *P. macrophylla*, *P. mlokosewitschii*, and *P. peregrina* crosses. A single pink, available from Caprice Farm.

'Sweet Melody' (Hollingsworth 1992). A semi-double pink lactiflora, available from Hollingsworth Peonies.

'Sweet Sixteen'. See 'Sweet 16'

'Sword Dance' (Auten 1933). A Japanese red lactiflora, available from Carroll Gardens; Viette Farm and Nursery; Hollingsworth Peonies; Ferncliff Gardens (Canada); Brickman's (Canada); and Klehm Nursery.

'Sylvia Saunders'. See 'Silvia Saunders'

'Tamate-Boku' (origin unknown). A Japanese pink lactiflora, available from Country Squires (Canada) and Maison des Fleurs (Canada).

'Tango' (Auten 1956). A single red lactiflora, available from Viette Farm and Nursery and Klehm Nursery.

'Tel Star' (Auten). A double red lactiflora, available from Klehm Nursery.

'Tempest' (Auten 1931). A semi-double red lactiflora, available from New Peony Farm; Hollingsworth Peonies; Sherman Nursery; and Country Squires (Canada).

'Terry Grudem' (Brand 1963). A Japanese red lactiflora, available from Brand Peony Farm; A & D Nursery; and Tischler Peony Garden.

'The Admiral' (Franklin 1940). A double white lactiflora, available from Busse Gardens and Wild and Son.

'The Belgian' (origin unknown). A single red hybrid, available from Viette Farm and Nursery.

'The Fawn' (Wright). A double pink lactiflora, available from Klehm Nursery.

'The Mighty Mo' (Wild 1950). A double red lactiflora, widely available.

'Therese' (Dessert 1904). A double pink lactiflora, available from Bluebird Nursery; Bluemount Nurseries; Ferncliff Gardens (Canada); and Brickman's (Canada).

'Thura Hires' (Nicholls 1938). A double white lactiflora, available from Busse Gardens; Klose (Germany); Wild and Son; and Cedar Creek (Canada).

'Tinkerbelle' (Krekler–R. Klehm). A single pink hybrid, available from Klehm Nursery.

'Tish' (Tischler 1980). A Japanese red lactiflora, available from Tischler Peony Garden and Caprice Farm.

'To Kalon' (Kelsey 1936). A double white lactiflora, available from Busse Gardens and Heschke Gardens.

'Tokio' (origin unknown pre-1910). A Japanese pink lactiflora, available from Brand Peony Farm; Tischler Peony Garden; Klose (Germany); and Ferncliff Gardens (Canada).

'Tom Eckhardt' (Krekler 1965). A Japanese pink lactiflora, available from Pivoinerie (France) and Klehm Nursery.

'Tondeleyo' (Lins 1942). A double pink lactiflora, available from Anderson Iris.

'Top Brass' (C. G. Klehm 1968). Linebred 'Charlie's White'. A double white, widely available.

'Top Hat' (Reynolds 1971). A Japanese red lactiflora, available from Busse Gardens.

'Topeka Coral' (Cousins–Bigger 1975). A double pink hybrid, available from Klehm Nursery.

'Topeka Garnet' (Bigger 1975). A single red lactiflora, available from New Peony Farm and Bigger Peonies.

'Torchsong' (origin unknown). A double red lactiflora, available from Ferncliff Gardens (Canada).

'Toro-No-Maki' (origin unknown pre-1928). A Japanese white lactiflora, available from Brand Peony Farm; Tischler Peony Garden; A & D Nursery; Klehm Nursery; Klose (Germany); Wild and Son; and Pivoinerie (France).

'Torpilleur' (Dessert 1913). A single red lactiflora, available from Kelways (U.K.); Klose (Germany); Terrace Peonies (New Zealand); and Pivoinerie (France).

'Tourangelle' (Dessert 1910). A double pink lactiflora, widely available.

'Trafford W. Bigger' (Bigger 1966). A Japanese red lactiflora, available from Bigger Peonies.

'Triomphe de l'Exposition de Lille' (Calot 1865). A double pink lactiflora, available from Gärtnerei und Staudenkulturen (Switzerland).

'Truly Yours' (Nicholls–Wild). A double pink lactiflora, available from Wild and Son.

'Truth' (Bigger 1968). A double white lactiflora, available from Bigger Peonies.

'Umbellata Rosea' (Dessert 1895). A double pink lactiflora, available from Busse Gardens.

'Uncle Tom' (Auten 1951). A semi-double red lactiflora, available from Wild and Son.

'Unknown Soldier' (origin unknown). A double red lactiflora, available from Ferncliff Gardens (Canada).

'Up Front' (Bigger 1970). A double pink lactiflora, available from Bigger Peonies.

'Valor' (Saunders 1939). A semi-double pink lactiflora, available from Busse Gardens.

'Valour'. See 'Valor'

'Vanity' (Brand 1951). A Japanese pink lactiflora, available from New Peony Farm and Tischler Peony Garden.

'Velvet Princess' (Bigger 1977). A 'Radiant Red' cross. A Japanese red, available from Bigger Peonies.

'Victoire de la Marne' (Dessert 1915). A double red lactiflora, widely available.

'Victoria Lincoln' (Saunders 1938). A cross between *Paeonia lactiflora* and *P. peregrina* 'Otto Froebel'. A semi-double or double pink, available from Cedar Creek (Canada).

'Victory' (Thompson 1944). A double white lactiflora, available from Busse Gardens and Anderson Iris.

'Victory Chateau Thierry' (Brand 1925). A double pink lactiflora, available from Brand Peony Farm; Viette Farm and Nursery; and Busse Gardens.

'Viette's Japanese White' (Viette). A Japanese white lactiflora, available from Viette Farm and Nursery.

'Viking Chief' (Krekler–R. Klehm). A semi-double pink lactiflora, available from Klehm Nursery.

'Ville de Nancy' (Calot 1872). A double rose lactiflora, available from von Zeppelin (Germany).

'Violet Dawson' (R. Klehm 1991). A third-generation, linebred 'Bowl of Cream'. A Japanese white, available from Klehm Nursery.

'Virginia Dare' (Newhouse 1939). A single white lactiflora, available from Busse Gardens and Klehm Nursery.

'Virginia Lee' (Auten 1939). A double blush lactiflora, available from Viette Farm and Nursery.

'Vivid Glow' (Cousins–R. Klehm pre-1988). A single pink hybrid, available from Klehm Nursery.

'Vivid Rose' (C. G. Klehm 1952). A double rose lactiflora, available from Caprice Farm; Klehm Nursery; Bluebird Nursery; Hildebrandt's; A & D Nursery; and Peony Gardens (New Zealand).

'Vogue' (Hoogendoorn 1949). A double pink lactiflora, available from New Peony Farm and Austin Roses (U.K.).

'W. F. Turner'. See 'William F. Turner'

'Walter E. Wipsom' (Murawska 1956). A cross between 'Frances Willard' and 'Le Cygne'. A double white, available from Reath's and Caprice Farm.

'Walter Faxon' (Richardson 1904). A double rose lactiflora, widely available.

'Walter Mains' (Mains 1957). Gold Medal. A Japanese red hybrid, available from Busse Gardens; Tischler Peony Garden; Bigger Peonies; and Cedar Creek (Canada).

'Walter Marx' (Marx–Rogers 1981). A single white lactiflora, available from Caprice Farm.

'Ward Welsh' (Neeley 1929). A double white lactiflora, available from Busse Gardens.

'Washington' (Guerin 1850). A double pink lactiflora, available from Pivoinerie (France).

'Waterlily'. See 'Marie Jacquin'

'Weisbaden' (Goos–Koenemann 1911). A double pink lactiflora, available from Austin Roses (U.K.); Klose (Germany); and Pivoinerie (France).

'West Elkton' (Krekler 1958). A Japanese red lactiflora, available from Peony Gardens (New Zealand); Heschke Gardens; and Klehm Nursery.

'West Hill' (Little 1938). A double pink lactiflora, available from Busse Gardens.

'Westerner' (Bigger 1942). Gold Medal. A Japanese pink lactiflora, widely available.

'White Cap' (Winchell 1956). Gold Medal. A Japanese rose lactiflora, available from Klehm Nursery; Hildebrandt's; Wild and Son; A & D Nursery; and Bigger Peonies.

'White Eagle' (Sass 1937). A double white lactiflora, available from Sherman Nursery.

'White Frost' (Reath 1991). A double white lactiflora, available from Reath's.

'White Gold' (Mann–van Steen 1936). A Japanese white lactiflora, available from Klehm Nursery.

'White Innocence' (Saunders 1947). A cross between *Paeonia emodi* and *P. lactiflora*. A single white, widely available.

'White Ivory' (R. Klehm 1981). Linebred 'Charlie's White'. A double white, available from Klehm Nursery and Viette Farm and Nursery.

'White Perfection' (Auten 1931). A single white lactiflora, available from Reath's and Bigger Peonies.

'White Sands' (Wild 1968). A Japanese white lactiflora, available from Carroll Gardens; Hollingsworth Peonies; A & D Nursery; Wild and Son; Caprice Farm; and Ferncliff Gardens (Canada).

'White Wings' (Hoogendoorn 1949). A single white lactiflora, available from Kelways (U.K.); Busse Gardens; Austin Roses (U.K.); Craigmore (New Zealand); Klehm Nursery; and Marsal (New Zealand).

'Whopper' (C. G. Klehm 1980). A 'Mons. Jules Elie' cross. A double pink, available from A & D Nursery; Klehm Nursery; Viette Farm and Nursery; and Hildebrandt's.

'Wilbur Wright' (Kelway 1909). A single red lactiflora, available from Klose (Germany).

'Wilford Johnson' (Brand 1966). A double rose lactiflora, available from Reath's; Caprice Farm; and Brand Peony Farm.

'William Cousins' (Cousins 1968). A double red lactiflora, available from Hildebrandt's.

'William F. Turner' (Shaylor 1916). A double red lactiflora, available from Pivoinerie (France).

'William Pickett' (origin unknown). A double white lactiflora, available from Tischler Peony Garden and Brand Peony Farm.

'Wind Chimes'. See 'Windchimes'

'Windchimes' (Reath 1984). A *Paeonia tenuifolia* cross. A single pink, available from Reath's and Klehm Nursery.

'Wine Red' (Gilbertson 1974). A double red lactiflora, available from New Peony Farm and Brand Peony Farm.

'Winged Victory' (Saunders 1950). Descended from *Paeonia lactiflora*, *P. macrophylla*, *P. mlokosewitschii*, and *P. peregrina* crosses. A single rose, available from Anderson Iris.

'Winnifred Domme' (Brand 1913). A double red lactiflora, available from New Peony Farm and Brand Peony Farm.

'Woodwardii'. Offered as a cultivar of *Paeonia veitchii*. A double red, available from Austin Roses (U.K.) and Caprice Farm.

'Wrinkles and Krinkles' (Wild 1971). A double pink lactiflora, available from Brand Peony Farm; Wild and Son; and American Daylily.

'Yellow King' (via Harding). A Japanese pink lactiflora, available from Wild and Son; Busse Gardens; and Ferncliff Gardens (Canada).

'Your Majesty' (Saunders 1947). A cross between *Paeonia lactiflora* and *P. peregrina*. A single red, available from Wild and Son.

'Zelda Gilbertson' (Gilbertson 1981). A double pink lactiflora, available from Brand Peony Farm.

'Zenith' (Krekler). A double pink lactiflora, available from Klehm Nursery.

'Zuzu' (Krekler 1955). A semi-double pink lactiflora, available from Klehm Nursery.

SUFFRUTICOSA TREE PEONY CULTIVARS

'Amateur Forest' (A. Rivière 1935). A semi-double rose suffruticosa, available from Rivière (France).

'Arahi No Sora' (ex Japan 1896). A double pink suffruticosa, available from Pivoinerie (France).

'Arashi-yama' (ex Japan). A double pink suffruticosa, available from Pivoin-
    erie (France).
'Asahi Yama'. See 'Arashi-yama'

'Baronne d'Ales' (Gombault). A double pink suffruticosa, available from
    Rivière (France).
'Beauty of Tokyo' (ex Japan). A single red suffruticosa, available from Riv-
    ière (France).
'Belle d'Orleans' (ex France). A double rose suffruticosa, Rivière (France).
'Best Student of Peonies' (ex China). A semi-double red suffruticosa, availa-
    ble from Cricket Hill.
'Big Deep Purple' (ex China). A double red-purple suffruticosa, available
    from Cricket Hill.

'Carnea Plena' (ex France). A double blush suffruticosa, available from
    Rivière (France).
'Caroline of Italy' (origin unknown pre-1846). A double red suffruticosa,
    available from Rivière (France).
'Charming Age'. See 'Howki'
'Choraku' (ex Japan). A single pink suffruticosa, available from Pivoinerie
    (France).
'Companion of Serenity' (Gratwick 1959). A single pink suffruticosa, avail-
    able from Reath's; Klehm Nursery; and Craigmore (New Zealand).
'Comtesse de Tuder' (origin unknown pre-1866). A double pink suffruti-
    cosa, available from Rivière (France).

'Duchesse de Morny' (ex France pre-1955). A double pink suffruticosa,
    available from Rivière (France).

'Eternal Camellias'. See 'Yachiyo-tsubaki'
'Eugene Verdier' (ex France). A double pink suffruticosa, available from
    Rivière (France).
'Ezra Pound' (Gratwick). Originally called 'Mistress of the Monastery'. A
    single or semi-double pink suffruticosa, available from Klehm Nursery.

'Feng dan bai' (ex China). A single white suffruticosa, available from Heze-
    Beijing (P.R.C.) and Piroche Plants (Canada).
'Flight of Cranes'. See 'Renkaku'

'Flora' (ex Japan). A single white suffruticosa, available from Rivière (France).

'Flower Rivalry'. See 'Hanakisoi'

'Fragrans Maxima Plena' (ex France pre-1955). A double pink suffruticosa, available from Rivière (France).

'Fuji No Mine' (ex Japan). A semi-double white suffruticosa, available from Pivoinerie (France).

'Gengioraku'. See 'Genjoraku'

'Genjoraku' (ex Japan). A semi-double white suffruticosa, available from Rivière (France).

'Georges Paul' (Seneclauze pre-1886). A double purple suffruticosa, available from Rivière (France).

'Gessekai' (ex Japan). Also sold as 'Kingdom of the Moon'. A semi-double or double white suffruticosa, available from Klehm Nursery; Reath's; and Austin Roses (U.K.).

'Godaishu' (ex Japan). A semi-double white suffruticosa, available from Craigmore (New Zealand); Rivière (France); Pivoinerie (France); and Piroche Plants (Canada).

'Goshozakura' (ex Japan). A semi-double pink suffruticosa, available from Pivoinerie (France).

'Green Dragon Lying in a Black Pool' (ex China). A semi-double rose suffruticosa, available from Cricket Hill.

'Guardian of the Monastery' (Gratwick 1959). A single lavender suffruticosa, available from Klehm Nursery and Reath's.

'Gunphoden' (ex Japan). A semi-double pink suffruticosa, available from Reath's.

'Haku Benru'. See 'Hakubanryu'

'Hakubanryu' (ex Japan). A semi-double white suffruticosa, available from Klehm Nursery and Rivière (France).

'Hakugan' (ex Japan). A single or semi-double white suffruticosa, available from Rivière (France).

'Hakuo Jishi'. See 'Hakuojishi'

'Hakuojishi' (ex Japan). Also sold as 'King of White Lion'. A semi-double white suffruticosa, available from Rivière (France); Pivoinerie (France); and Austin Roses (U.K.).

'Hana Daijin'. See 'Hanadaijin'

'Hana Kisoi'. See 'Hanakisoi'

'Hanadaijin' (ex Japan pre-1910). Also sold as 'Magnificent Flower'. A semi-double purple suffruticosa, available from Reath's; Rivière (France); Pivoinerie (France); Piroche Plants (Canada); and Austin Roses (U.K.).

'Hanakisoi' (ex Japan 1926). Also sold as 'Flower Rivalry'. A semi-double pink suffruticosa, widely available.

'Hatsu Garashu'. See 'Hatsugarashu'

'Hatsugarashu' (ex Japan pre-1929). A single red suffruticosa, available from Rivière (France).

'Higurashi' (ex Japan pre-1929). A single red suffruticosa, available from Rivière (France).

'Higure' (ex Japan). A double pink suffruticosa, available from Klehm Nursery and Reath's.

'Hinode-sekai' (ex Japan). A semi-double red suffruticosa, available from Klehm Nursery and Pivoinerie (France).

'Hinode-Seki'. See 'Hinode-sekai'

'Hisiana Alba' (Mouchelet). A semi-double white suffruticosa, available from Rivière (France).

'Hoki' (ex Japan). A semi-double red suffruticosa, available from Reath's and Pivoinerie (France).

'Hooki'. See 'Hoki'

'Horakumon' (ex Japan). A semi-double lavender-red suffruticosa, available from Klehm Nursery.

'Howki' (ex Japan). Also sold as 'Charming Age'. A double red suffruticosa, available from Klehm Nursery and Austin Roses (U.K.).

'Hu Hong' (ex China). A double pink suffruticosa, available from Heze-Beijing (P.R.C.).

'Hu's Family Red' (ex China). A semi-double red suffruticosa, available from Cricket Hill.

'Imitation of a Lotus Flower' (ex China). A semi-double pink-rose suffruticosa, available from Cricket Hill.

'Intoxicated Celestial Peach' (ex China). A double pink suffruticosa, available from Cricket Hill.

'Isabelle Rivière' (A. Rivière 1975). A single red suffruticosa, available from Rivière (France).

'Itaou' (ex Japan). A single or double red suffruticosa, available from Piroche Plants (Canada).

'Iwato-kagami' (ex Japan pre-1895). A semi-double pink-red suffruticosa, available from Reath's and Pivoinerie (France).

'Jealousy of One Hundred Flowers' (ex China). A double red suffruticosa, available from Cricket Hill.
'Jeanne d'Arc' (Seneclauze pre-1889). A double pink suffruticosa, available from Rivière (France).
'Jewelled Screen'. See 'Tama Sudare'
'Jitsu Getsu-nishiki'. See 'Jitsugetsu-nishiki'
'Jitsugetsu-nishiki' (ex Japan pre-1927). A semi-double red suffruticosa, available from Rivière (France).

'Kamada Brocade'. See 'Kamata-nishiki'
'Kamada Fuji'. See 'Kamata-fuji'
'Kamada Nishiki'. See 'Kamata-nishiki'
'Kamata-fuji' (ex Japan pre-1893). A double purple suffruticosa, available from Reath's.
'Kamata-nishiki' (ex Japan 1893). Also sold as 'Kamada Brocade'. A semi-double purple suffruticosa, available from Klehm Nursery; Reath's; Rivière (France); Pivoinerie (France); and Austin Roses (U.K.).
'Kao'. See 'Kaow'
'Kao's Cap Purple' (ex China). A double purple suffruticosa, available from Cricket Hill.
'Kaow' (ex Japan). Also sold as 'King of Flowers'. A semi-double red suffruticosa, available from Rivière (France); Pivoinerie (France); Austin Roses (U.K.); and Reath's.
'Kikubotan' (ex Japan pre-1919). A semi-double rose suffruticosa, available from Rivière (France).
'King of Flowers'. See 'Kaow'
'King of White Lion'. See 'Hakuojishi'
'Kingdom of the Moon'. See 'Gessekai'
'Kinpukurin' (ex Japan). A single red suffruticosa, available from Rivière (France).
'Kirin No Tsuka' (ex Japan 1892). A double red suffruticosa, available from Pivoinerie (France).
'Kishu Caprice' (ex Japan via Rogers 1991). A double pink suffruticosa, available from Caprice Farm.
'Koikagura' (ex Japan pre-1926). A semi-double red suffruticosa, available from Pivoinerie (France).

'Kokamon' (ex Japan). A semi-double red suffruticosa, available from Klehm Nursery.

'Kokuryu Nishiki'. See 'Kokuryu-nishiki'

'Kokuryu-nishiki' (ex Japan pre-1905). A semi-double purple suffruticosa, available from Pivoinerie (France) and Rivière (France).

'Kumagai' (ex Japan). A double red suffruticosa, available from Pivoinerie (France).

'Lactea' (David or Guerin 1839). A double white suffruticosa, available from Rivière (France).

'Lady of the Lake'. See 'Lilith'

'Lambertiana' (Makoy). A double purple suffruticosa, available from Rivière (France).

'Lilith' (Gratwick). Originally called 'Lady of the Lake'. A single pink suffruticosa, available from Klehm Nursery.

'Louise Mouchelet' (Mouchelet 1860). A double pink suffruticosa, available from Rivière (France).

'Madame Andre de Villers' (A. Rivière 1955). A double rose suffruticosa, available from Klehm Nursery and Rivière (France).

'Madame Emile Joubert' (M. Rivière 1990). A double rose suffruticosa, available from Rivière (France).

'Madame Victor Gillier' (ex France 1899). A double pink suffruticosa, available from Rivière (France).

'Magnificent Flower'. See 'Hanadaijin'

'Mistress of the Monastery'. See 'Ezra Pound'

'Mizukage' (ex Japan). A single rose suffruticosa, available from Rivière (France).

'Mont Vesuve' (Seneclauze pre-1899). A double red suffruticosa, available from Rivière (France).

'Naniwa Brocade'. See 'Naniwa-nishiki'

'Naniwa Nishiki'. See 'Naniwa-nishiki'

'Naniwa-nishiki' (ex Japan pre-1929). Also sold as 'Naniwa Brocade.' A semi-double rose suffruticosa, available from Reath's; Rivière (France); and Austin Roses (U.K.).

'Nigata Tenn'yionomai'. See 'Niigata Ten'nyonomai'

'Nihonko' (ex Japan). A semi-double rose suffruticosa, available from Rivière (France).

'Niigata Ten'nyonomai' (ex Japan). A semi-double pink suffruticosa, available from Rivière (France).

'Nishigetsunishiki' (ex Japan). A single or semi-double red suffruticosa, available from Pivoinerie (France).

'Nishoo' (ex Japan 1934). A semi-double pink suffruticosa, available from Pivoinerie (France).

'Ohfujinishiki' (ex Japan). A single or semi-double purple suffruticosa, available from Pivoinerie (France) and Rivière (France).

'Osirus' (origin unknown). A double purple suffruticosa, available from Rivière (France).

'Palace of Gems'. See 'Shugugyokuden'

'Pride of Taishow Dynasty'. See 'Taishono-hikari'

'Prince de Troubetskoy' (Guerin). A double purple suffruticosa, available from Rivière (France).

'Princess Amelie' (ex France). A single purple suffruticosa, available from Rivière (France).

'Reine des Violettes' (ex China). A double purple suffruticosa, available from Rivière (France).

'Reine Elisabeth' (origin unknown pre-1846). A double rose suffruticosa, available from Rivière (France) and Craigmore (New Zealand).

'Renkaku' (ex Japan 1931). Also sold as 'Flight of Cranes'. A semi-double white suffruticosa, available from Austin Roses (U.K.); Klehm Nursery; Reath's; Craigmore (New Zealand); Rivière (France); and Pivoinerie (France).

'Rimpou' (ex Japan pre-1926). A double purple suffruticosa, available from Rivière (France).

'Sahohime' (ex Japan). A semi-double blush suffruticosa, available from Pivoinerie (France).

'Samarang' (origin unknown). A double red suffruticosa, available from Rivière (France).

'Savii' (ex France). A double pink suffruticosa, available from Rivière (France).

'Saygio-Sakura' (ex Japan). A semi-double red suffruticosa, available from Rivière (France).

'Seven Gods of Fortune'. See 'Shichifukujin'

'Shendan lu' (ex China). A single or double pink suffruticosa, available from Piroche Plants (Canada).

'Shen's Brilliant' (ex China). A double pink suffruticosa, available from Cricket Hill.

'Shichifukujin' (ex Japan 1896). Also sold as 'Seven Gods of Fortune'. A semi-double pink suffruticosa, available from Rivière (France) and Pivoinerie (France).

'Shima Daijin'. See 'Shimadaigin'

'Shimadaigin' (ex Japan). A semi-double purple suffruticosa, available from Reath's.

'Shin Kumagai' (ex Japan pre-1926). A double purple suffruticosa, available from Pivoinerie (France).

'Shinkumagai'. See 'Shin Kumagai'

'Shintenchi' (ex Japan pre-1931). A semi-double pink suffruticosa, available from Klehm Nursery and Reath's.

'Shiuden' (ex Japan). A double purple suffruticosa, available from Rivière (France).

'Shugugyokuden' (ex Japan). Also sold as 'Palace of Gems'. A semi-double red suffruticosa, available from Austin Roses (U.K.).

'Souvenir de Madame Knorr' (van Houtte 1853). A double pink suffruticosa, available from Rivière (France).

'Stolen Heaven' (Smirnow). A semi-double white suffruticosa, available from Reath's.

'Sylphide' (M. Rivière 1992). A single red suffruticosa, available from Rivière (France).

'Syun Koo Den' (ex Japan 1935). A double lavender suffruticosa, available from Pivoinerie (France).

'Taisho No Hikari'. See 'Taishono-hikari'

'Taishono-hikari' (ex Japan 1936). Also sold as 'Pride of Taishow Dynasty'. A semi-double or double red suffruticosa, available from Pivoinerie (France) and Austin Roses (U.K.).

'Taiyo' (ex Japan pre-1931). A semi-double red suffruticosa, available from Reath's; Klehm Nursery; and Rivière (France).

'Tama Fuyo'. See 'Tamafuyo'

'Tama Sudare' (ex Japan). Also sold as 'Jewelled Screen'. A semi-double white suffruticosa, available from Reath's; Pivoinerie (France); and Austin Roses (U.K.).

'Tamafuyo' (ex Japan pre-1919). A semi-double white suffruticosa, available from Reath's and Pivoinerie (France).

'Tamasudare' (ex Japan pre-1919). A semi-double pink suffruticosa, available from Klehm Nursery; Rivière (France); and Pivoinerie (France).

'Teikan' (ex Japan). A semi-double pink suffruticosa, available from Klehm Nursery; Rivière (France); and Pivoinerie (France).

'Teni'. See 'Ten'i'

'Ten'i' (ex Japan). A semi-double blush suffruticosa, available from Reath's.

'The Beauty of Practical Living' (ex China). A double rose suffruticosa, available from Cricket Hill.

'Toichi Ruby' (Domoto–R. Klehm pre-1988). A semi-double rose suffruticosa, available from Klehm Nursery.

'Triomphe de van der Malen' (van der Malen 1849). A double rose suffruticosa, available from Rivière (France).

'Twin Beauty' (ex China). A semi-double red-pink suffruticosa, available from Cricket Hill.

'Ubatama' (ex Japan pre-1929). A single or semi-double red suffruticosa, available from Pivoinerie (France).

'Valse de Vienne' (M. Rivière 1983). A single pink suffruticosa, available from Rivière (France).

'Very Double Cherry'. See 'Yae Zakura'

'White Light in the Night' (ex China). A semi-double white suffruticosa, available from Cricket Hill.

'Wilhelmine' (origin unknown). A double red suffruticosa, available from Rivière (France).

'Wu long peng-sheng' (ex China). A semi-double red suffruticosa, available from Heze-Beijing (P.R.C.) and Piroche Plants (Canada).

'Yachiyo Jishi'. See 'Yachiyojishi'

'Yachiyojishi' (ex Japan). A semi-double or double pink suffruticosa, available from Rivière (France).

'Yachiyo Tsubaki'. See 'Yachiyo-tsubaki'

'Yachiyo-tsubaki' (ex Japan pre-1931). Also sold as 'Eternal Camellias'. A semi-double pink suffruticosa, available from Klehm Nursery; Caprice Farm; Reath's; and Pivoinerie (France).

'Yae Zakura' (ex Japan pre-1931). Also sold as 'Very Double Cherry'. A semi-double pink suffruticosa, available from Reath's; Pivoinerie (France); and Austin Roses (U.K.).

'Yaezakura'. See 'Yae Zakura'

'Yagumo' (ex Japan 1940). A semi-double purple suffruticosa, available from Pivoinerie (France).

'Yao's Family Yellow' (ex China). A double yellow suffruticosa, available from Cricket Hill.

'Ying Luo's Precious Pearl' (ex China). A double red-pink suffruticosa, available from Cricket Hill.

'Zenobia' (origin unknown). A double purple suffruticosa, available from Rivière (France).

'Zhao's Family Pink' (ex China). A semi-double pink suffruticosa, available from Cricket Hill.

'Zhuang yuan hong' (ex China). A single or double pink suffruticosa, available from Piroche Plants (Canada).

HYBRID TREE PEONY CULTIVARS

'Adriane' (Daphnis). A semi-double peach-rose hybrid, available from Klehm Nursery.

'Age of Gold' (Saunders 1948). Gold Medal. A semi-double gold hybrid, available from Klehm Nursery; Reath's; Caprice Farm; Craigmore (New Zealand).

'Alhambra' (Saunders 1948). A semi-double gold hybrid, available from Klehm Nursery; Reath's; Caprice Farm; Craigmore (New Zealand); and Pivoinerie (France).

'Alice Harding' (Lemoine 1935). Also sold as 'Kinko'. A cross between *Paeonia lutea* and 'Yaso Okina'. A semi-double yellow, available from Caprice Farm; Rivière (France); Craigmore (New Zealand); and Pivoinerie (France).

'Amber Moon' (Saunders 1948). A single yellow hybrid, available from Reath's.

'Anglet' (Saunders). A single yellow and rose hybrid, available from Klehm Nursery and Pivoinerie (France).

'Anna Marie' (Seidl 1984). A cross between a Daphnis seedling and Reath's A197. A single lavender, available from Caprice Farm.

'Artemis' (Daphnis). A 'White Queen' cross. A single yellow, available from Reath's and Pivoinerie (France).

'Aurora' (Daphnis). A 'Wings of the Morning' cross. A semi-double yellow, available from Klehm Nursery.

'Banquet' (Saunders 1941). A semi-double red hybrid, available from Klehm Nursery; Reath's; Caprice Farm; Craigmore (New Zealand); and Pivoinerie (France).

'Black Panther' (Saunders 1948). A semi-double red hybrid, available from Klehm Nursery; Reath's; Caprice Farm; and Pivoinerie (France).

'Black Pirate' (Saunders 1948). A single or semi-double red hybrid, available from Klehm Nursery and Reath's.

'Boreas' (Daphnis). A semi-double red hybrid, available from Klehm Nursery; Reath's; Craigmore (New Zealand); and Pivoinerie (France).

'Brocade' (Saunders 1941). A single yellow hybrid, available from Reath's.

'Canary' (Saunders 1940). A single yellow hybrid, available from Reath's.

'Chinese Dragon' (Saunders 1948). Gold Medal. A single or semi-double red hybrid, available from Reath's; Klehm Nursery; and Caprice Farm.

'Chore' (Gratwick). A single lavender hybrid, available from Klehm Nursery.

'Chromatella' (Lemoine 1920). Also sold as 'Kinshi'. A cross between *Paeonia lutea* and 'Yaso Okina'. A double yellow, available from Rivière (France) and Pivoinerie (France).

'Coronal' (Saunders 1948). A semi-double white and rose hybrid, available from Klehm Nursery.

'Corsair' (Saunders 1948). A single red hybrid, available from Reath's.

'Dare Devil' (Saunders 1948). A single red hybrid, available from Klehm Nursery.

'Flambeau' (Lemoine 1930). A double red hybrid, available from Rivière (France).

'Gauguin' (Daphnis). A 'Shintenchi' cross. A single yellow and red, available from Caprice Farm and Reath's.

'Gold Finch' (Saunders 1948). A single yellow hybrid, available from Klehm Nursery.

'Gold Sovereign' (Saunders 1949). A semi-double gold hybrid, available from Caprice Farm; Klehm Nursery; Reath's; and Pivoinerie (France).

'Golden Bowl' (Saunders 1948). A single yellow hybrid, available from Reath's; Klehm Nursery; and Pivoinerie (France).

'Golden Era' (Reath 1984). 'Golden Isles' crossed with mixed Daphnis pollen. A single yellow, available from Reath's.

'Golden Hind' (Saunders 1948). A double gold hybrid, available from Reath's.

'Golden Isles' (Saunders 1948). A semi-double yellow hybrid, available from Reath's.

'Golden Mandarin' (Saunders 1952). A double gold hybrid, available from Klehm Nursery.

'Golden Vanitie' (Saunders pre-1960). A single yellow hybrid, available from Klehm Nursery and Pivoinerie (France).

'Happy Days' (Saunders 1948). A semi-double yellow and red hybrid, available from Klehm Nursery and Pivoinerie (France).

'Harvest' (Saunders 1948). A semi-double gold hybrid, available from Reath's and Pivoinerie (France).

'Helios' (Daphnis). A 'Golden Hind' cross. A semi-double yellow, available from Reath's.

'Hephestos' (Daphnis). A semi-double red hybrid, available from Reath's.

'Hesperus' (Saunders 1948). A 'Thunderbolt' cross. A single pink, available from Klehm Nursery; Reath's; and Caprice Farm.

'High Noon' (Saunders 1952). Gold Medal. A semi-double yellow hybrid, available from Caprice Farm; Klehm Nursery; Reath's; Rivière (France); and Pivoinerie (France).

'Icarus' (Daphnis). A single red hybrid, available from Klehm Nursery and Reath's.

'Infanta' (Saunders 1948). A single white hybrid, available from Reath's.

'Iphigenia' (Daphnis). A 'Daioh' cross. A single red, available from Klehm Nursery and Reath's.

'Kinkaku'. See 'Souvenir de Maxime Cornu'
'Kinko'. See 'Alice Harding'
'Kinshi'. See 'Chromatella'

'Kronos' (Daphnis). An 'Ubatama' cross. A semi-double red, available from Klehm Nursery and Reath's.

'L'Aurore' (Lemoine 1935). A single red hybrid, available from Rivière (France).

'L'Esperance' (Lemoine 1909). A cross between *Paeonia lutea* and 'Yaso Okina'. A single yellow, available from Rivière (France).

'La Lorraine' (Lemoine 1913). A double pink hybrid, available from Rivière (France).

'Leda' (Daphnis). A 'Kokamon' cross. A semi-double lavender-rose, available from Reath's; Klehm Nursery; and Caprice Farm.

'Madame Louis Henry' (Henry 1907). A single rose hybrid, available from Rivière (France).

'Marchioness' (Saunders 1942). A single mauve-rose hybrid, available from Reath's; Klehm Nursery; and Rivière (France).

'Marie Laurencin' (Daphnis). A 'White Queen' cross. A semi-double lavender, available from Reath's.

'Mine d'Or' (Lemoine 1943). A single yellow hybrid, available from Rivière (France) and Pivoinerie (France).

'Mystery' (Saunders 1948). A single or semi-double lavender hybrid, available from Reath's; Klehm Nursery; and Pivoinerie (France).

'Nike' (Daphnis). A single pink hybrid, available from Klehm Nursery.

'Orion' (Saunders 1948). A semi-double gold hybrid, available from Klehm Nursery.

'Persephone' (Daphnis). A 'White Queen' cross. A semi-double yellow, available from Klehm Nursery and Reath's.

'Phoenix' (Saunders 1941). A single or semi-double red hybrid, available from Klehm Nursery.

'Princess' (Saunders 1941). A single rose hybrid, available from Reath's.

'Red Rascal' (Gratwick). A semi-double red hybrid, available from Klehm Nursery.

'Redon' (Daphnis). A 'Shintenchi' cross. A single or semi-double pink, available from Klehm Nursery and Reath's.

'Regent' (Saunders 1945). A double yellow and red hybrid, available from Klehm Nursery.

'Renown' (Saunders 1949). A single red hybrid, available from Reath's; Klehm Nursery; and Pivoinerie (France).

'Right Royal' (Saunders 1950). A semi-double yellow and rose hybrid, available from Klehm Nursery.

'Roman Gold' (Saunders 1941). A single gold hybrid, available from Klehm Nursery; Reath's; and Pivoinerie (France).

'Rose Flame' (Saunders 1952). A double rose hybrid, available from Reath's.

'Sang Lorraine' (Lemoine 1939). A cross between *Paeonia delavayi* and a suffruticosa tree peony. A semi-double red, available from Rivière (France).

'Satin Rouge' (Lemoine 1926). A double rose hybrid, available from Rivière (France).

'Savage Splendor' (Saunders 1950). A single white, rose, and lavender hybrid, available from Klehm Nursery; Reath's; and Pivoinerie (France).

'Silver Plane' (Saunders 1948). A single yellow hybrid, available from Klehm Nursery.

'Silver Sails' (Saunders 1940). A single yellow hybrid, available from Reath's and Klehm Nursery.

'Souvenir de Maxime Cornu' (Henry 1919). Also sold as 'Kinkaku'. A cross between *Paeonia lutea* and 'Ville de Saint Denis'. A double yellow and red, available from Klehm Nursery; Craigmore (New Zealand); Rivière (France); and Pivoinerie (France).

'Spring Carnival' (Saunders 1944). A single gold and rose hybrid, available from Klehm Nursery and Rivière (France).

'Summer Night' (Saunders 1949). A semi-double rose and yellow hybrid, available from Klehm Nursery.

'Surprise' (Lemoine 1920). A double yellow and red hybrid, available from Rivière (France).

'Terpsichore' (Daphnis). An 'Amber Moon' cross. A single pink, available from Klehm Nursery.

'Tessera' (Daphnis). A semi-double orange hybrid, available from Klehm Nursery.

'Themis' (Daphnis). A 'White Queen' cross. A semi-double pink, available from Craigmore (New Zealand) and Caprice Farm.

'Thunderbolt' (Saunders 1948). A single red hybrid, available from Klehm Nursery; Reath's; and Pivoinerie (France).

'Tiger Tiger' (Saunders 1948). A single or semi-double red and yellow hybrid, available from Reath's and Caprice Farm.

'Tria' (Daphnis). A single yellow hybrid, available from Klehm Nursery; Reath's; and Caprice Farm.

'Vesuvian' (Saunders 1948). A double red hybrid, available from Klehm Nursery; Reath's; and Caprice Farm.

'Zephnos'. See 'Zephyrus'

'Zephyrus' (Daphnis). Also sold as 'Zephnos'. A semi-double pink hybrid, available from Klehm Nursery; Reath's; and Caprice Farm.

ITOH (INTERSECTIONAL) HYBRIDS

The following cultivars are the intersectional hybrids of *Paeonia lactiflora* and tree peonies.

'Bartzella' (Anderson 1986). A double yellow, available from Beaux Jardins.

'Border Charm' (Hollingsworth 1984). A cross between tree peony 'Alice Harding' and *Paeonia lactiflora*. A semi-double yellow, available from Hollingsworth Peonies and Caprice Farm.

'Cora Louise' (Anderson 1986). A semi-double white and raspberry, available from Beaux Jardins.

'Court Jester' (Anderson 1992). A single gold, available from Beaux Jardins.

'First Arrival' (Anderson 1986). A semi-double pink, available from Beaux Jardins.

'Garden Treasure' (Hollingsworth 1984). A cross between tree peony 'Alice Harding' and *Paeonia lactiflora*. A semi-double yellow, available from Hollingsworth Peonies and Caprice Farm.

'Hidden Treasure' (Seidl 1989). A single or semi-double yellow, available from Caprice Farm.

'Julia Rose' (Anderson 1991). A single or semi-double red, available from Beaux Jardins.

'Little Darlin' (Anderson 1986). A single pink, available from Beaux Jardins.

'Morning Lilac' (Anderson 1992). A single or semi-double lavender, available from Beaux Jardins.

'Prairie Charm' (Hollingsworth 1992). A semi-double yellow, available from Hollingsworth Peonies.

'Rose Fantasy' (Seidl 1989). A cross between 'Chinese Dragon' and 'Harriet Olney'. A single fuchsia-rose, available from Caprice Farm.

'Tinge of Yellow' (Anderson 1992). A double or semi-double yellow, available from Beaux Jardins.

'Yellow Crown' (Itoh–Smirnow 1974). A cross between tree peony 'Alice Harding' and 'Kakoden'. A semi-double yellow, available from Reath's and Caprice Farm.

'Yellow Dream' (Itoh–Smirnow 1974). A cross between tree peony 'Alice Harding' and 'Kakoden'. A semi-double yellow, available from Caprice Farm and Reath's.

'Yellow Emperor' (Itoh–Smirnow 1974). A cross between tree peony 'Alice Harding' and 'Kakoden'. A semi-double yellow, available from Reath's; Caprice Farm; and Beaux Jardins.

'Yellow Heaven' (Itoh–Smirnow 1974). A cross between tree peony 'Alice Harding' and 'Kakoden'. A semi-double yellow, available from Caprice Farm and Reath's.

Appendix II

Nursery Sources

All growers offer bare-root peonies. Mail order is available unless otherwise noted.

A & D Peony and Perennial Nursery
6808 180th S.E.
Snohomish, Washington
    98290 U.S.A.
retail

Adamgrove
Route 1, Box 246
California, Missouri 65018 U.S.A.
retail

Aimers
81 Temperance Street
Aurora, Ontario, Canada L4G 2R1
retail

Ambergate Gardens
8015 Krey Avenue
Waconia, Minnesota 55387 U.S.A.
retail

American Daylily and Perennial
Box 210
Grain Valley, Missouri 64029 U.S.A.
retail

Anderson Iris Gardens
22179 Keather Avenue N.
Forest Lake, Minnesota 55025 U.S.A.
retail

David Austin Roses
Bowling Green Lane
Albrighton, Wolverhampton
West Midlands WV7 3HB U.K.
wholesale and retail

Les Beaux Jardins
W6658 Sunset Lane
Fort Atkinson, Wisconsin 53538 U.S.A.
retail

Bigger Peonies
201 North Rice Road
Topeka, Kansas 66616 U.S.A.
retail

Bluebird Nursery
Box 460
Clarkson, Nebraska 68629 U.S.A.
wholesale

Bluemount Nurseries
2103 Blue Mount Road
Monkton, Maryland 21111 U.S.A.
wholesale

Boughen Nurseries, Ltd.
Box 1955
Nipawin, Saskatchewan,
    Canada S0E 1E0
retail

K. Bourgondien and Sons
Box 1000
Babylon, New York 11702 U.S.A.
wholesale

Brand Peony Farm
Box 862
Saint Cloud, Minnesota 56302 U.S.A.
retail

Breifne Flowers
Clothiers Road, Eyreton
Kaiapoi No. 2 R.D., New Zealand
retail

Brickman's Botanical Gardens
R.R. 1
Sebringville, Ontario, Canada N0K 1X0
retail

Busse Gardens
Box N
Cokato, Minnesota 55321 U.S.A.
wholesale and retail

Cannon Nurseries
383 Dundas Street E., Box 832
Waterdown, Ontario,
    Canada L0R 2H0
retail; no mail order

Caprice Farm Nursery
15425 SW Pleasant Hill Road
Sherwood, Oregon 97140 U.S.A.
wholesale and retail

Carroll Gardens
444 East Main Street, Box 310
Westminster, Maryland 21157 U.S.A.
retail

Cedar Creek Farm
R.R. 4
Rockwood, Ontario,
    Canada N0B 2K0
retail

Cheyenne Tree Farms
Box 8704, Station L
Edmonton, Alberta,
    Canada T6C 4J5
retail; no mail order

Coopers Garden
212 West County Road
Roseville, Minnesota 55113 U.S.A.
retail

Corn Hill Nursery Ltd.
R.R. 5, Route 890
Petitcodiac, New Brunswick,
    Canada E0A 2H0
wholesale

Country Squires Garden
2601 Derry Road W., R.R. 3
Campbellville, Ontario,
    Canada L0B 1B0
retail; no mail order

Craigmore Peonies
No. 2 R.D.

Timaru, New Zealand
wholesale and retail

Cramer Nursery Inc.
1101 Don Quichotte
Ile Perrot, Quebec, Canada J7V 5V6
retail; no mail order

Cricket Hill Garden
670 Walnut Hill Road
Thomaston, Connecticut
    06787 U.S.A.
retail

Cruickshank's Inc.
1015 Mt. Pleasant Road
Toronto, Ontario,
    Canada M4P 2M1
retail

Dominion Seed House
Georgetown, Ontario,
    Canada L7G 4A2
retail

Eagle Lake Nurseries Ltd.
Box 819
Strathmore, Alberta,
    Canada T0J 3H0
wholesale and retail; no mail order

Edgewood Gardens
Route 2, Box 505
Warrenton, Virginia 22186 U.S.A.
retail

Ferncliff Gardens
8394 McTaggert Street, S.S.1
Mission, British Columbia,
    Canada V2V 5V6
retail

Gardenimport Inc.
Box 760
Thornhill, Ontario,
    Canada L3T 4A5
retail

Gärtnerei und Staudenkulturen
Wildensbuck CH-8465 Switzerland
retail

Granville Hall
Route 6, Box 7365
Gloucester, Virginia 23061 U.S.A.
retail

Harrison's Garden Center
Box 460
Carnduff, Saskatchewan,
    Canada S0C 0S0
retail

Heschke Gardens
11583 77th Street S.
Hastings, Minnesota 55033 U.S.A.
wholesale and retail

Heze-Beijing Nong Feng
Peony Development Company Ltd.
Heze, Shandong Province
    P.R.C. 27400
wholesale

Hildebrandt's Iris Garden
HC 84, Box 4
Lexington, Nebraska 68850 U.S.A.
retail

Hillier Nurseries (Winchester) Ltd.
Ampfield, Romsey
Hampshire SO51 9PA U.K.
wholesale and retail; no mail order

Holden Clough Nursery
Holden, Bolton-by-Bowland
Clitheroe
Lancashire BB7 4PF U.K.
wholesale and retail

Hollingsworth Peonies
Route 3, Box 27
Maryville, Missouri 64468 U.S.A.
retail

Homestead Nurseries Ltd.
4262 Wright Road
Clayburn, British Columbia,
    Canada V0X 1E0
wholesale and retail

Hortico Inc.
723 Robson Road, R.R. 1
Waterdown, Ontario,
    Canada L0R 2H0
retail

Keinosen Puutarha
Peijonniemi 82660
Uusi-Vartsila 9KP-F0 Finland
retail

Kelways Nurseries Ltd.
Langport
Somerset TA10 9SL U.K.
wholesale and retail

Kiwi Gardens
R.R. 7
Perth, Ontario,
    Canada K7H 3C9
wholesale; no mail order

Klehm Nursery
4210 North Duncan Road
Champaign, Illinois 61821 U.S.A.
wholesale and retail

Staudengärtnerei Heinz Klose
Rosenstrasse 10
34253 Lohfelden, Frankfurt, Germany
retail

Langthorns Plantery
High Cross Lane W.
Little Canfield, Dunmow
Essex, CM6 1TD U.K.
retail; no mail order

Wolfgang Linnemann
Rheindorfer Strasse 49
5300 Bonn-Beuel, Germany
wholesale and retail

Long Lane Farm
R.D. 1, Box 178B
Spring Mills,
    Pennsylvania 16875 U.S.A.
wholesale and retail

La Maison des Fleurs Vivaces Enr.
807 Boulevard Sauve, C.P. 264
Saint-Eustace, Quebec,
    Canada J7R 4K6
wholesale

Marsal Paeonies
Old South Road
R.D. Dunsandel
Canterbury, New Zealand
wholesale and retail

McConnell Nurseries
Port Burwell, Ontario,
    Canada N0J 1T0
retail

Mcfayden
30 Ninth Street, Box 1060
Brandon, Manitoba, Canada R7A 6A6
retail

Milaeger's Gardens
4838 Douglas Avenue
Racine, Wisconsin
    53402-2498 U.S.A.
retail

Mount Arbor Nurseries
Shenandoah, Iowa 51601 U.S.A.
wholesale

New Peony Farm
Box 19235
St. Paul, Minnesota 55118 U.S.A.
retail

Park Seed Co.
Cokesbury Road, Box 46
Greenwood, South Carolina
    29648-0046 U.S.A.
retail

The Peony Gardens
Lake Hayes, No. 2 R.D.
Queenstown, New Zealand
retail

Pepieniere Charlevoix
345 Fraser
La Malbaie, Quebec,
    Canada G5A 1A2
wholesale and retail

W. H. Perron and Co. Ltd.
2914 Labelle Boulevard
Chomedey Laval, Quebec,
    Canada H7P 5R9
retail

Piroche Plants Inc.
20542 McNeil Road
Pitt Meadows, British Columbia,
    Canada V3Y 1Z1
wholesale

La Pivoinerie
Latrenne
47380 Monclar d'Agenais, France
retail

M. Putzer Hornby Nursery Ltd.
7314 Sixth HNE
Hornby, Ontario, Canada L0P 1E0
wholesale; no mail order

L. J. Rambo Wholesale Nurseries
10495 Baldwin Road
Bridgman, Michigan 49106 U.S.A.
wholesale

Reath's Nursery
County Road 577, N-195
Vulcan, Michigan 49892 U.S.A.
wholesale and retail

Pivoines Michel Rivière
La Plaine
26400 Crest, France
retail

Saekinoen Co. Ltd.
5-13-5 Komazawa
Setagaya-ku, Tokyo, Japan
wholesale

Sakatanotane Co. Ltd.
3-1-7 Nagata-higashi
Minami-ku, Yokohama, Japan
wholesale

Sarcoxie Nurseries
1510 Joplin Street
Sarcoxie, Missouri 64862 U.S.A.
wholesale

Sevald Nursery
4937 Third Avenue S.
Minneapolis, Minnesota 55409 U.S.A.
retail

Sheridan Nurseries
R.R. 4, Tenth Line
Georgetown, Ontario,
    Canada L7G 4S7
wholesale

Sherman Nursery Co.
Charles City, Iowa 50616 U.S.A.
wholesale

Stauobuki-bussan Co. Ltd.
Yatsuka Town
Yatsuka-gun, Shimane Prefecture,
    Japan
wholesale

Sunny Border Nursery
Box 86
Kensington, Connecticut 06037 U.S.A.
wholesale

Swedberg Nurseries
Box 418
Battle Lake, Minnesota 56515 U.S.A.
retail

T & T Seeds Ltd.
Box 1710
Winnipeg, Manitoba, Canada R3C 3P6
wholesale and retail

The Terrace Peonies
Mount Grey Road
Leithfield R.D.
North Canterbury, New Zealand
retail

Tischler Peony Garden
1021 East Division Street
Faribault, Minnesota 55021 U.S.A.
retail

J. van Hoorn
Box 814
Island Lake, Illinois 60042 U.S.A.
wholesale

Steve Varner
Route 3, Box 5
Monticello, Illinois 61856 U.S.A.
retail

André Viette Farm and Nursery
Route 1, Box 16
Fishersville, Virginia 22939 U.S.A.
wholesale and retail

Walters Gardens
Box 137
Zeeland, Michigan 49464 U.S.A.
wholesale

Wayside Gardens
Hodges, South Carolina
    29653 U.S.A.
retail

Weston Nurseries Inc.
East Main Street
Hopkinton, Massachusetts
    01748-0186 U.S.A.
retail

White Flower Farm
Litchfield, Connecticut
    06759-0050 U.S.A.
retail

White House Perennials
R.R. 2
Almonte, Ontario,
    Canada K0A 1A0
retail; no mail order

Gilbert H. Wild and Son
112 Joplin Street
Sarcoxie, Missouri 64862 U.S.A.
wholesale and retail

Yatsuka-gun Agricultural Cooperative Assn.
Yatsuka Town
Yatsuka-gun, Shimane Prefecture, Japan
wholesale

Staudengärtnerei Gräfin von Zeppelin
79295 Sulzburg, Laufen/Baden, Germany
retail

Appendix III

Landscaping with Peonies: An Illustrated Essay by Linda Engstrom

Dedicated gardeners, especially those who specialize over the years and are known by others as experts on a particular plant group, are often avid collectors. They are frequently driven to acquire every species of a particular genus or are so enamored of plants in general that anything the least bit unusual becomes a "must have." Such compulsive collecting usually leads to a disastrous garden design. Collector's gardens all too often become a labeled collection of plants simply laid out in alphabetical rows, or a haphazard assortment based on date of acquisition. In both cases those design principles necessary to transform a collection of plants into a horticultural paradise are missing. The difference between a collection of plants and a garden is comparable to the difference between a list of words and an eloquent poem. A designed garden is made up of individual plants each possessing unique characteristics arranged in a unified spatial sequence, evoking a special mood and emotional response. The person who puts it all together is a mix of architect, historian, poet, musician, ecologist, horticulturist, and painter.

The peony has quite a distinct personality that has made it a prima donna in world gardens for centuries. I have wonderful memories of the peonies growing in my grandmother's garden on Long Island, New York, at the public park where I ran and played as a child, and in the bouquets I admired on my aunt's kitchen table. Unlike most plants with relatively neutral characters, the peony stands out in my memory. A parallel can be found in the case of a person who illuminates a party, commanding attention and response. With sufficient analysis, one can usually understand why such an individual stands out. An analogous character analysis leads to an understanding of why the peony has been valued for so many centuries. Adjectives that best describe the peony for me include the following: magnificent, bold, elegant, textured, showy, paperlike, sculptural, velvety, silky, frilled, wispy, crinkled, sensual, fragrant, and sumptuous. In order to design with peonies, the adjectives finally settled upon by the gardener must reflect a sense of the soul of the plant, its character.

For many gardeners, collecting peonies is a satisfying endeavor considered part of a learning process. Yet placing peonies in an organized spatial sequence leads a step beyond education to a sense of real fulfillment.

Elements and principles of design

Let me describe why it is that one garden elicits a magical, comfortable, euphoric feeling, inspiring exclamations at every turn, while another yields no excitement and quickly fades from memory. It isn't simply a question of the collective plants or number of garden objects that leads us to a respond in one way or another, but rather the way these objects define the space experienced. A successful garden evokes a positive response. It contains plants of contrasting character that fill space and define a harmonious ordering of that space. The basic design elements of line, form, texture, and color play crucial roles in the design of garden spaces.

This art form differs from others, such as painting or drawing, in that a garden is always in flux. It constantly changes, so cannot be dealt with as a static entity. It changes with time, with light, with rain or snow, as the plants grow and as the seasons progress. As with sculpture, it can also be viewed from a variety of different vantage points.

A basic consideration is that of the scale of the environment in which a garden is to be situated—the buildings, water, distant views, or horizon. Most of us have become accustomed to a human scale derived from the interior spaces of the homes in which we live. This scale is best used in planning a landscape. Without such a sense of human scale, a garden becomes an uncomfortable place. To limit the obvious sense of vastness in outdoor space, ceilings can be created using tree canopies, walls by using shrubs and other mid-sized plant material, and floor covering by using various textured ground covers. A sense of movement through such a garden space is created by the pathways that connect the plant-defined spaces, just as hallways and door openings connect the rooms of a house. Attention to this question of scale as well as to existing structures, such as walls, fences, and seating areas, leads to an intimate, comfortable garden.

Designing a garden involves all the senses. Each is intricately related to the garden design elements of line, form, texture, scent, and color. Informed attention to these aesthetic principles leads to an exciting, rich, personal space that is an extension of its creator's lifestyle. By understanding how these design elements affect space and create a specific response, the confusion arising out of the conflicting compendia of landscaping rules offered by various "experts" can be avoided. With attention to the materials and design principles, each gardener can mold a satisfying space of his or her own choosing.

Since the space that the garden occupies is three-dimensional, the starting point of design is to get inside that space and create it from within. The developing space needs to evolve to accommodate the use, comfort, and pleasure of its creator. The design elements are then employed to determine the way space will be perceived.

Line is impressed upon all of us from earliest childhood—remember defining objects with connect-the-dots drawings, or carefully coloring inside the lines? Later one learned to write letters on a straight line and discovered just what the horizon line meant. In garden design, the form of a line creates a sense of direction as well as a sense of movement. The eye automatically follows a garden line, whether it be the edge of a walkway, the curve of a flower bed, or the outline of plant materials. The character of a line yields specific responses. Gentle, slow curves and horizontal lines tend to be experienced as restful, while jagged diagonals or vertical lines create more excitement and tension.

Form—the shape defined by line—is probably the most enduring element in garden design. It is what is seen when one first looks at a garden from a distance. Every plant has a distinct growth habit, a unique mass and volume, that develops and changes as the plant matures. These shapes, whether pyramidal, weeping, columnar, spreading, or round, divide and define the spaces in the garden. Some forms are more dramatic than others and so attract attention. The siting of a specific plant may block a view, or open a sightline, or alter the view depending on the maturity, nature, and growth habit of the plant—herbaceous, evergreen, or deciduous, open or compact. These plant qualities often change with the seasons and restructure the lines of the garden. The form of the plants selected and their placement are critical to creating comfortable, dynamic spaces and pleasing silhouettes.

Texture in the garden creates sensual and visual excitement. It is generally read as the mass and void of foliage, bark, or flowers and changes with the light during the day and with the seasons. Up close, the size and shape of the leaves and twigs become the predominant textural elements of a plant. From a distance, it is the quality of light and shadow on the entire form—the patterns of light and dark—that translates as texture. Rough, coarse textures tend to create an informal mood and are visually dominant, while fine, smooth textures are associated with formal, elegant, subdued moods and are visually more passive. Since fine-textured plants are visually translated as being farther away, fine textures can be a tool for providing a sense of perspective in a small garden and making the space appear larger. A predominance of coarse-textured plants makes a garden space appear smaller. Strong textural contrasts add drama and interest to a garden.

Scent in a garden is often neglected. Introducing a variety of fragrances will bring an extra dimension to the garden by expanding sensory awareness. If the garden is exposed, fragrant plants may need to be located in a sheltered location. The scent of delicately fragrant plants is also more appreciated if they are located near a path or at the edge of a patio or entry area. Specific fragrances, like colors, evoke emotional responses and can help create a certain mood or sense of time in the garden.

Color is often a confusing and puzzling design element for gardeners, and yet it seems to be the one and only element some consider when planning a garden. Although color is a key element in the design of a garden, many give it too great an importance and fret continually about the often complex rules that some designers have propounded.

One of three widely employed formulas for planning color in the garden is best used. The first is to design in a green monotone with only an occasional splash of another color, as exemplified in traditional Japanese gardens. The second is to translate from nature, using harmonies of colors or the kaleidoscopic patterns of a wildflower meadow. Finally, one can use the artist's color wheel and paint pictures in the palette-gardening approach made famous by Gertrude Jekyll.

The gardener's final choice of a formula is dictated by location, the size of the garden, and the kind of garden wanted. Living in the countryside just outside of Portland, Oregon, I prefer to translate from nature so that my garden blends in with the natural beauty of the area. But since I also have acres of ground at my disposal, I have room for many flower and mixed borders. In designing them I develop specific color schemes using the palette approach, creating for example, a white garden or a blue border. Generally, the larger the area to be dealt with, the more complex the color scheme can be. A garden created in limited space will be more dramatic if the color scheme is kept as simple as possible.

Research has identified the emotional responses specific colors can be counted upon to generate. The bright reds, yellows, and oranges tend to excite. The softer blues, pinks, greens, and violets produce a calming, tranquil effect. This is one reason the monochromatic green gardens of the Japanese are so revered. The "music of the color green" is a phrase often heard in reference to this basic garden color and its numerous tones, ranging from blue-green to yellow-green. White tends to be the great unifier, providing a neutral, yet somewhat uplifting spirit. Gardeners need to employ an awareness of color responses when planning the functional needs of garden spaces. In general, warm colors—red, yellow, and orange—attract the eye, standing out or advancing. Cool colors—blue, most violets, and some greens—recede into the landscape. Color therefore contributes to a sense of depth by defining spatial relationships. Remember too that colors in the landscape are not static but change with the time of day, cloud cover, and season. Color intensity directly relates to the amount of reflected light. Flower color is transient, while foliage, bark, seed pods, and berries provide color highlights and interest at other times of the year, and so must loom large in design considerations.

To create a garden space satisfying to the senses and imparting a feeling of unity with the environment, gardeners must also consider six basic principles of design: repetition, variety, balance, emphasis, sequence, and scale.

Repetition is the continuing thread in a garden and is generally defined as duplication. When any design element is repeated, the mind is better able to understand the composition as a whole and so a sense of order is introduced. It is the qualities or character of an object—line, form, texture, scent, or color—that are usually repeated. Repeating finely textured plants in a garden helps to unify the design and impart a powerful sense of simplicity. Repetition is simply a matter of holding one design quality constant while varying the others. A word of caution: if repetition is carried to extremes, the garden will become either monotonous or so subtle that the viewer only sees disorder.

Variety is the life of the garden. The design qualities of line, form, texture, scent, and color are changed and contrasted to provide diversity and avoid uniformity. Diversity develops tension, which helps to hold the observer's attention while creating excitement and enjoyment. Variety is the opposite of repetition. But when it is overdone by adding too many elements, chaos results, so a very fine balance between repetition and variety is needed to achieve unity in a landscape.

Balance refers to the stability or repose of the garden; it is realized by creating an equilibrium between the parts that make up the whole. Line, form, texture, scent, and color all attract our attention, so these sensual energies must be gauged and then balanced out. One form of balance relates to layout along a preconceived central axis. That axis can either be informal or formal in its arrangement. Formal or symmetrical arrangements are exactly the same on either side of the axis, while informal or asymmetrical arrangements are unlike on either side of the axis. Another way of conceiving an axis is in the vertical dimension. Natural, informal landscapes—which are increasingly popular—depend upon balancing vertical and horizontal elements, or small, dense masses and large, diffuse groupings. In all cases the elements being balanced must hold the same importance in the eye.

Emphasis refers to the garden elements that initially seize attention and to which the eye continually returns. It is the creation of the more important and the less important elements in the garden. The parts of any composition should not be equal in their visual interest. Certain parts should be different, perhaps larger than the rest, or of a contrasting color, form, fragrance, or texture, depending on the function of the design. Again, if too many elements are introduced the effect is lost. Emphasis can be achieved only by limiting the number of dominant design elements.

Sequence is the movement of the garden. It is the rhythms that develop when line, form, texture, and color are changed in a consistent way to lead in a particular direction or to a point of focus. Sequence helps to connect the various design elements. It can be achieved through carefully planned repetition (if care is taken to avoid monotony), through progression (such as using textures in graded steps from fine to coarse), or through alternation (a repetition of two or more contrasting features).

Scale within the garden, as distinct from the overall scale of the garden, refers to the harmony of the garden. That is, all the elements of a garden should agree in the sense they convey of the size of the whole. The actual size of an object is different from its relative scale or proportion in relation to other neighboring objects, so scale is concerned with the relation between the size of an object and the size of the other objects within the same composition. Thus, a tiny alpine plant is out of scale among tall trees, just as it would be planted next to a large building.

With these general principles in mind, applied in connection with the elements of line, form, texture, scent, and color, let me now turn to incorporating peonies in well-designed gardens.

Foliage

Peony foliage is generally tidy and unobtrusive, one of the plant's best traits. Individual plants are usually chosen simply for flower form and color, yet flowers are transient. It is the foliage that provides the more enduring element of texture in the garden. There is much about peonies to be enjoyed both before the flowers have arrived and after they have faded. Foliage interest in the herbaceous peonies begins in the early spring when the red shoots emerge from the ground and catch the morning light. And their visual interest continues through the growing season until the first heavy frost. Tree peony foliage often turns shades of bronze and purple in the fall.

The tree peonies, with persistent woody stems and large forms, generally produce an airy and graceful foliage with a dull finish on the top surface of the leaves. Leaves also tend to be deeply cut into three to five lobes. *Paeonia lutea* var. *ludlowii*, for example, has deeply cut foliage, giving the plant an almost tropical look. This foliage can attain a spread of 12 feet in a mature plant. This species, because it is larger, bushier, and more dramatic than the popular Chinese and Japanese suffruticosa cultivars, deserves a special place in the garden as a specimen plant.

The herbaceous peony leaf usually has a much heavier, coarser texture overall, with a slight sheen to the surface. The brilliant red-flowered 'Carina' and the larger, pale yellow 'Prairie Moon' both exhibit these typical herbaceous foliage traits. Some notable exceptions are 'Early Windflower' and 'Late Windflower', herbaceous peonies whose deeply cut, lobed leaves emerge just weeks apart in early spring. *Paeonia tenuifolia*, commonly known as the fernleaf peony, does indeed have extremely fine, fernlike foliage. Some of the dwarf peonies, such as 'Earlybird', 'Little Red Gem', and 'Windchimes' (all tenuifolia hybrids), also have narrow, finely cut foliage. Other peonies with distinct foliage include 'Elizabeth Cahn', 'Laddie', 'Nosegay', and 'Picotee', as well as all the Itoh hybrids.

One consideration in siting peonies is the foliage texture of adjacent plants. A variety of textures is usually desirable. The fine texture of a hemlock, *Tsuga canadensis* 'Pendula', for example, placed next to a medium- to coarse-textured peony emphasizes the individual textures of both plants. Strong contrasts—coarse next to extremely fine—create visual excitement in the garden. The coarse-textured foliage of peonies, iris, and *Euphorbia characias* 'Wulfenii' creates a pleasing contrast with the finer-textured foliage of phlox, dianthus, myosotis, and alyssum, while at the same time the swordlike form of the iris foliage contrasts with the compound leaf form of the peony. Slender spiky plants, such as lupine, veronica, and foxglove, contrast well with the more solid clumps of peonies.

Repetition of similar fine or medium textures creates a restful atmosphere. The larger, coarser-textured peonies will be more dominant in the landscape and are best used as accent plants rather than in large massed plantings. Foliage texture can also suggest movement in the garden by providing a visual sequence, moving from coarse to fine or the reverse.

When siting peonies it is important to remember that typical foliage die-back differs from one species or cultivar to the next. Peony foliage is often used as a backdrop for other plants, so a midsummer decline creates gaps. *Paeonia tenuifolia*, the fernleaf peony, which is often placed at the front of the border due to its small size and scale, tends to die back earlier than most of the other perennials used in borders. Some cultivars, such as 'Cytherea', tend to develop rather shabby foliage by late August and so must be cut back at that time. Many hybrids of *P. peregrina* also have this tendency. When planting a row or hedge of peonies, place those whose foliage tends to decline earlier at the ends of the row, to avoid gaps in the bed.

Gardeners can effectively use the foliage of peonies to conceal the unattractive, dying foliage of early spring-flowering bulbs. Such a planting becomes a layered garden with one plant coming in as another declines. Using this layering principle, a small-flowered clematis, such as *Clematis alpina* 'Pamela Jackman' or *C. texensis* 'Gravetye Beauty', can be planted nearby to grow over the peony foliage as the peony flowers fade. Layered gardens present a moving tapestry and add greatly to the visual excitement and interest of the space.

Accent

A specimen peony chosen for its magnificent flower color and growth habit is useful in punctuating a landscape. It leads viewers to stop or at least pause to take in its beauty. It is usually seen from a distance. Trees are most commonly used as landscape accents because of their enduring and dominant forms, yet the large and often fragrant flowers of the peony, their foliage texture, and attractive form all command attention. The peony is an excellent candidate for accent planting and is particularly suitable for gardens of a smaller scale. A bold peony provides the needed emphasis in a flower border by drawing attention to a particular section. Plants used as accents in the garden are necessarily few in number; too many simply cancel each other out just as too many stars tarnish a production. The flowers of 'Gay Paree' are true showstoppers—vibrant pink outer petals surrounding a ruffled ball of creamy white. Other candidates for accent plants include 'Centerpoint', 'Coral Charm', 'Old Faithful', and 'Red Charm'. Remember though that it is not simply the flower color but the unusual form or foliage of the peony as well that provides the contrast and visual strength necessary to qualify as an accent plant. The tall peony 'Prairie Moon', with large, creamy yellow flowers and bright glossy green foliage, is a standout when surrounded by the dwarf forms of red barberry and blue iris. Peonies offer relief from an overabundance of conifers and broad-leaved evergreens, which can easily engulf a house with dark, heavy forms. Peonies provide variety of texture and form while maintaining a distinct measure of authority.

A sunny entrance garden, either along the walkway or in the courtyard, is often a comfortable space with its human scale and sense of shelter. In cities, where an entry garden must necessarily be the focus, a single potted plant next to the door can be used to represent the whole of nature. What better place for an accent peony, either tree types or herbaceous.

Tree peonies, which can often reach diameters of 4–6 feet, quite naturally demand singular treatment and are best not massed together. Their opulent flowers and dramatic size demand that space be given them, allowing each to be considered individually. One approach is to plant a tree peony in a large container, which can be moved from one location to another.

As with any container planting, regular watering by hand or with a drip system must be maintained. Japanese tree peonies, which in time can develop a spread of 4 feet or more, are sufficiently distinguished to flank even large formal entrances. Hybrids of *Paeonia lutea*, with their dark, thick foliage, give a sense of great strength and are particularly successful when placed on either side of wide steps or walkways. If temperatures dip well below 30°F, the container must be moved into a greenhouse or a protected environment to prevent winter damage.

Herbaceous peonies also make fine potted specimens. 'Picotee', with its distinct flowers—single pale petals edged with a deep pink band—and perfect mound of large, heavily textured, dark green leaves, is an ideal size for smaller situations at 18 inches. Other herbaceous peonies comfortable in a movable pot are *Paeonia tenuifolia*, 'Bouquet Perfect', 'Ludovica', 'Sanctus', and 'Sunlight'.

The hard surfaces typical of an entrance area can be effectively softened by using peonies with open, relaxed forms. Both 'Early Windflower' and 'Late Windflower' have excellent design qualities and provide year-round interest. Their single white flowers with yellow centers appear very early and stand up well above the foliage. Even a heavy rain or wind does not seem to bother them, unlike some cultivars, especially those bearing large double flowers, which are easily broken. The leaves of both cultivars are deeply cut and tinged red in the fall. As the winged seed pods develop, they appear like red butterflies dancing over the leaves. One of my favorite plant associations is a grouping of an 'Early Windflower' peony, *Rhododendron* 'P. J. M.', and *Thymus serpyllum* 'Mother-of-Thyme', carpeting the hard edge of a walkway.

Bring all the senses into play when working with an entry space, walkway, or courtyard. Scented peonies, like roses, need to be planted where people can catch the scent. 'Audrey', 'Mt. St. Helens', 'Sea Shell', 'Top Brass', and 'Vivid Rose' are just a sampling of peonies with an old-rose fragrance.

Color

Foliage and stem color, not surprisingly, add a good deal of vitality and interest to the garden. 'Picotee', for example, has beautiful red stems with red veins running through its dark green leaves.

Hybridization has led to a multitude of colors in the peony flower. The dominant reds, pinks, and whites typical of my grandmother's garden are now joined by an ever-increasing procession of salmons, yellows, corals, oranges, apricots, and raspberrys.

How color is used in a landscape often reflects the temperament of the gardener, mirroring each person's particular moods. Color inclinations undoubtedly spring from obscure and primitive sources, leading to quite distinctive individual choices. I would not consider using intense colors—deep purples and bright pinks, for instance—in my home, yet I use them in the garden frequently. In part, a difference such as this is a function of the light source, for sunlight tends to lighten and soften color. Greens or the more neutral gray-browns predominate in a garden and therefore influence the value of other colors brought into the garden. In a natural setting, intense colors set against the larger background of less-intense colors creates a pleasing balance.

Colors that share the same pigment—red, violet, and blue, for example—are said to be analogous and tend to harmonize. Analogous colors appear next to each other on the color wheel or circle. The human eye tends to move between analogous colors easily because they share the same pigment.

The reverse is true of complementary colors, which do not share a common pigment and appear opposite each other on the color wheel. Examples are the color pairs of orange and blue, red and green, and yellow and violet. When complementary colors are used together, the eye must continually refocus, creating a restless, disruptive effect, often positively exciting.

Once the selection of plants is made, the major landscaping objective is to place the plants so they produce differing color harmonies between analogous colors and contrasts between the complementary colors. Placing colors in this way creates splashes of color without causing visual confusion. Large blocks of intense colors should generally be avoided save in large or public display gardens. Rather, a kaleidoscopic pattern of intense colors should be broken up into smaller fragments interspersed among the neutral background colors. Look to the colorists among artists—Matisse, Cézanne, Renoir, Monet, and their fellows—for inspiration in planning a garden color scheme. Color harmonies in paintings translate quite successfully to the garden. To continue the analogy, foliage, stonework, and neutral ground colors provide the framing that unifies the design.

It is of great design importance that people wandering through a garden see the various elements from both a distance and at close range. Colors and forms are therefore observed from many different angles, viewpoints, and perspectives. Repeated colors should be sequenced to draw visitors into the garden and entice them to explore.

Light pastel colors can be seen from greater distances as they possess greater reflective quality and so contrast especially well against green foliage. These same pale colors are outstanding when viewed in the less intense light of morning or early evening. Plants bearing such colors are best placed toward the back of the garden to lead the viewer in.

Dark, blue-based red flowers cannot be relied upon to be noticed from a distance as their color value is quite close to that of the green foliage. Recent cultivar introductions have increased the range in red flowers considerably, with more yellow-based red hybrids providing colors that stand out better from darker colored foliage. An example is 'Flame', which comes close to orange in color. Plants bearing flowers in the dark orange range should be planted where they can readily be seen.

Single peony flowers also appear much brighter than the double forms, since the sunlight shines through the petals and is not dispersed into the deep shadows created by the multiple petals of the doubles. 'Golden Glow' is a marvelous example of the display a single flower makes. In early spring it produces huge, deep red buds resembling giant satin balls shimmering in the sunlight. As the flower petals open, the red color appears translucent and the center cluster of yellow stamens simply glows. As the flower ages, the papery petals turn an intense pink and eventually drop to the ground, leaving patches of color to linger on the garden floor.

Gray-leaved plants, such as *Santolina chamaecyparissus*, *Senecio greyi*, and *Artemisia ludoviciana*, augment contrasts, accentuating the brightness of adjacent colors and heightening color effect. An example of this principle can be seen when *Nepeta mussinii*, with its billowing gray foliage and misty blue flowers, is placed in front of a pale pink peony, such as 'Blushing Princess'. The gray leaves accentuate the pale peony flowers making them appear more brilliant. For a bolder effect, the large gray leaves of the globe artichoke, *Cynara cardunculus*, provide both a color and an architectural companion to a sturdy peony.

Working in the opposite direction, the purple-foliaged plants of *Prunus*, *Cotinus*, and *Berberis* tone down contrasts because their foliage and stems are darkly colored and give weight and balance to a potentially overpowering color scheme. The impact of *Paeonia peregrina* 'Otto Froebel' (sometimes offered as 'Sunshine'), with its salmon-orange flowers, is moderated when surrounded by bronze- and purple-leaved plants. In such a background, a scattering of red and pink oriental poppies can be added without creating visual shockwaves.

Some especially lovely soft-color combinations include 'Sunlight', a single pale yellow with a distinct pink cast on the outside of the petals, combined with the double pale pink flower of 'Audrey' and the single white of 'Seraphim'. 'Claire de Lune', an upright pale yellow, combines beautifully with 'Salmon Glow', a peony with an open, weeping form, salmon petals, and yellow stamens. The colors relate to one another while the forms contrast. The creamy pink flower of 'Sugar n' Spice' harmonizes well with the more intense plum of 'Rivida' since their colors are analogous. Other perennial genera suitable for inclusion in this color scheme include *Heuchera*, *Digitalis*, *Lupinus*, *Cistus*, and *Aquilegia* with flower shades of pink, lavender, and white.

A very dramatic scheme of contrasting colors results from placing the cherry-red flowers of 'Carina' next to a large clump of clear blue iris against the soft maroon foliage of a Japanese maple such as *Acer palmatum* 'Bloodgood'. A truly dramatic color treatment is the white garden. Using a spectacular white peony, such as 'Moonstone' or 'Gardenia', with *Spiraea*, *Cornus*, *Deutzia*, *Lilium*, *Syringa*, *Rosa*, or *Rhododendron* (including azaleas) can create a magical place.

The possibilities with color are endless. The garden designer can use and control color to enhance both mood and function in the three-dimensional, atmospheric space of the garden.

Edges and hedges

Peonies are ideal for hedges or edging plants in particular situations. In this role the strength of their form and foliage emphasizes line and direction in the garden. Repetition of form and color guides people visually and physically through the defined space. The most dramatic use with the greatest visual impact is created by using the same type of peony the length of the bed. Such a planting maintains an even appearance throughout the season with its repetition of form, texture, and color. As noted earlier, foliage die-back is a real design problem. A planting of the same peony prevents the opening of gaps in the hedgerow and an uneven visual line. A peony hedge is particularly attractive as a continuous line that converges on or leads to a focal point in the distance.

Dwarf peonies, such as 'Bouquet Perfect', 'Mandarin's Coat', 'Picotee', and 'Sanctus', all ranging 18–24 inches in height, make wonderful low borders edging flower beds and paths. Used as a low edging along a walkway, the flowers are a visual standout during the early summer, with the neat masses of dark foliage emphasizing the line during the later months. The medium-sized peonies (24–36 inches in height) with dense foliage, such as 'Fire Opal', 'Heidi', or 'Firelight', make attractive low hedges and guide visitors in or through various areas of the garden.

Evergreens provide an unusually strong complementary background for peonies. Siting peonies in front of a bed or border of junipers or other evergreens adds a linear emphasis all year long and creates a rich, complex composition during the growing season.

The medium to tall peonies make good screens and privacy barriers. These informal screens not only create enclosures within the garden but make superb backdrops for later blooming plants as well. 'Walter Marx', a tall (36–40 inches), fragrant peony with single, white flowers, makes a spectacular hedge as well as a stunning screen when placed against the simple backdrop of stone wall or wooden fence. 'Coral Charm', a vigorous semi-double coral-peach, is another excellent choice for a tall hedge. Some of the tree peonies grow to 6 feet or more. The white-flowered *Paeonia rockii* (also sold as 'Joseph Rock' or 'Rock's Variety') and the yellow, semi-double 'High Noon', which has a tendency to rebloom in the fall, make excellent screens. 'Kishu Caprice', a tree peony with magnificent pink flowers and a spreading, horizontal growth habit, can be planted along the top of a wall or successfully sited among rockery on a slope. 'Festiva Maxima', a huge, frilly, white peony with red flecks hidden among the petals, softens the edges and lines of a fence that would otherwise dominate the landscape.

Some cultivars create such a presence that more than one might prove overpowering. A single tree peony—such as 'Renkaku', a tall suffruticosa with huge, white flowers—may be of such dense habit that it is able to create a substantial screen all by itself. At maturity 'Renkaku' can easily reach a width and height of 5 feet.

The height and shape of the peonies selected for edging and hedges affects the character of the space. Since peonies are generally not pruned and develop a variety of habits, they serve well as informal elements in the garden. However, symmetrical arrangements of the same cultivars make a formal element in the garden. Conversely, asymmetrical groupings of peonies of various height and colors impart a casual mood. A formal treatment is readily achieved by framing another section of the garden or a particular piece of garden art with two large peonies. Screen plantings with regularly spaced gaps not only create a formal rhythm but tempt visitors with periodic glimpses of other areas. Beds edged with boxwood (*Buxus sempervirens*) and planted with peonies and low ground covers create a more formal mood.

Companion plants and the mixed border

A mixed border, one containing shrubs and perhaps a few small trees together with herbaceous perennials and annuals, creates a much stronger impression than one consisting exclusively of perennials. Shrubs and trees give balance, vigor, and weight to the bed, adding variety of texture, form, and interest throughout the year. In such a design the herbaceous plants are fillers, providing a constantly changing pattern of colors and a variety of moods. Part of the joy of a mixed border derives from selecting plant material that provides a sequence of interest throughout the seasons.

Peonies play a transitional role within the structural hierarchy of a mixed bed. While their magnificent flowers are fleeting, their form, size, and strong foliage texture add substance to the landscape. Because they are commonly used as transition plants, they should be sited in front of taller, later-blooming plants, or used as a foliage backdrop for smaller, finer textured plants. Both peony foliage and flowers can serve as a unifier. Many flowering herbaceous plants possess rather nondescript forms, undistinguished foliage, and similarity in flower scale. By virtue of their attractive habit, peonies provide a strong backbone, helping both to tie the border together and to relate it to the rest of the garden.

Peonies are best placed in mixed borders in groups of no more than two or three, since they need substantial room to develop. Plantings of one to three specimens impart strength and cohesion to a mixed border. Adjacent foliage color must be attended to for they help determine how strong a statement the peony flowers and foliage make.

In early spring, as the herbaceous peonies are pushing up new growth in shades of red, copper, and bronze, early tulips, narcissus, and other spring bulbs can be used to fill the beds with splashes of bright color. When the bulbs have finished their show the peony leaves remain to hide the declining bulb foliage.

Paeonia tenuifolia combines well with dwarf iris and species tulips to create a small-scale, foreground planting. *Helleborus orientalis* and *Euphor-*

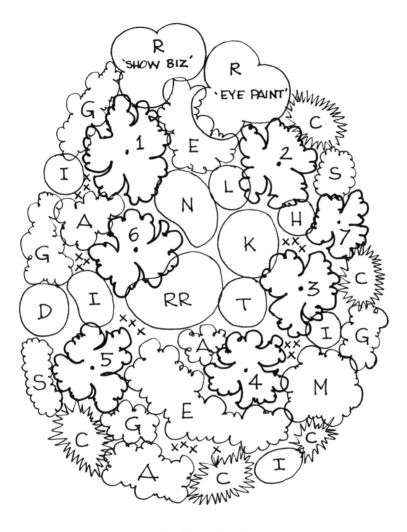

An oval island bed for all seasons.

Featured peonies: 1. 'Gold Sovereign' (specimen tree peony); 2. 'Heidi'; 3. 'Golden Glow'; 4. 'Prairie Moon'; 5. 'Carina'; 6. 'Prairie Moon'; 7. 'Vivid Rose'. Other plantings: A—*Aster ×frikartii*; C—*Crocosmia*; D—*Hemerocallis*; E—*Euphorbia polychroma*; G—*Geranium sanguineum*; H—*Heliopsis helianthoides*; I—*Iris*; L—*Lilium* (Asiatic red); M—*Acer palmatum* 'Dissectum'; N—*Nicotiana*; R—*Rosa* ('Show Biz' and 'Eye Paint'); RR—*Rosa rubrifolia*; S—*Santolina chamaecyparissus*; T—*Thalictrum speciosissimum*; ×—*Narcissus, Tulipa*.

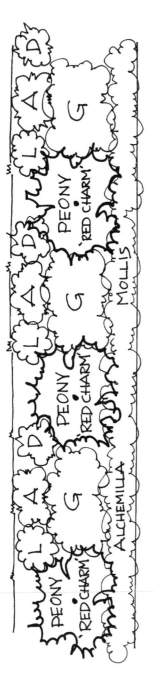

A bold border of red, white, and blue.

Featured peony: 'Red Charm'. Other plantings: *Alchemilla mollis*; A—*Artemisia* 'Powis Castle'; D—*Delphinium* (blue); G—*Geranium himalayense*; L—*Lilium* (Asiatic white).

bia polychroma combine nicely with the larger peonies and help to unify the spots of early perennial growth emerging from the ground. The billowing yellow mounds of *Euphorbia polychroma* add a glow of color to that provided by the early spring bulbs and eventually become a light-green foliage blanket under the taller peonies and later perennials. *Helleborus orientalis* and *Epimedium grandiflorum* with *Paeonia lutea* var. *ludlowii* make a lovely combination in a north-facing border. In early spring, the double white *Arabis caucasica* 'Flore Plena' circles the emerging muted pink and green new growth of Japanese suffruticosa tree peonies. *Arabis* is a light feeder, has shallow roots, and provides a fine-textured carpet for the peony foliage after flowering.

In a white garden, *Paeonia* 'Campagna', 'Elsa Sass', or 'Gardenia' can be combined with the evergreen azalea *Rhododendron* 'Everest' used as a foreground plant. For a succession of bloom into fall, the spring bloom of these plants may be followed by an underplanting of white lilies and *Anemone* ×*hybrida*, whose long stems weave nicely through the denser peony foliage. Persian lilac (*Syringa* ×*persica*), *Viburnum carlesii*, and mock orange (*Philadelphus coronarius*) are all worthy background companions to the early-blooming white peonies.

As summer approaches, the low ground covers of *Alyssum saxatile*, *Iberis sempervirens*, and *Phlox subulata* work well planted near or under larger peonies. The hardy geraniums—*Geranium himalayense*, *G. macrorrhizum*, *G. sanguineum*, and others—offer a midlevel of foliage and harmonious flower color. A spectacular spring combination can be seen at Hidcote Manor Garden in Gloucestershire, England, in a border of red peonies and blue hardy geraniums. The geraniums spill out over the gravel pathway punctuating the contrasting upright foliage of the peonies. The bright red peony flowers complement the paler, smaller, blue flowers of the geranium and the soft variations of green foliage balance the entire color scheme.

The new coppery growth of some rhododendrons also makes a wonderful understory for peony blooms. One of the more unusual plantings I have seen consists of a regal suffruticosa tree peony with large, ruffled, pink blooms climbing out of the top of a mature hedge planting of *Rhododendron* 'Bow Bells'. Even before the peony flowers appear, the coppery new growth on the rhododendron harmonizes beautifully with its upperstory neighbor. Another association that benefits both companions is planting peonies in front of clematis, allowing the peony foliage to provide shade for the roots of the clematis, while their combined flowers create a pleasing bouquet.

In June the lactiflora hybrids combine well with *Papaver orientale* and iris. The taller meadow rues, *Thalictrum delavayi*, *T. rochebrunianum*, and *T. speciosissimum*, together with *Rosa rubrifolia* provide soft masses of blue-gray foliage. These combined with the frothy chartreuse blooms of *Alchemilla mollis* can act as unifiers to the wide range of colors appearing in the summer garden. An interesting tree that fits well in the mixed border is the fringe tree (*Chionanthus virginicus*). Sweet-scented white flowers appear in June and give the slow-growing tree the appearance of a white lilac.

As summer progresses, contrasts for the deep green peony foliage can be provided by the silver-gray leaves of artemisias and the rich purple leaves of *Heuchera* 'Palace Purple'. The many colorations of the ornamental grasses provide contrast and also add striking contrast in overall form and texture. The architectural *Euphorbia wulfenii* with its yellow-green bracts combines beautifully with pink peonies such as the late-blooming 'Sea Shell'. The many colors of daylilies (*Hemerocallis*) combine well with peonies and provide an interesting variation in leaf form.

Consider interplanting lilies, delphiniums, verbenas, and some of the tall, strong-stemmed perennials with peonies since they help support the large flowers. In July and August, the peony foliage covers the sparse and fading lower foliage of the lily stems so the lily blooms appear to float above the peonies. Another lovely effect results from nestling the large peony 'Prairie Moon', with its huge, cream-colored blooms, among and supported by the cascading branches of *Rosa rubrifolia*. The blue-gray foliage and small pink and white flowers of the rose weave through the peony foliage, creating a hazy tapestry. The soft yellow- or cream-flowered peonies also harmonize well with the stronger yellows of *Coreopsis grandiflora* and the green-stemmed shrub *Kerria japonica*.

As winter approaches, seed pods glow and bronze-tinged foliage makes a final parting statement. *Aster novi-belgii* and *Boltonia asteroides* can then share the spotlight with the waning foliage. Red peony stems start to relax, supported perhaps by an adjacent *Rhododendron* 'P. J. M.' or the stiff branches of a shrub rose with lingering rose hips. It is time to rest. With dying foliage cleaned away and tall perennial stems cut back, the mixed border reveals its skeleton and a promise of what will come. Empty spaces exist to be slowly filled with new emerging shoots, and the cycle will begin again.

Planning the garden

A gardener may have all the ingredients for a great garden—a hospitable climate; excellent soil; an assortment of outstanding plant material, including peonies; a beautiful site with a variety of landforms; access to rock, wood, and paving materials; and an ample supply of time and money—but still end up with a lackluster garden. Such an unhappy outcome is the inevitable consequence of the failure to carefully attend to the principles of sound landscape design.

A successful garden is first of all a personal garden, reflecting the gardener's way of being. It should be comfortable, functional, enjoyable, and inspiring to its creator. A successful garden is outdoor space organized to meet specific objective and subjective needs. I start garden planning by defining the types of spaces I feel comfortable in. It sometimes helps to remember the places of retreat favored as a child—a bedroom alcove, a sunny window seat, the shaded canopy under the mulberry tree, or, perhaps, a perch up in the branches of an old apple tree. But most often, such favored spaces change with maturity; adult spaces are usually more complex, and I often find myself high on a hill overlooking a spectacular view or sitting under a rose-covered pergola, surrounded by a multitude of colors and enclosed by tall hedges. In order to shape and organize outdoor space to suit one's needs the gardener generally forms boundaries and enclosures and develops vistas and focused views.

Secondly, the garden must maintain the integrity of the site. One's relationship to the natural environment is surely one element of what gardening is all about. The designer must respect nature and learn from it. Further, the gardener must be sensitive to delicate ecosystems, for a man-made garden is the most fragile ecosystem of all. In short, the garden should reflect an awareness of the regional differences that make each area of our planet unique. This guiding principle has been termed "regionalism" but is actually shorthand for this advice: Don't fight nature. Trying, for example, to grow lush tropicals in the desert or cacti in a rainforest is simply unwise and unprincipled.

Gardens are typically sited either in close proximity to a house or other structure with a human scale, or alternatively to a larger, more monumental structure that dwarfs the human body. In either case, the garden needs to relate in a proportionate way back to the scale-determining structure. Unity between the structures and the garden is a requisite of landscape

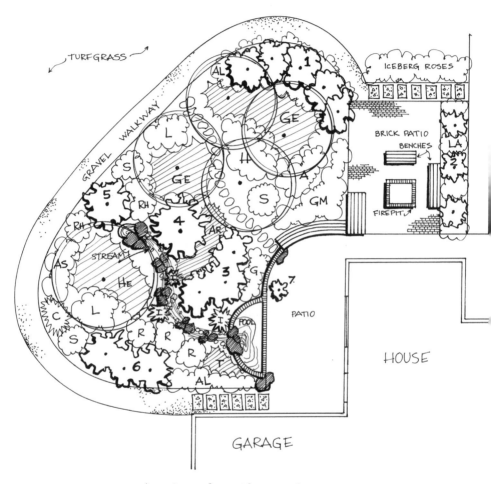

A patio garden with water feature.

Featured peonies: 1. 'Bouquet Perfect' (low hedge of five plants); 2. 'Blaze' (three plants); 3. 'Picotee' (three plants); 4. 'Kishu Caprice' (specimen tree peony); 5. 'Early Windflower'; 6. 'Heidi' (three plants); 7. 'Gay Paree' (in container). Trees: ornamental cherries (five specimens, position represented on plan by dots within large circles). Other plantings: A—*Astilbe*; AL—*Alchemilla mollis*; AR—*Arabis*; AS—*Aster*; C—*Crocosmia*; GE—*Geranium endressii*; GM—*Geranium macrorrhizum*; H—*Hosta*; HE—*Helleborus*; I—*Iris*; L—*Leucothoe*; LA—*Lavandula*; R—Meidiland roses; Iceberg roses; RH—*Rhododendron* 'P. J. M.'; S—*Sedum* 'Autumn Joy'; T—*Thymus serpyllum*.

planning. As Dean Joseph Hudnut of Harvard University wrote in 1948, "That which the house tells us, the garden must reaffirm." In the same essay he also noted that "art instantly alters the pattern of its environment." In short, adjacent elements mutually influence each other.

Any structure added following the creation of the garden creates a new spatial quality, and therefore the plantings, bed contours, and accessories of the landscape that coexist in the same space must be adjusted to the new relationship. Simple patterns and shapes boldly define the character of the design and best establish a solid relationship with the garden structures.

Patios, courtyards, wood decks, walkways, and the like often serve as a transition zone between the hard, rectilinear quality of most structures and the soft, rounded quality of the beds and the growing plants in them. In general, as a person moves further away from the structure, the garden should become less detailed and defined, the patterns more open, and the character more relaxed. Natural landscapes form simple, strong, and bold patterns and relationships.

It is very helpful, economical, less labor-intensive, and much less frustrating to plan a garden on paper before getting out the shovel and rearranging soil and plants. Start with a basic framework, the general logic of the design, in an easily understood format. Many people cannot readily picture three-dimensional constraints so a two-dimensional plan during the initial designing process often proves most useful. Garden design kits and computer software programs have helped in the making of landscape plans, but a few sheets of paper, a pencil and some simple measuring tools are still basic to getting the job done.

Measure the dimensions of the built structures, the topography of the space, other fixed features such as existing plants, walkways, or hardscaping that may be kept, and the garden boundaries, and then draw all these features to an appropriate scale. At this point, like the writer faced with a blank piece of paper, the designer needs an outline or framework to carry the design forward.

A visual relationship between the structure and the site can be found by establishing a ground pattern or grid of intersecting equally spaced lines that serves to unify the two elements, at least on paper. Grid size is best determined by employing some common denominator that holds the architecture together, such as the rhythm of measurement between the window openings, or the width of a prominent structural feature. This measurement is then translated to a pattern of squares, which forms the basis for all the shapes and lines in the garden. A simple house on a small lot may have a 4-foot grid while a large complex estate may best be done on a 10-foot or 12-foot grid. Because the scale of the grid harmonizes with that of the structure, a rhythm is developed that translates into a comfortable, proportionate garden space. The shapes of the planting bed and flower borders, the size of the pathways, and perhaps the curving edges of any lawn areas are all incorporated into the grid pattern.

Architects and artists commonly develop an arrangement of shapes consisting of both straight lines and curves within a grid system; the same principle is advocated here. The primary difference is that a garden is not static—it grows and changes with time and so requires ongoing design modifications, becoming a never-ending project. One of my favorite quotes is from Russell Page's classic 1962 garden autobiography, *The Education of a Gardener*:

> Like clouds moving across the sky dissolving and reforming, now in towering rounded masses, now in long streamers or curling wraiths, now jagged and torn or neatly spread in fish scale pattern over the sky, my garden's patterns shape and reshape themselves.

Once the grid is in place and the main patterns of the garden are determined, then the detailed work, the very fabric of the garden—the plant textures, colors, and forms that will occupy space—can begin. A garden is often compared to a tapestry, I suppose because it is composed of a rich mix of color and form. And like the warp threads that hold a tapestry together, the grid holds a landscape design together.

When the shapes of the planting beds have been carved out of the garden space, when the walkways and patios have been constructed, then the individual plants can be placed. This can be done on paper first, using graphic symbols, or, secondly, by actually placing potted plants in their rough position and then finally arranging them to suit.

Each plant is influenced by its neighbor, so it is wise to start at the top. Decide where all the trees in the design are or will be. These are the large, architectural plants that best link the garden and the house or other structures and will provide the dominant, year-long features. Next in order come the evergreen and larger shrubs that form the skeletal backbone and also provide winter interest. These shrubs usually also form the backdrop for other plants, provide screening, and enclose private spaces. The plants used to provide foliage and flower color interest are placed last; these include the herbaceous perennials and the transitory annuals, which act as filler plants and unifiers.

The peony commonly fits into this last group but not infrequently finds a legitimate place in the second position on the hierarchical ladder, that of the shrubs. It keeps excellent and comfortable company with the hydrangeas, lilacs, deutzias, and viburnums, as well as with the perennials and annuals. It is in this larger context that sequential bloom and variety of plant character play a determining role. But restraint is called for at this point to keep the design simple enough to savor each element, to repeat pleasing elements, and to maintain a unified style.

It is wisest, although not always possible, to design the entire garden as a unit rather than treating each area as a separate entity. By creating such a working master plan, the garden can be installed over time without appearing fragmented, and, at least as importantly, the design can be changed as needs and wishes change without destroying the very fabric of the design.

The peony contributes a unique quality in any well-planned garden just as an eloquent word contributes to and embellishes a poem. If it is genuinely good, it bears repeating in several settings.

Appendix IV

Useful Conversions

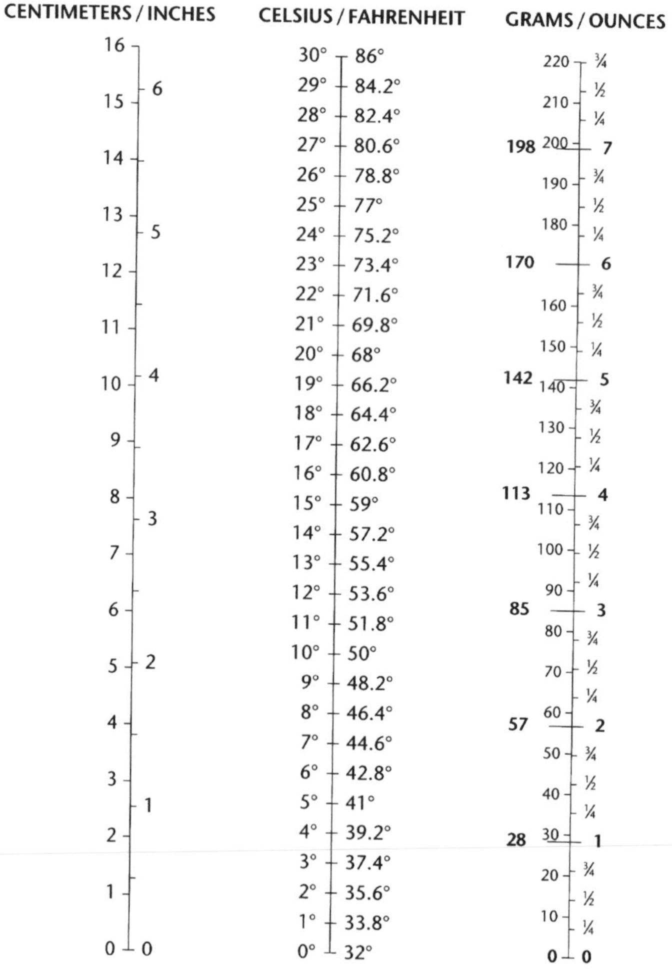

CENTIMETERS / INCHES	CELSIUS / FAHRENHEIT	GRAMS / OUNCES
16	30° — 86°	220 — ¾
15 — 6	29° — 84.2°	½
	28° — 82.4°	210 — ¼
14	27° — 80.6°	198 200 — 7
	26° — 78.8°	190 — ¾
13	25° — 77°	½
— 5	24° — 75.2°	180 — ¼
12	23° — 73.4°	170 ——— 6
	22° — 71.6°	160 — ¾
11	21° — 69.8°	½
	20° — 68°	150 — ¼
10 — 4	19° — 66.2°	142 140 — 5
	18° — 64.4°	130 — ¾
9	17° — 62.6°	½
	16° — 60.8°	120 — ¼
8	15° — 59°	113 110 — 4
— 3	14° — 57.2°	¾
7	13° — 55.4°	100 — ½
	12° — 53.6°	¼
6	11° — 51.8°	90 —
	10° — 50°	85 ——— 3
5 — 2	9° — 48.2°	80 — ¾
	8° — 46.4°	70 — ½
4	7° — 44.6°	¼
	6° — 42.8°	57 60 — 2
3	5° — 41°	50 — ¾
— 1	4° — 39.2°	40 — ½
2	3° — 37.4°	¼
	2° — 35.6°	28 30 — 1
1	1° — 33.8°	20 — ¾
	0° — 32°	½
0 — 0		10 — ¼
		0 — 0

Appendix V

Hardiness Map

RANGE OF AVERAGE ANNUAL MINIMUM
TEMPERATURES FOR EACH ZONE

	Fahrenheit	Celsius
ZONE 1	Below −50	−46
ZONE 2	−50 to −40	−46 to −40
ZONE 3	−40 to −30	−40 to −34
ZONE 4	−30 to −20	−34 to −29
ZONE 5	−20 to −10	−29 to −23
ZONE 6	−10 to 0	−23 to −18
ZONE 7	0 to 10	−18 to −12
ZONE 8	10 to 20	−12 to −7
ZONE 9	20 to 30	−7 to −1
ZONE 10	30 to 40	−1 to 4
ZONE 11	Above 40	Above 4

Recommended Reading
and Sources

The following is a select list of the bibliographic sources and references used in the preparation of this book.

Adams, David. 1992. *Ornamentals Newsletter*. Aurora, Oregon: North Willamette Research and Extension Center.

American Peony Society. 1991. *Handbook of the Peony*. 6th ed. Hopkins, Minnesota: American Peony Society.

Andersen Horticultural Library. 1993. *Source List of Plants and Seeds: A Completely Revised Listing of 1990–92 Catalogues*. Chanhassen, Minnesota: Andersen Horticultural Library.

Aoki, N., and S. Yoshino. 1984. Effects of duration of cold storage. *Journal of the Japanese Society for Horticultural Science* 4, no. 52:450–457.

Ashley, A., and P. Ashley. 1992. *The Canadian Plant Source Book 1992–93*. Ottawa: Self-published.

Benoit Rivière. 1911. Catalog (in French).

Boyd, James, ed. 1928. *The Manual of the American Peony Society*. Robinsdale, Minnesota: American Peony Society.

Brand Peony Farms. 1923. *Brand Peony Manual*. Faribault, Minnesota.

Bretschneider, E. 1898. *History of European Botanical Discoveries in China*. London: Sampson Low, Marston and Co.

Byrne, T. C., and A. H. Halevy. 1986. Forcing herbaceous peonies. *J. Amer. Soc. Hort. Sci.* 111, no. 3:379–383.

Capon, Brian. 1990. *Botany for Gardeners*. Portland, Oregon: Timber Press.

Chen, Junyu. 1992. Personal communication. Ornamental Plants, Beijing Forestry University, Beijing, P.R.C.

Coates, Peter. 1970. *Flowers in History*. New York: Viking Press.

Cooper, F. C. 1970. Peony flower pigments. American Peony Society Bulletin 197.

Cooper, Ray. 1988. *Survey of the Paeonia Species in the Light of Recent Literature*. Oldham, England: Self-published.

Cornere, J. H. 1946. Centrifugal stamens. *Journal of the Arnold Arboretum*. Cambridge, Massachusetts.

Cullen, J., and V. H. Heywood. 1964. Notes on the European species of *Paeonia*. *Feddes Repertorium* 69:32–35.

———. 1964. *Flora Europaea*. Edited by T. Tutin et al. Vol. 1. London: Cambridge University Press.

Davidson, J. G. N. 1991. *History, Management and Recommended Varieties of Peonies in the Peace River Region*. Beaverlodge, Alberta, Canada: Agriculture Canada, Northern Research Group.

Eames, A. J. 1946. *Morphology of the Angiosperms*. New York: McGraw-Hill.

Ellis, Andrew. 1992. Personal communication. American College of Traditional Chinese Medicine, San Francisco.

Foster, Stephen, and Yue Chongxi. 1992. *Bringing Chinese Medicine to the West*. Rochester, Vermont: Inner Traditional International.

Frank, Reinhilde. 1989. *Paonien: Pfingstrosen*. Stuttgart, Germany: Eugen Ulmer Verlag.

Hao, H., D. Zang, M. Han, and C. Fan. 1992. *An Introduction to Heze Peony of China*. Heze, P.R.C.: Heze Peony Research Institute.

Harding, Alice. 1917. *The Book of the Peony*. New York: J. B. Lippincott.

———. 1923. *Peonies in the Little Garden*. New York: Atlantic Monthly Press.

———. 1993. *The Peony: Alice Harding's* Peonies in the Little Garden *and* The Book of the Peony. Introduced and updated by Roy G. Klehm. Portland, Oregon: Sagapress/Timber Press.

Harris, R. A., and S. H. Mantell. 1991. Micropropagation of tree peonies. *Journal of Horticultural Science* 66, no. 1:95–102.

Harrison, C. S. 1907. *The Peony.* York, Nebraska: Self-published.

Hashida, Ryoji. 1990. *A Book of Tree and Herbaceous Peonies in Modern Japan* (in Japanese with English summaries). Tatebayashi City, Japan: Japan Botan Society.

Haw, S. G. 1985. The garden. *Journal of the Royal Horticultural Society* 110:54–159.

Haw, S. G., and L. A. Lauener. 1990. A review of the intraspecific taxa of *Paeonia suffruticosa* Andrews. *Edinburgh Journal of Botany* 47:273–281.

Haworth-Booth, Mark. 1963. *The Moutan or Tree Peony.* New York: St. Martin's Press.

Hong, T., J. Zhang, J. Li, W. Zhao, and M. Li. 1992. Study of the Chinese wild woody peonies. Bulletin of Botanical Research 12:223–234.

Hosaki, T. 1992. Personal communication. Faculty of Agriculture, Shimane University, Shimane, Japan.

Hutton, B. 1992. Personal communication. Mt. Macedon, Victoria, Australia.

Huxley, A., 1992. *The New Dictionary of Gardening.* Vol. 3. London: Royal Horticultural Society.

International Bureau for Plant Taxonomy and Nomenclature. 1980. *International Code of Nomenclature for Cultivated Plants.* Utrecht, The Netherlands: International Bureau for Plant Taxonomy and Nomenclature.

Jenvons, J. 1974. *How to Grow More Vegetables.* Berkeley, California: Ten Speed Press.

Kessenich, Greta, ed. 1976. *History of the Peonies and Their Originations.* Hopkins, Minnesota: American Peony Society.

——, ed. 1979. *American Peony Society: Seventy-Five Years.* Hopkins, Minnesota: American Peony Society.

——, ed. 1987. *Peonies 1976–1986.* Hopkins, Minnesota: American Peony Society.

Kessenich, Greta, ed., and Don Hollingsworth. 1990. *The American Hybrid Peony.* Hopkins, Minnesota: American Peony Society.

Li, H. L. 1959. *The Garden Flowers of China.* New York: Ronald Press.

Moffitt, R. 1989. *Preserving Flowers.* Wilmington, Delaware: Self-published.

Nehrling, Arno, and Irene Nehrling. 1960. *Peonies, Outdoors and In.* New York: Hearthside Press.

Nowak, Joanna, and Ryszard M. Rudnicki. 1990. *Postharvest Handling and Storage of Cut Flowers, Florist Greens, and Potted Plants.* Portland, Oregon: Timber Press.

Phillips, Roger, and Martyn Rix. 1989. *The Random House Book of Shrubs.* New York: Random House.

——. 1991. *The Random House Book of Perennials.* Vol. 1, *Early Perennials.* New York: Random House.

Rivière, Michel. 1992. *Le monde fabuleux des pivoines.* Massy, France: Floraprint.

Rockwell, F. F. 1933. *The Home Garden Handbooks—Peonies.* New York: Macmillan.

Sinnes, A. C. 1979. *All About Fertilizers, Soils and Water.* San Francisco: Ortho Books.

Smith, Donald R., ed. 1994– . *Paeonia.* West Newton, Massachusetts. (Newsletter).

Stearn, William T., and Peter H. Davis. 1984. *Peonies of Greece.* Kifissia, Greece: The Goulandris Natural History Museum.

Stebbins, A. G. L. 1939. *Notes on Some Systemic Relationships in the Genus Paeonia.* University of California Publications in Botany 19:7.

Steiner, R. 1958. *Agriculture.* Kimberton, Pennsylvania: Bio Dynamic Farming and Gardening Association.

Stern, Frederick C. 1946. *A Study of the Genus Paeonia.* London: Royal Horticultural Society.

Xin, Jiguang, ed. 1986. *The Peony in Luoyang.* Beijing: China Pictorial.

Wilson, J. 1990. *Masters of the Victory Garden.* Boston: Little Brown.

Wister, John C., ed. 1962. *The Peonies.* Washington, D.C.: American Horticultural Society. Includes Section II *The Tree Peonies* by John C. Wister and H. E. Wolfe, originally published in 1955 in *National Horticultural Magazine* 34:1–61.

Wyman, D. Tree peonies. *Arnoldia* 29:25–32.

Zhang, Yuexian. 1992. Personal communication. Heze Mudan Research Institute, Heze, P.R.C.

Index
of Cultivars

'Polar Star' 209
'Pom Pom' 209
'Port Royale' 209
'Postilion' 81, 209
'Pottsi Plena' 209
'Prairie A Fire'. See 'Prairie Afire'
'Prairie Afire' 209
'Prairie Belle' 209
'Prairie Charm' 240
'Prairie Moon' 23, 81–82, 120, 209, 254,
    263, 266; Plate 112
'Prairie Princess' 209
'President Feuillet' 210
'President Lincoln' 210
'President Poincare' 210
'President Roosevelt' 210
'President Taft' 210
'President Wilson' 210
'Pride of Blasdell' 210
'Pride of Langport' 210
'Pride of Shenandoah' 210
'Pride of Taishow Dynasty'. See 'Taishono-
    hikari'
'Primevere' 28, 33, 173, 210
'Prince de Troubetskoy' 231
'Prince of Darkness' 210
'Princess' 237
'Princess Amelie' 231
'Princess Margaret' 30, 31, 82, 210;
    Plate 113
'Princess Margaret Rose' 210
'Princess of Darkness'. See 'Prince of
    Darkness'
'Professeur Jean-Marie Duvernay' 210
'Promenade' 210
'Pure Joy' 210

'Quality Folk' 210
'Queen of Hamburg' 211
'Queen of Sheba' 211
'Queen Rose' 211

'R. A. Napier' 211
'R. W. Auten'. See 'Robert W. Auten'
'Rachel' 211

'Radiant Red' 82, 212, 222
'Ramona Lins' 211
'Raoul Dessert' 211
'Rapture' 211
'Rare China' 211
'Rashoomon' 211
'Raspberry Charm' 211
'Raspberry Ice' 211
'Raspberry Rose' 211
'Raspberry Sundae' 26, 69, 82, 143, 211;
    Plate 114
'Ray Payton' 211
'Red Beauty' 211
'Red Bird' 211
'Red Carpet' 211
'Red Charm' 24, 28, 68, 74, 82, 141, 142,
    212, 264; Plate 115
'Red Comet' 82, 142, 212
'Red Dandy' 212
'Red Dragon in Red Pool' 212
'Red Ensign' 212
'Red Flag' 212
'Red Giant' 212
'Red Glory' 68, 82, 120, 212; Plate 116
'Red Goddess' 143, 212
'Red Grace' 212
'Red Imp' 212
'Red Japanese' 212
'Red Rascal' 237
'Red Red Rose' 34, 120, 212; Plate 117
'Red Romance' 212
'Red Triumph'. See 'Pfeiffer's Red Triumph'
'Redon' 237
'Regent' 238
'Reine Deluxe' 212
'Reine des Violettes' 231
'Reine Elisabeth' 231
'Reine Hortense' 212
'Reliance' 213
'Renato' 213
'Renkaku' 88, 231, 261; Plate 118
'Renown' 89, 238
'Requiem' 35, 82, 213; Plate 119
'Reverend H. N. Traggitt' 213
'Reward' 213

'Tempest' 220
'Teni'. See 'Ten'i'
'Ten'i' 233
'Terpsichore' 238
'Terry Grudem' 220
'Tessera' 238
'The Admiral' 221
'The Beauty of Practical Living' 233
'The Belgian' 221
'The Fawn' 221
'The Mighty Mo' 221
'Themis' 89, 238
'Therese' 221
'Thunderbolt' 236, 239
'Thura Hires' 221
'Tiger Tiger' 239
'Tinge of Yellow' 240
'Tinkerbelle' 221
'Tish' 221
'To Kalon' 221
'Toichi Ruby' 23, 233
'Tokio' 221
'Tom Eckhardt' 221
'Tondeleyo' 221
'Top Brass' 6, 85, 221, 257; Plate 134
'Top Hat' 221
'Topeka Coral' 221
'Topeka Garnet' 221
'Torchsong' 221
'Toro-No-Maki' 221–222
'Torpilleur' 222
'Tourangelle' 222
'Trafford W. Bigger' 222
'Tria' 22, 89, 239; Plate 135
'Triomphe de l'Exposition de Lille' 222
'Triomphe de van der Malen' 233
'Truly Yours' 222
'Truth' 222
'Twin Beauty' 233

'Ubatama' 233, 237
'Umbellata Rosea' 222
'Uncle Tom' 222
'Unknown Soldier' 222
'Up Front' 222

'Valor' 222
'Valour'. See 'Valor'
'Valse de Vienne' 233
'Vanity' 222
'Velvet Princess' 222
'Very Double Cherry'. See 'Yae Zakura'
'Vesuvian' 89, 239; Plate 136
'Victoire de la Marne' 6, 222
'Victoria Lincoln' 222
'Victory' 222
'Victory Chateau Thierry' 223
'Viette's Japanese White' 223
'Viking Chief' 223
'Ville de Nancy' 223
'Ville de Saint Denis' 238
'Violet Dawson' 223
'Virginia Dare' 223
'Virginia Lee' 223
'Vivid Glow' 223
'Vivid Rose' 68, 85, 92, 223, 257, 263; Plate 137
'Vogue' 223

'W. F. Turner'. See 'William F. Turner'
'Walter E. Wipsom' 92, 223
'Walter Faxon' 223; Plate 138
'Walter Mains' 85, 223
'Walter Marx' 29, 108, 115, 134, 139, 223, 261; Plate 139
'Ward Welsh' 223
'Washington' 223
'Waterlily'. See 'Marie Jaquin'
'Weisbaden' 224
'West Elkton' 224
'West Hill' 224
'Westerner' 19, 85, 118, 224
'White Cap' 85–86, 224
'White Eagle' 224
'White Frost' 31, 134, 224
'White Gold' 224
'White Innocence' 7, 35, 61, 86, 224; Plate 140
'White Ivory' 224
'White Light in the Night' 233
'White Perfection' 195, 224